THE MISTREATMENT OF ELDERLY PEOPLE

THE MISTREATMENT OF ELDERLY PEOPLE

edited by

Peter Decalmer and Frank Glendenning

SAGE Publications
London · Newbury Park · New Delhi

First published 1993
Reprinted 1994

 SAGE Publications Ltd
6 Bonhill Street
London EC2A 4PU

SAGE Publications Inc
2455 Teller Road
Newbury Park, California 91320

SAGE Publications India Pvt Ltd
32, M-Block Market
Greater Kailash – I
New Delhi 110 048

British Library Cataloguing in Publication Data

Mistreatment of Elderly People
  I. Decalmer, Peter.   II. Glendenning, Frank
  362.6

  ISBN 0–8039–8712–9
  ISBN 0–8039–8713–7 (pbk)

Library of Congress catalog card number 92–050906

Typeset by Type Study, Scarborough
Printed and bound in Great Britain by
Biddles Ltd, Guildford and King's Lynn

Contents

List of Contributors

Dudley Ainsworth is Community Nurse Liaison Officer for the Elderly (Psychiatry), North Manchester Health District.

Robert Bamlett is Team Manager (Mental Health), North Manchester Social Services.

Jan Cowley is Clinical Nurse Specialist for the Elderly (Psychiatry), North Manchester General Hospital.

Michael Davies is Director of Post Basic/Continuing Education, Hertfordshire College of Health Care Studies.

Peter Decalmer is Consultant in Psychiatry for the Elderly, North Manchester General Hospital, and a part-time Lecturer in the Department of Psychiatry and Social Work, University of Manchester.

Frank Glendenning is Honorary Senior Research Fellow, Centre for Social Gerontology, University of Keele and Visiting Professor, Program in Gerontology, University of Waterloo, Ontario.

Aled Griffiths holds a degree in law and is Principal Lecturer in Social Policy, Y Coleg Normal, Bangor and a Visiting Lecturer, University of Wales, Bangor.

Jill Manthorpe is Lecturer in Social Policy, University of Hull.

Alison Marriott is Principal Clinical Psychologist, Department of Psychiatry for the Elderly, Manchester Royal Infirmary.

Michael Nolan is Senior Lecturer in Nursing Research, Faculty of Health Studies, University of Wales, Bangor.

John F. Noone is a General Practitioner and Clinical Tutor in General Practice, Post-Graduate Medical Centre, North Manchester General Hospital.

Chris Phillipson is Professor of Applied Social Studies and Social Gerontology, University of Keele.

viii   *The Mistreatment of Elderly People*

Gwyneth Roberts holds a degree in law and is Senior Lecturer in Social Policy, University of Wales, Bangor.

John Williams is Senior Lecturer in Law, University of Wales, Aberystwyth.

Preface

We met through a series of study days on elder abuse, organized by the British Association for Service to the Elderly, which took place throughout England and Wales from the late 1980s onwards. The absence of any theoretical text on elder mistreatment, abuse and neglect led us to conceive this volume of essays.

We have cause to be grateful to numerous people: to Professor Chris Phillipson for his support and encouragement; to Aled Griffiths, Alison Marriott and Dr Gwyneth Roberts, whose cooperation went far beyond the call of duty; to Michael Davies for his considerable contribution to the checklist on indicators of physical abuse in Chapter 2; to Dr Maggie Pearson; to Phyllis Mallinson, formerly Chief Librarian at North Manchester Post-Graduate Medical Centre; to Gillian Crosby and her colleagues at the library of the Centre for Policy on Ageing in London; and to all those who have contributed to this volume.

We are fully aware that we have not made specific reference to the abuse and neglect of older people in black and ethnic minority communities. The reason for this is twofold. First, we are unaware of any relevant studies and, secondly, although case studies are available to us, we are reticent about including such personal material lest it be misinterpreted and used as a stereotype. It is clear that the abuse and neglect of old people within the black and ethnic minority communities requires special attention. As within the white indigenous population in Britain, it certainly exists, but specific studies are required which relate to specific cultural backgrounds.

Typing and word processing skills have been in abundance. Anne Jennings has been a model of patience, and Wendy Heap also has made a special contribution. We are grateful also to Sue Allingham and Margaret Tiplady. Paul Davies contributed the graphics in Appendix 6.1. We are grateful to Dr T.F. Johnson for permission to reproduce Table 2.3. Finally, we thank Sue Ashton, and Rosemary Campbell and Karen Phillips of Sage Publications, who watched over us with great skill and considerable patience.

Peter Decalmer and Frank Glendenning

1
What is Elder Abuse and Neglect?

Frank Glendenning

The neglect and abuse of old people is not new. What is new is the attempt, since the end of the 1970s, to find out why it happens. It is established that miscare, mistreatment, physical, emotional or material abuse takes place. It is what Bennett (1992a) has called 'another iceberg phenomenon'. This collection of essays will attempt to describe recent developments in our understanding of the issues involved. The focus of this opening chapter will be to examine what has been written about the mistreatment, abuse and neglect of older people in three countries. For it is from the United States of America, Canada and Britain that the main thrust and exchange of ideas about abuse and neglect has come.

In the USA and Britain, about 5 per cent of older people live in institutional settings (Hudson and Johnson, 1986; Fennell et al., 1988). In Canada, the figure is approaching 9 per cent (Forbes et al., 1987). There is chilling evidence that these elderly people are more likely to be at risk than the 95 per cent or 91 per cent who live in the community. However, although the vast majority of elderly people are cared for and tended with affection at home, a considerable amount of violence takes place within the family. Whitehead, for instance, has written in a British nursing journal: 'Interest and concern about non-accidental injury grew out of a general awareness that individuals sometimes assaulted people close to them and then either forced or conspired with them to make out that the resulting injuries were sustained accidentally.' (Whitehead, 1983: 32–3)

It is unclear whether there is a connection between child abuse and elder abuse, but it is singular that several times in the literature there appears, with minor syntactical changes, the anonymous verse which from folk memory presents such a view:

When I was a laddie,
I lived with my granny,
And many a hiding me granny gi'ed me.
Now I am a man,
And I live with my granny.

And I do to my granny,
What she did to me.

The connection, however, remains to be substantiated. What can be said is that commentators such as Pillemer and Wolf (1986), Wolf (1988) and Wolf and Pillemer (1989) have been urging an increased study of family dynamics. Brubaker (1990) has pointed out that we must be sensitive to later life family relationships, recognizing that there can be both a positive and a negative side. Steinmetz (1990: 194) has considered family relationships in previous centuries and concluded that 'The romantic view of close-knit, multi-generational families of yesteryear is a mythical representation rather than an accurate account of family life in the past.' Steinmetz suggests that evidence from family papers and civic records indicates that the traditional belief that care was always provided for elderly people by their family requires examination. Similarly, Laslett's study of English social structure has led him to the conclusion that 'there never was a time when all elderly English people lived in large, extended households' (Laslett, 1989: 112).

During the past 10 years, in particular, society has become more overtly aware of the existence of elder abuse and neglect. Observers agree that the quantity (not the proportion) of abuse and neglect will inevitably rise, as will the actual numbers of those suffering from senile dementia of the Alzheimer type, because of the demographic changes taking place. In Britain, in 1901, there were half a million people over 75 and 57,000 over 85. By 1981, these numbers had increased to over three million and just over half a million. In Canada, nearly 900,000 people were over 75 in 1981 and just under half a million were over 80. In the USA, in 1901, less than one million were aged over 75 and only 100,000 were over 85. By 1988, nearly 12.5 million were over 75 and nearly 2,900,000 over 85 (see Table 1.1).

Hudson and Johnson, writing in 1986, believed that between 4 and 10 per cent of the elderly population in the USA were abused, primarily within a family context and they suggested that certain questions needed to be addressed:

(1) How do families who abuse or neglect their elders differ from those who do not? (2) How can families at risk for elder neglect or abuse be identified? (3) What are the circumstances in family settings that generate elder neglect and abuse? (4) How can families be helped to effectively prevent or control neglectful and abusive situations? (Hudson and Johnson, 1986: 113)

Even in the 1960s in Scotland, an examination of the hypothesis that old people are less well cared for by the 'younger generation' led to

Table 1.1 *Elderly population in Great Britain, Canada and USA (in thousands)*

	65+	%	75+	%	85+	%
Great Britain						
1901	1,734	4.7	507	1.4	57	0.15
1981	7,985	15.0	3,053	5.7	552	1.03
Projections (1989 based)						
1989	8,758	15.7	3,850	6.9	819	1.5
2001	9,022	15.7	4,324	7.5	1,149	2.0
2041	12,468	21.2	6,365	10.8	1,715	2.9
2051	11,586	20.0	6,139	10.6	2,010	3.5
Canada						
1901	272	5.1	–	–	–	–
1981	2,360	9.7	–	–	–	–
Projections						
1981	2,360	9.7	883	3.6	451	1.9
2001	3,883	12.8	1,794	5.9	1,000	3.3
2041	7,744	20.7	4,346	11.6	2,708	7.2
2051	7,555	19.5	4,104	10.6	2,766	7.1
USA						
1901	3,080	–	less than 1,000		100	–
1980	25,704	11.3	10,051	4.4	–	–
1988	30,367	12.3	12,470	5.1	–	–
Projections						
2000	34,882	13.0	16,639	6.2	–	–
2010	39,362	13.9	18,323	6.5	–	–

Sources: For Britain: 1901–81: Census Data OPCS; Projections: Government Actuary OPCS PP2 No. 17. For Canada: Denton et al. (1987). For USA: Statistical Abstract of the United States, US Department of Commerce, Bureau of Census, 1990.

the conclusion that as between 1959 and 1966 out of 1,500 patients discharged from a geriatric unit, in only 12 cases was home care by relatives unreasonably refused. The hypothesis could not be sustained (Lowther and Williamson, 1966). A subsequent study, however, showed that the generalized actuality was not as they had thought. Isaacs studied 612 patients in another Department of Geriatric Medicine in Scotland between 1966 and 1967 and concluded that 'the prolonged survival of many severely disabled and ill people into advanced old age . . . has created unprecedented strain on our family and social system' (Isaacs, 1971: 286). Four years later, Baker reported the ill-treatment of elderly people and this was perhaps the first time that the term 'granny battering' was used (Baker, 1975; Burston, 1975). Later, Burston wrote:

> Hitting elderly people is not a new phenomenon; there can be little doubt that old people have been subjected to physical violence since time began . . . It is in the community that the trouble starts. The majority of elderly patients are not known to the primary health care team as a whole . . . In the past the medical profession has disregarded the problems of old age and must accept a share of responsibility for those who are subsequently physically assaulted . . . The catalyst seems to be the continued and continual presence of the older person. (Burston, 1977: 54–5)

The main thrust for the next ten years in Britain came from Eastman, a practising social worker in London, who enabled a growing number of professional social workers to admit the existence of elder abuse. The terms 'granny battering' and 'granny bashing' in Britain (Baker, 1975; Burston, 1975; Eastman and Sutton, 1981, 1982; Eastman, 1983) changed in the mid-1980s to 'old age abuse': *Old Age Abuse* became the title of Eastman's book in 1984. Rich in case material, but lacking the sophistication of the American and Canadian studies, this volume stands as a landmark in the British literature. With the support of Age Concern England, Eastman brought the British Geriatrics Society firmly into the debate in 1988 with their conference on elder abuse which was attended by some 400 people. General practitioners in Britain are nevertheless still slow to respond to the problem.

Eastman's approach was challenged by Cloke (1983) who regarded his work in relation to problem-solving as being underdeveloped. Stevenson (1989: 28) reflected that Eastman's

> concern about the issue does not seem to be adequately conceptualised nor related to more general issues concerning the strains on family life. To separate consideration of old age abuse from the range of powerful emotions, positive and negative, which are present in those who depend and those who care, and which affect all interactions, is both limiting and stigmatising.

The same can be said about Pritchard (1989, 1990a,b, 1992).

'There is no systematic research reported from the UK or the rest of Europe' (Fisk, 1991: 901; but see Ogg and Bennett, 1991: 15–16). 'Old age abuse' is still in use as a term, as is the term 'elder abuse' and the 'abuse or mistreatment of elderly (or 'older') people'.

In America, in 1975, Robert Butler wrote in *Why Survive?* of the 'battered old person syndrome'. One of the first American academic studies was never published, although it is referred to frequently in the American and Canadian literature: 'The battered elder syndrome: an exploratory study' by Block and Sinnott (1979). Conducted in Maryland, with 24 agencies, 427 professionals (randomly selected) and 443 elders (randomly selected), the response rate was very low (17 per cent overall, including 4 per cent from the agencies, i.e. one agency), and typifies the climate of opinion 12 years ago. They found 26 cases of elder abuse, the majority of which had been reported to the relevant agency. Little action was taken and, not surprisingly, the study went no further.

The Canadians during the past decade, like the British, have been highly dependent on the American material. According to Hudson (1988), serious interest in elder abuse has only existed since the 1980s. The first study was that of Shell in Manitoba in 1982. Gnaedinger published a detailed discussion paper in 1989 for the National Clearing House on Family Violence. Podnieks and Pillemer carried out the second major study which was a national study of prevalence (the Ryerson Study) which reported in 1989. In 1991, the Canadian National Advisory Council on Aging, which advises the Minister of National Health and Welfare, published a report on elder abuse (Wigdor, 1991).

Just as child abuse entered the general public's consciousness in the 1960s, followed by spouse abuse in the 1970s, the 1980s brought us face to face with the abuse of older people. Several myths about the family have been shattered (Gnaedinger, 1989). The Schlesingers (1988) identified over 200 North American research papers relevant to elder abuse and neglect and some of these will be referred to in order to outline the argument.

Definitions

During the 1980s, there were many definitions of elder abuse and elder neglect, and there is wide recognition that they lacked clarity and precision (Hudson, 1988; Pillemer and Finkelhor, 1988; Wolf, 1988; Filinson, 1989; Stevenson, 1989; Wolf and Pillemer, 1989; Bennett, 1990a; McCreadie 1991). A clear difficulty has been that investigators have approached elder abuse from different perspectives: the victim, the carer, the physician, the nurse, the agency, the social worker, social policy; and, as a result, there has been a lack of clarity. In addition, by 1988 some 32 investigations had been completed and every state in the USA except one had legislation dealing with the maltreatment of adults. Yet the basic critical questions were still unanswered. 'What is, and is not elder abuse? Elder neglect? Exploitation? Self-abuse? Who should define these terms?' (Hudson, 1986: 160).

Typologies of domestic abuse
From the beginning there was a distinction between those who sought to establish a typology of various kinds of elder abuse and neglect and

Table 1.2   *Definitions of elder abuse and neglect*

Investigators	Typologies
Lau and Kosberg, 1979	Physical, psychological, material abuse and violation of rights
Block and Sinnott, 1979	Physical, psychological, material and medical abuse
Kimsey et al., 1981	Physical, psychological, material and fiscal abuse
Hickey and Douglass, 1981b	Passive neglect, active neglect, verbal and emotional abuse, physical abuse
Chen et al., 1981	Physical, psychological, sexual, social/environmental abuse
Sengstock and Liang, 1982	Physical, psychological, financial abuse; physical and psychological neglect
Rathbone-McCuan and Voyles, 1982	Physical assault, verbal and psychological assault, misuse of money or property, theft, misuse or abuse of drugs, not providing care
Eastman, 1984b	Systematic maltreatment, physical assault, emotional or financial abuse, threatening behaviour, neglect, abandonment, sexual assault
Hirst and Miller, 1986	Maltreatment divided into types of abuse and neglect
Pillemer and Finkelhor, 1988	Physical violence, psychological, emotional, mental abuse; neglect
Bexley Social Services, 1988	Assault, deprivation of nutrition, administration of inappropriate drugs, deprivation of prescribed drugs; emotional and verbal abuse, sexual abuse, lack of help in performing acts of daily living; involuntary isolation; financial abuse
Wolf and Pillemer, 1989	Physical, psychological, material abuse; active and passive neglect
Steinmetz, 1990	Financial exploitation, neglect, emotional, sexual and physical abuse; self-abuse and self-neglect

those who attempted to conceptualize elder abuse and neglect (see Tables 1.2 and 1.3). From 1979 onwards, there was some understanding of what the discussion was about. Physical abuse involved being hit, sexually assaulted, burned or physically restrained, while psychological abuse involved the abused person being insulted, frightened, humiliated, intimidated or treated as a child (Hickey and Douglass, 1981b). Medical abuse involved the withholding of, or careless administration of, drugs (Block and Sinnott, 1979). Social and environmental abuse included the deprivation of human services, involuntary isolation and financial abuse (Chen et al., 1981). Material abuse included misuse of property or money, theft, forced entry into a nursing home, financial dependence and exploitation (Rathbone-McCuan and Voyles, 1982). Passive neglect referred to

Table 1.3 *Definitions of elder abuse and neglect*

Investigators	Concepts
O'Malley et al., 1979	The wilful infliction of physical pain, injury or debilitating mental anguish, unreasonable confinement or deprivation by a caretaker of services which are necessary to the maintenance of mental and physical health.
Rathbone-McCaun, 1980	A heretofore unrecognized form of intra-family violence.
O'Malley et al., 1983	Active intervention by a caretaker such that unmet needs are created or sustained with resultant physical, psychological or financial injury . . . Failure of a caretaker to intervene to resolve a significant need despite awareness of available resources.
Johnson, 1986	A state of self-inflicted or other-inflicted suffering unnecessary to the maintenance of the quality of life of the older person.
Fulmer and O'Malley, 1987	The actions of a caretaker that create unmet needs . . . The failure of an individual responsible for caretaking to respond adequately.
Wolf, 1988	Not only is it impossible to compare the findings from the early studies, because of variations in the meaning of elder abuse, but it is also not possible to compare or aggregate data obtained from state reporting systems.
Wolf and Pillemer, 1989	We believe it is necessary to include . . . the more general literature on relations between spouses and between elderly parents and adult children . . . The determinants of the quality of family relationships of the elderly can provide important insights into elder abuse, especially in concert with family violence research.
Filinson, 1989	Because the lack of empirical work is an intrinsically significant feature of the transformation of elder abuse into a social issue, the implications for practice and policy in the light of the paucity of sound data are considerable . . . The complexity of the elder abuse phenomenon and the various motivations and circumstances for abuse suggest that a multi-faceted approach to dealing with the problem is needed.

the elderly person being left alone, isolated or forgotten (Hickey and Douglass, 1981b). Active neglect involved the withholding of items that were necessary for daily living (food, medicine, companionship, bathing), the withholding of life resources and not providing care for the physically dependent person (Rathbone-McCuan and Voyles, 1982). Eastman (1984b: 23) defined old age abuse as 'the systematic maltreatment . . . of an elderly person by a care-giving relative. This may take the form of physical assault, threatening behaviour, neglect and abandonment (when the relative is either thrown onto the street with their belongings, or is put in a room with no furniture), or sexual assault.'

Hudson and Johnson (1986: 114) commented on the nature of these developing typologies: 'Physical and psychological mistreatment are consistently included, whereas inclusion of separate classifications of neglect (active and passive), financial or material abuse, self-neglect, violation of rights, sexual abuse and medical abuse, vary from study to study.' Investigators were using different words and different descriptions of categories of abuse. Hudson and Johnson noted that Lau and Kosberg (1979) referred to 'physical abuse' as 'withholding personal care', while Sengstock and Liang (1982) applied 'withholding personal care' to 'psychological neglect'.

These discrepancies might be explained by variations in sampling techniques and differences in research design, but there is a certain incongruity when investigators do not work with definitions that have an accepted meaning. The situation caused Cloke (1983: 2), writing from a British perspective, to say: 'There has been a tendency to include such a wide range of abuses within the overall term "old age abuse" that the concept becomes almost meaningless as a heuristic tool.' Nevertheless, the issue was now unmistakably in the public domain. In the years to come, not only was the medical profession to become in principle more involved, but more honesty was to be asserted both in relation to domestic abuse and neglect, and also in relation to abuse taking place, sometimes in horrific circumstances, in institutions.

Conceptualization

Some investigators attempted to conceptualize the issues. Some of these attempts are listed in Table 1.3. O'Malley et al. (1979) sought to place abuse and neglect within the wider context of inadequate care. They defined elder abuse as 'the wilful infliction of physical pain . . . mental anguish . . . or deprivation by a caretaker of services which are necessary to the maintenance of mental and physical health' (1979: 2). Hudson and Johnson (1986) criticized this definition because the label of abuse could only be applied if it was clear that the carer or caregiver intended to do the harm. The assumption is also that the patient is dependent, thus excluding independent older people who may also become victims of abuse.

In a paper written in 1983, O'Malley et al. simplified the conditions of abuse to 'physical, psychological or financial injury' and developed a new definition for neglect: 'the failure of a caretaker to intervene to resolve a significant need despite awareness of available resources' (1983: 1,000). In 1984, they wrote:

> The terms 'elder abuse and neglect' are being applied to situations in which an elderly person is subject to battering, rough handling, verbal abuse, denial of rights, neglect of care needs, infantilization, abandonment or misuse of resources . . . The terms used to describe cases of family mediated abuse and neglect emphasize the behavior of the individual alleged to be responsible for the abuse and neglect. (O'Malley et al., 1984: 362)

Hudson and Johnson (1986) suggested that here abuse was an act of commission and neglect an act of omission. Rathbone-McCuan (1980: 296) broached the hypothesis that elder abuse is a formerly unrecognized form of intra-family violence: 'Conceptual confusion . . . is reinforced by rapidly changing norms and values, social policies and definitions that are applied to describe the social problems faced by the elderly.' Her conclusion was that 'the brief history of clinical intervention in intrafamily violence in the United States is very discouraging' (Rathbone-McCuan and Voyles, 1982: 192).

Lack of consensus

Investigators continued to publish their findings without a consensus emerging. Hirst and Miller (1986) argued that to include too many broad types of abuse would result in an overstatement of the problem, making it impossible to determine the aetiology of abuse. They suggested a general heading of maltreatment, subdivided into various types of abuse and neglect. This, however, proved to be merely cosmetic.

    Pillemer and Finkelhor (1988) noted the failure of an expert conference in the USA in 1986 to reach agreement on a definition of elder abuse. They spoke of 'definitional disarray' and found 'no generally accepted definitions of elder abuse and neglect'. They believed, however, that a consensus had been established about types of mistreatment. These they stated to be: physical violence; psychological, emotional or mental abuse; and neglect (the failure of a clearly constituted caregiver to meet the needs of an elder). Tomlin (1989: 5) follows a similar path and quotes a working party of Bexley Social Services Department (1988): assault (including force-feeding); deprivation of nutrition; administration of inappropriate drugs and deprivation of prescribed drugs; emotional and verbal abuse; sexual abuse; deprivation of help in performing activities of daily living (glasses, hearing aid etc.); involuntary isolation and confinement; and financial abuse. (However, Hildrew (1991a) noted that this working party was in abeyance.) Since 1982, Callahan has consistently suggested that the definitional problem is so great that it would be prudent to abandon the concept (Callahan, 1982, 1986, 1988). He admitted in 1988 that elder abuse 'may have reached a new plateau of legitimacy' by appearing on the front page of the *Wall Street Journal* (4 February 1988), but he continued to question the need to elevate elder abuse as a central concern of social policy. While it is an urgent concern for the victim, it only affects a relatively small number of people, he maintained, although he recognized that this might be the result of under-reporting.

Pointers to future developments
Wolf (1988: 758) refers favourably to Johnson's (1986) study of definitions and her definition of elder mistreatment as: 'a state of self-inflicted or other-inflicted suffering unnecessary to the maintenance of the quality of life of the older person' (Johnson, 1986: 180). Later, Johnson was to add to this definition: '[older person] by means of abuse and neglect caused by being overwhelmed' (Johnson, 1991: 4). The discussion had now shifted to what is important, namely, avoiding labels and seeking a consensus about care. Wolf also added her weight to those criticizing the continuing search for definitions: 'Not only is it impossible to compare the findings from the early studies because of the variations in the meaning of "elder abuse", but it is also not possible to compare or aggregate data obtained from the state reporting systems' (Wolf, 1988: 758). And Filinson (1989: 17) wrote that 'the implications for practice and policy in the light of the paucity of sound data are considerable.'

Wolf and Pillemer (1989) and Godkin et al. (1989) use the following as a classification of abuse and neglect in their review of the Three Models Project (Massachusetts, Syracuse and Rhode Island, set up in 1981): *physical abuse* (the infliction of physical pain or injury, physical coercion, sexual molestation, physical restraint); *psychological abuse* (the infliction of mental anguish), and *material abuse* (the illegal or improper exploitation and/or use of funds or resources); *active neglect*: refusal or failure to undertake a caretaking obligation (including a conscious and intentional attempt to inflict physical or emotional distress on the elder); *passive neglect*: refusal or failure to fulfil a caretaking obligation (excluding a conscious and intentional attempt to inflict physical or emotional distress on the elder). Gnaedinger (1989) follows the same classification in Canada.

It was not surprising then that Bennett (1990a: 53) said: 'The difficulty in defining elder abuse is a major thread throughout the published literature.' It is mainly the Americans who have sought to clarify our understanding of the abuse and neglect of older people. But the case material is perfectly recognizable elsewhere. American investigators have been largely concerned with domestic abuse. Very little work has been done on abuse and neglect in institutional settings in the USA and Canada, but in Britain as a result of official boards of inquiry, episodes involving the ill-treatment of patients and poor standards of care in hospitals and residential homes are well documented. There was a procession of reports in Britain on the abuse of old people in institutions in the 1970s and 1980s: Ely Hospital, Cardiff (National Health Service, 1969); Besford House, Shropshire (Medd, 1976); Moorfield, Salford (Hytner, 1977); Stonelow Court (Derbyshire County Council, 1979); Nye Bevan Lodge, Southwark (Gibbs et al., 1987), and there have continued to be others since. They are, however, not analysed, apart from Clough's unpublished evidence to the Wagner Committee on residential care in 1988.

In summary, then, there is uncertainty as to the relation between domestic and institutional abuse, and an unresolved question is whether elder abuse has characteristics which distinguish it from the abuse of other adults. We also have too little information about the relation between neglect and other forms of abuse. Definitions of abuse so far vary according to the purpose for which they are needed, although Pillemer, Finkelhor and Wolf have probably reached an important stage in reaching workable definitions.

How much abuse and neglect is there?

Domestic abuse

There has been no major study of the prevalence or incidence of elder abuse in Britain. By 'prevalence' is meant 'the number of cases . . . in a given population at a specific point in time'. By 'incidence' is meant 'the number of new cases occurring in a given population within a defined period of time' (Victor, 1991: 4–5). Tomlin (1989), writing the report of the British Geriatrics Society, quotes the figure of 500,000. Eastman and Sutton arrived at this figure in their paper 'Granny Battering' saying that in the USA, 42 per cent of the over-65s were being supported by caregiving relatives and that 'evidence from the United States indicates that ten per cent of such people supported by family members are at risk' (1982: 12). They concluded, on that assumption, that nearly 500,000 were at risk in Britain. Hocking (1988), who pioneered a study of non-accidental injury (NAI) found in old people in the 1970s, claims that one in 10 is at risk and one in 1,000 suffers physical abuse, but she provides no source for this figure. Ogg and Bennett (1992a: 63) have ventured an estimate (translated from American figures) of 'eight elderly people who are [subjected to] abuse or inadequate care within a patient register of 200'. These estimates seem to be misleading and to apply American statistics elsewhere is an unsafe procedure. Very recent figures given by Ogg and Bennett at the end of 1992 (based on an omnibus survey by the Office of Populations, Censuses and Surveys in May of that year, with 2,130 interviews) suggested that in the experience of the over-60s in the sample, verbal abuse was much more significant than physical or financial abuse. But they cautioned against taking their findings 'in isolation from other attempts to systematically identify elder abuse' (Ogg and Bennett, 1992b: 998).

McPherson, one of Canada's leading sociologists, suggests that 'it is difficult to identify either the incidence per 1,000 elders, or the absolute number of cases that may be present in a given community or society . . . [because] most elder abuse and neglect is hidden or unreported' (1990: 360). However, he refers to Shell's Manitoba study (1982) and suggests that, transposed onto a national basis, this represents about 22 cases per 1,000 elders; and in the Ryerson national study, Podnieks and Pillemer (1989) found that about 40 persons per 1,000 experienced some form of mistreatment: that is to say, 98,000 people. Regional variations were discovered also. British Columbia, at 53 per 1,000 was much higher than the Prairies with 30 per 1,000. Health and Welfare Canada (the government Ministry) has estimated that 100,000 elderly Canadians were abused (Brillon, 1987).

The methods for obtaining estimates of prevalence rates in the USA have not been satisfactory. Among the early attempts to estimate the prevalence of elder abuse and neglect, Block and Sinnott (1979) found 40 per 1,000 in Maryland, and Gioglio and Blakemore (1983) 15 per 1,000 in New Jersey. As in the case of the Ryerson survey, these regional variations require further study. The Block and Sinnott (1979) survey gave rise to the widely cited figure of 4 per cent of elderly people suffering abuse, but it has to be said that there are no reliable statistics because of the lack of uniformity in state reporting laws and in the keeping of records. Definitions of elder abuse are unclear with the use of professional and agency reports rather than interviews with victims and the failure to use rigorous research designs (for example, random sample surveys and case-comparison studies) (Pillemer and Finkelhor, 1988). With the exception of the work of Wolf, Pillemer and their associates, it is now recognized that much of the early American work has inbuilt weaknesses.

The first large-scale random sample survey of elder abuse and neglect was by Pillemer and Finkelhor (1988) in Boston involving over 2,000 older people. Their prevalence findings showed that the sample translated into a rate of 32 per 1,000. 'If a survey of the entire

United States were to find a rate similar to the one in Boston, it would indicate between 701,000 and 1,093,560 abused elders in the nation' (Pillemer and Finkelhor, 1988: 54). The rates for types of mistreatment were: physical violence, 20 per 1,000; verbal aggression, 11 per 1,000; and neglect, four per 1,000. Wolf and Pillemer (1989) remark that these rates are lower than other forms of family abuse. The rate for child abuse in the USA is 110 children per 1,000. Nevertheless, there are potentially over a million abused elders in the United States.

It is worth noting Stevenson's remarks in her *Age and Vulnerability* (1989: 22): 'There seems little point in wasting research time on the incidence of old age abuse; as with child abuse, it can lead to a kind of spurious precision, in which figures are cited which will not bear scrutiny.' She gives three reasons. First, without agreement on definitions, we may be attempting to compare different phenomena. Secondly, estimates are likely to be based on reported abuse, which is dependent on the highly variable practices of agencies and practitioners. Thirdly, much abuse is likely to be hidden and difficult to discover.

Abuse in institutions

The Americans have been slow to investigate abuse and neglect in residential settings. During the 1970s and early 1980s, there were several qualitative reports which were based on case studies. These did not show the prevalence rates for mistreatment of elderly patients. Lau and Kosberg (1979) studied 404 elderly patients seen in one year at the Chronic Illness Center in Cleveland, Ohio. They found that 9.6 per cent were abused in some way. Seventy-five per cent of this group had severe physical or mental impairments. Doty and Sullivan (1983) found that 7 per cent of skilled nursing facilities were deficient in patients' rights, policies and procedures.

Pillemer and Moore (1989) surveyed a random sample of 577 nurses and nursing aides who were working in long-term care facilities. They do not translate physical and psychological abuse from their findings into a national or regional rate but they affirm that 'abuse is sufficiently extensive to merit public concern' and 'may be a common part of institutional life' (1989: 318). Cowell (1989) cites Nusberg's (1985) study of the consumer's perspective on the quality of care in nursing homes, which was conducted under the auspices of the National Citizens' Coalition for Nursing Home Reform. She also describes the progress made in California during the 1980s, which instituted its own studies of the quality of care in nursing homes. These led to legislation to deal with alleged abuse and neglect in health care facilities that received state medical insurance payments. But Cowell suggests that legislation alone cannot bring about change.

In Canada, investigators have paid no special attention to institutional abuse, although Podnieks (1983) witnessed it with some distress. McPherson (1990) regards it as a fact, and relies on the American work of Pillemer and Moore (1989). Wigdor (1991: 8) suggests that 'the fact that mandatory reporting of mistreatment of residents in institutions has become law in a number of provinces can be taken as evidence that claims of abuse have been real and frequent enough to require legislative action.'

In Britain, a distinction is drawn between individual acts of abuse in institutions and institutional abuse. In recent years there have been several official inquiry reports (to which we have already referred), but prevalence and incidence rates are not available.

Who are the victims and who are the perpetrators?

Tomlin (1989), in the British Geriatrics Society report on elder abuse, suggested that the most vulnerable elderly people are those with whom it is difficult to communicate and who show fluctuating disabilities. Those with dementia or Parkinson's disease, she remarked, are more likely to be abused than others. (No source is given for this statement.) She quotes Hocking (1988) as saying that those who are particularly vulnerable are women over 80 with dementia, Parkinson's disease or cerebrovascular disease, who may have communication difficulties, hearing impairment, immobility and/or incontinence. She also reports that 'American studies have shown the classic victim to be an elderly person over the age of seventy-five, female, roleless, functionally impaired, lonely, fearful and living at home with an adult child' (Tomlin, 1989: 5). Eastman (1984b: 41) writes that 'the majority are female over eighty and are dependent as a result of physical or mental incapacity . . . They are not confined to any particular social group, but are to be found in all social classes.' (Steuer and Austin (1980) had made this latter point also in America.) Horrocks (1988: 10850) spoke of the abused victim being 'over seventy-five, female, physically heavy, often immobile, incontinent, aphasic and dementing'. Bennett (1990b: 46) wrote that victims were more likely to be 'female, average age 76, living in houses with spouse or family'. The age differs from case study to case study, but the contexts are similar. There is a generality here in all these claims, and the lack of specificity as to how these conclusions were arrived at is noticeable.

Perpetrators are frequently seen as being the victims of stress and isolation and Tomlin gives a useful summary of the caring process

(Tomlin, 1989), as does Eastman (1984b). But there are no studies in Britain that illuminate this problem apart from Homer and Gilleard (1990a), who reported from their sample that all carers who committed some form of abuse lived with their victim. Abuse was significantly associated with alcohol consumption. Abusers who admitted physical and verbal abuse scored significantly higher on the depression subscale of the questionnaire than did the non-abusive carers. There was poor communication between victim and perpetrator. Abusive caregivers were likely to have stopped work in order to care for their relative. Non-abusers by and large had not.

The Manitoba and Ryerson studies

In Canada, certainly until 1988, when the Schlesingers published their book *Abuse of the Elderly*, practitioners were almost entirely dependent on American sources. Shell (1988), however, in the Manitoba study had found that two-thirds of victims were women aged 80–84 who had lived with a family for 10 years or more. Vadasz (1988) believed from the literature up to 1983 that victims were most likely to be female, over 75, confused and physically dependent. The caregiver is seen as being driven to a sense of helplessness, rage and frustration. Podnieks and Pillemer in the Ryerson study (1989) found little to distinguish between the abused and the non-abused as far as gender, marital status and living arrangements were concerned; and, according to McCreadie (1991), Podnieks found that victims of material abuse were more likely to live at home, while 40 per cent of the perpetrators of material abuse were known to the victim. Those who were abused physically or verbally were likely to be married, or married and living with an adult child.

Early observations in the USA

Responses to the question 'who are the victims?' in the American literature are frequently scarce and, as in Britain, based on the observation of case material. The majority of the early investigators did not use a case-comparison or control group method but simply looked at what material was available in aggregate. Thus, 'based on an analysis of case materials', Rathbone-McCuan (1980: 300) listed (without explanation) the victim's characteristics: female, over 65, functionally dependent, a history of alcoholism, retardation or psychiatric illness for either the victim or the caregiver, a history of intra- and inter-generational conflict, a previous history of related illnesses. She does not build up a profile of the perpetrator, but regards him/her as a member of the family. She believes that there is a background of intra-family violence, with all that that implies. Abusive behaviour may be associated with alcohol. There is an intolerance of dependency and members of the family may reinforce the violent behaviour of others. Rathbone-McCuan's conclusion was that the position of abused elders was similar to that of wives and children who are abused and neglected, which seems a simplistic view from our perception 12 years later. The tendency merely to extend the concepts relating to other forms of family violence will not go far enough in a study of elder abuse (Wolf and Pillemer, 1989). We need to extend the study of family relationships and older people alongside research into family violence.

The early debate about elder abuse and neglect was still in its infancy 10 years ago and many of the early investigators found themselves in a cloud of uncertainty and ignorance. Hence Hickey and Douglass (1981b) were not specific beyond 'family members' and made a plea for 'in-depth studies of victims and their families', believing that abusive behaviour was probably triggered by parental dependency which recalled parent–child hostilities of earlier life. They also reported that in 63 per cent of cases of physical abuse, the abuser was suffering from alcohol and/or drug abuse and severe stress. Douglass (1983), cited in Schlesinger and Schlesinger (1988: 6), described victims as 'the older elderly persons, frail, mentally or physically disabled, female and living with the person responsible for the abuse'. Gesino et al. (1982) were interested in spouse abuse which existed throughout married life and spoke of the dearth of knowledge about spouse abuse in later life.

O'Malley et al. (1983) were responsible for one of the earliest surveys (of the reports of professionals and paraprofessionals) in Massachusetts. Their analysis of existing reports from professionals concluded that the victims were chiefly over 75 and female and that 75 per cent had significant mental or physical impairment. Sengstock and Liang (1983: 198) reported from their survey that the age-span was from 60 to over 90 and predominantly female. More whites were involved than blacks and 80 per cent were in receipt of an income of less than $10,000 a year. Taler and Ansello (1985) agreed on the basis of their records that the majority of victims were female, over 75, widowed and unable to be financially independent, with at least one physical or mental impairment. Similar responses came from Hirst and Miller (1986) and Mildenberger and Wessman (1986), but over 65; Soule and Bennett (1987), over 70; and Powell and Berg (1987), over 75.

O'Malley et al. (1983), turning to the perpetrators, found them to be caregivers, suffering from stress, and/or the products of domestic violence which had become learned behaviour and normative for them. The abusers, in O'Malley's study, frequently suffered from drug and alcohol abuse or were pathologically violent people. Taler and Ansello (1985) noticed that 40 per cent of perpetrators in their sample were spouses of victims and 50 per cent were children or grandchildren. Hirst and Miller (1986) identify daughters as abusers, with marital conflict, alcohol or drug abuse and ineffective coping patterns. Mildenberger and Wessman (1986) describe the daughters as white, middle-aged and middle class.

The Boston study
Alongside this scrutiny of the records, Pillemer and Wolf (from 1981) were involved in their major study. Among their findings were the results of the first large-scale rigorous random survey, involving 2,020 elderly people in Boston who were interviewed by telephone and included interviews with abused persons, which we have already mentioned in another context. Here the profile was quite different from previous studies. Pillemer and Finkelhor (1988) noted that no longer were the results showing that elderly women were being mistreated by an adult child. Instead, in older people living in the community, abused men outnumbered abused women by 52 per cent to 48 per cent. Of the perpetrators, 58 per cent were spouses and 24 per cent were children. Because more elders live with spouses than with adult children, the chances of being mistreated by a spouse rather than an adult child is greater. If that is so, they suggest, it may account for the greater visibility of abused older women in previous surveys and trawls, because they suffer more severe injury and are more likely to report or be reported to a service agency.

Some of the other findings confirmed the picture painted by previous investigators. Abused elderly people were likely to be living with someone else. They were more likely to be in poor health. Neglected elders tended to have no one to turn to for support. In previous studies (Johnson et al., 1985; Hudson, 1986) as Pillemer and Finkelhor point out, victims appeared to come more from the older and disadvantaged sections of the community. They draw attention also to two more 'striking differences' between their study and earlier reports of elder abuse. There were high rates of spouse abuse and of men as victims. This study established that elder abuse in future could be the subject of general population surveys. Until Wolf, Pillemer, Finkelhor, Kosberg et al., most of the results of surveys, with the possible exception of O'Malley et al., had been obtained through unsound methodology. The findings were, for this reason, un-reliable.

Later observations
Throughout the 1980s, some commentators emphasized the dependency of the victim on the perpetrator (Steinmetz, 1983; Quinn and

Tomita, 1986), together with the stress to the carer that results. Wolf and Pillemer disputed this in 1989, maintaining that few research findings supported this view. They pointed out that while a large number of elderly people are dependent on relatives, only a small minority of these are abused. Therefore, they claimed, no direct correlation between the dependence of an elderly person and abuse could be established. Similarly, they continued, many elderly people are physically impaired, but without case comparison and control groups, it is inadequate to claim that abuse victims have some physical dependency. There had in the past been a tendency to generalize and Wolf and Pillemer exercised caution, concluding that 'a better way to conceptualize the issue is to view a serious imbalance of dependency in either direction as a potential risk factor' (Wolf and Pillemer, 1989: 27).

There is little information in the literature about victims and perpetrators in nursing homes, residential homes and hospitals. We have already pointed to the effect of stressful working situations, burn-out, dissatisfaction, the nature of staff–patient conflict, attitudes to ageing and lack of resources. There are clear instances of sadism in the reports of official inquiries and this element must be a subject for further study.

Indicators of abuse

In domestic cases
Burston's letter to the *British Medical Journal* in 1975 drew attention to the physical abuse of old people (who, he said, often had mental impairment). We had entered the world of 'granny battering' as he called it. Eastman, from the early 1980s, listed 'signs of facial bruising, grip marks on limbs, burns (caused perhaps by cigarettes), cuts or fractures' (1984b: 58). In addition, as examples of abuse he lists sexual abuse, the misuse of medication, recurring or unexplained injuries, physical constraints (tying people to beds or chairs), malnutrition and/or dehydration, lack of personal care. There may be responses from both the abused person and the abuser. Both men and women who have been abused may cower when approached (Hocking, 1988).

The early literature from America had moved quite quickly to describe the manifestations of abuse and neglect of older people (Block and Sinnott, 1979; Lau and Kosberg, 1979; O'Malley et al., 1979; Steuer and Austin, 1980; Hickey and Douglass, 1981a,b; Rathbone-McCuan and Voyles, 1982). Their descriptions are strikingly similar to those from Britain. In the USA, Hall (1989) studied a sample of 284 cases of abuse and mistreatment with, by this time, a considerably more sophisticated analysis of what was happening. Hall found 43 separate acts or situations which related to the 284 cases. Two elements appeared in 15 per cent of the cases and 63 per cent contained two or more elements of mistreatment. Furthermore, the most frequently recurring items were (*a*) care of the person and the immediate living area, and (*b*) not seeking medical care. The items concerning self-care and health status accounted for 38 per cent of the recorded elements in this study: what Hall defined as personal maintenance (hygiene, clothing, food), care of the immediate living area, medication problems and food.

He went on to suggest that there may be a core of deterioration in the victim which makes the more extreme forms of mistreatment easier to commit. Abuse of elders' resources (theft, misuse of resources and/or coercion) constituted 14 per cent of the whole. Hall identified the most common indicators of abuse as 'not caring for health or seeking medical care'; the theft of material resources; physical abuse (including beating up, pushing, shoving, grabbing and slapping, kicking, hitting, sexual molestation), emotional and psychological abuse (calling names, insulting, swearing at, abandonment for long periods of time, threats, non-specific verbal aggression, restraint, locking up); and violation of elders' rights (forms of restraint, imposition and abandonment). Such a list exemplifies the great variety of acts of mistreatment that may be present and which were being increasingly recognized during the 1980s.

O'Malley et al., whose work in Massachusetts was discussed approvingly by Wolf (1988), developed an identification chart in 1983 which provides a good summary:

Conditions that may be manifestations of abuse or neglect
Recurring or unexplained injuries
Non-treatment of medical problems
Poor hygiene
Malnutrition
Dehydration
Depression, withdrawal or fearfulness
Imposed social or physical isolation
Over-sedation or misuse of medication

Conditions associated with high risk of abuse or suggesting potential for abuse
Severe cognitive impairment
Severe physical impairment requiring heavy care
Depression
Mention of punishment by elder or caretaker

Family norm of violence
Isolation of caretaker
Refusal of outside services
Control of elder's financial affairs or assets by another
Inconsistency of information by family or caretaker

They also included a useful flow chart to assist decision-making, which asked the following questions:

Does the elder want to remain at home?
Are the reasons sound and justifiable?
Can the needs be met by the family and others?
Are the family and the patient willing to accept inadequate care to remain at home?
Either provide support services which involve one or more of home health aide, homemaker/chore services, transportation, medical nursing care, counselling, respite care.
Or, explore the choices, and counsel the family and the patient.
Or, explore alternative living arrangements for the patient, with another member of the family: foster care, residential home, nursing home.

O'Malley et al. emphasized that in domestic cases of abuse and neglect it is useful to divide them into two categories, those in which the elderly person has physical or mental impairments and is dependent on the family for daily care needs and those in which care needs are minimal and are overshadowed by the pathological behaviour of the caregiver. They emphasize that access and intervention must be negotiated with both the abuser and the abused, neither of whom may desire help. The aim must be to benefit the elderly person, and in the negotiation it should be emphasized that services will resolve unmet needs for the patient while providing support to the caregiver.

American commentators continued to write about how to recognize the indicators of abuse (Hudson, 1986; American Medical Association, 1987; Soule and Bennett, 1987; Kosberg, 1988). The papers were numerous. Extended studies were virtually non-existent apart from the longitudinal studies of Pillemer and Wolf, who were cautious to report, until the end of the 1980s. Breckman and Adelman (1988) included in their list of physical indicators: unexplained genital infections; soiled bed linen or clothing; unexplained or unexpected deterioration in health; absence of glasses, hearing aid and/or dentures. They suggest some indicators for psychological abuse: insomnia, sleep deprivation, need for excessive sleep, change in appetite, unexplained weight gain or loss, tearful-ness, unexplained paranoia, low self-acceptance, excessive fears, ambivalence, confusion, resignation and agitation. Indicators of financial mistreatment may be the elderly person's inability to pay bills; an unexplained or sudden withdrawal of money from the elderly person's account; a disparity between assets and satisfactory living conditions; an unusual interest by family members in the older person's assets.

They also set out a detailed protocol (devised by Tomita, 1982) for identification and assessment. This takes the reader (the worker) step by step, question by question, through the procedure and also lists a thorough raft of options as did Podnieks (1988). Kingston (1990) investigated identification procedures in health authorities in Britain. Unlike the USA, where there is universal support for 'screening instruments', by mid-1990 two health authorities had a policy and seven had draft guidelines. Four authorities followed child abuse guidelines. In mid-1991, Hildrew (1991a) reported that 11 social services departments had approved guidelines and 26 were well advanced in their plans. It is, however, 17 years since Burston wrote to the *British Medical Journal*.

A promising development in the USA in relation to the treatment of elder abuse and neglect is the work of the neighbourhood justice centres (also referred to as mediation centres). They attempt to solve personal disputes between people who have a continuing relation-ship. Their techniques include counselling, mediation and arbitration (Nathanson, 1983). Mediation developed quite quickly in America in the 1980s and is now beginning to be discussed in Britain.

In residential settings

The difficulty in obtaining reliable information about abuse and neglect in residential settings has already been referred to. Hala-mandaris (1983) presented a cavalcade of abuse in nursing homes in the USA, which included theft of patients' funds, false claims on the part of 'carers' to Medicare and Medicaid, trading in real estate, fraudulent therapy and pharmaceutical charges, even involvement in organized crime. Stathopoulos (1983) similarly reported financial abuse, denial of civil rights (lack of privacy, lack of voting rights, removal from private or semi-private rooms to three- or four-bed wards), neglect, psychological abuse, maltreatment in various ways. Pillemer and Moore also reported discouraging findings in American nursing homes:

Despite increases in federal and state regulation of nursing homes over the past two decades, some staff are nevertheless able to behave inappropriately toward patients . . . This study presents a picture of staff who are working in highly stressful, difficult environments. By reducing this stress, while increasing the ability of staff to resolve conflicts in more positive ways, nursing homes may become more humane environments. (1989: 319)

Britain has had its quota of official inquiries into the conduct of abusive practices in residential homes, as we have noted. One of the most infamous scandals took place at Nye Bevan Lodge, in South-wark, London and one commentator wrote: 'It is self-evident that when elderly, often confused residents are made to eat their own faeces, left unattended, physically manhandled, forced to pay money to care staff and even helped to die, something is seriously wrong' (Vousden, 1987: 19). Clough has suggested that abuse of residents is more likely when:

> there have been a series of complaints over a long period and relate to more than one member of staff; the establishment is run down and basic arrangements for laundry and hygiene are poor, for example a pervasive smell of urine; there are staff shortages and staff sickness; senior staff are on holiday; interaction between resident and worker takes place in private; there is little supervision of staff and they are able to develop their own patterns of work (we know little of what happens at night time); staff have been in charge of the unit with considerable autonomy for a long time; there is a high turnover of staff; staff drink alcohol regularly during breaks or when on duty; there is uncertainty about the future of the establishment; there are few visitors; residents are highly dependent on staff for personal care; residents go out little or have few contacts; a particular resident has no one taking an active interest in him or her; there is discord among the staff team or between staff and managers; the task or the people being cared for are ascribed little worth; the residents are troublesome, when their care makes very heavy demands or when the task to be carried out is unpleasant. (1988: 7)

Horrocks (Tomlin, 1989) analysed 12 consecutive Health Advisory Service reports of long-stay wards in hospitals. Their findings included:

> the wards were too large, unhomely, open, revealing few personal possessions;
> custodial;
> overcrowded and the beds were too close together;
> furniture was often referred to as dilapidated;
> absence of carpets;
> excessive use of restraint;
> privacy was widely threatened (even with inspectorate teams present, patients were openly toileted, dressed, washed and bathed);
> half the units inspected had no written policies about continence;
> catering was poor and lacked choice;
> the last meal was often served at 5 p.m. to suit the needs of the institution;

the drawing up of individual care plans had been discussed in some units, but had only been implemented in one;
nurses were too few and lacked help from doctors and other disciplines;
a complete lack of mental stimulation. (Tomlin, 1989: 11–12)

Tomlin (1989) commented: 'These examples reflect passive abuse on a massive scale.'

Establishing a theory

Most of the reasons given for abuse are reminiscent of the typology in relation to definitions. In cases of domestic abuse, there were those who stressed psychological and psychosocial causes, concerned with family relationships, violence and family history. Others suggested a variety of other possibilities.

Reasons advanced for elder abuse by selected investigators

Psychological and psychosocial causes
Rathbone-McCaun, 1980; Steuer and Austin, 1980; Hickey and Douglass, 1981b; Cloke, 1983; O'Malley et al., 1983; American Medical Association, 1987; Hudson, 1988; Godkin et al., 1989; Homer and Gilleard, 1990a.

Other possibilities
Drugs and/or alcohol (Mildenberger and Wessman, 1986; Homer and Gilleard, 1990a)
Chronic medical problems (O'Malley et al., 1983)
Financial problems (Hickey and Douglass, 1981b)
Dependency of victim (Hickey and Douglass, 1981b; American Medical Association, 1987; Soule and Bennett, 1987; Hudson, 1988)
Provocation by the victim (Mildenberger and Wessman, 1986)
Internal stress of the caregiver (Block and Sinnott, 1979; Rathbone-McCuan, 1980; Soule and Bennett, 1987; Hudson, 1988)
External stress of the caregiver: age, financial, work or unemployment (Soule and Bennett, 1987; Hudson, 1988; Godkin et al., 1989)
Social isolation (Godkin et al., 1989)

In the case of abuse in institutional settings, much less has been achieved. Hudson (1988) and Stevenson (1989) have suggested that the abusing caregiver may also be dealing with unresolved conflict. Pillemer and Moore (1989) have pointed to frustration engendered through long hours of work, low pay and low prestige; Kimsey et al. (1981) to discouragement, understaffing, underfunding and inadequate facilities, a point echoed by the American Medical Association

(AMA) (1987) and by Pillemer and Moore (1989) who also pressed for a study of conflictual staff–patient relationships. Block and Sinnott (1979) pointed to internal stress; Hudson (1988) to external stress and negative attitudes towards older people. The AMA (1987) also suggested that formal caregivers often had pessimistic attitudes towards life and death, which frequently resulted in callousness.

None of these suggestions alone, however, provides a theoretical base which has been empirically tested. As early as 1981, Hickey and Douglass wrote of the need for a model that was free from professional bias from which could be developed appropriate crisis intervention and prevention techniques.

The situational model
Phillips (1986) explored three theories of elder abuse and the way in which they reflected the empirical data. The earliest theory of elder abuse was the 'situational model'. The premiss fits easily within an intervention framework and is derived from a theoretical base associated with child abuse and less strongly with other forms of family violence:

> as the stress associated with certain situational and/or structural factors increases for the abuser, the likelihood increases of abusive acts directed at a vulnerable individual who is seen as being associated with stress. The situational variables that have been linked with abuse of the elderly have included (1) elder-related factors such as physical and emotional dependency, poor health, impaired mental status, and a 'difficult' personality; (2) structural factors such as economic strains, social isolation and environmental problems; and (3) caregiver-related factors such as life crisis, 'burn-out' or exhaustion with caregiving, substance abuse problems, and previous socialization experiences with violence. (Phillips, 1986: 198)

However, Phillips had difficulties in relating this model to the empirical data, mainly because of the lack of clarity over definitions of elder abuse and the confusion between physical, emotional, neglect and other forms of abuse. Existing samples have differed from agency to professional to victim. Few studies used comparison groups. Usually, studies have described a sample of abused elders and then generated a theory to explain the observed data. The assumption that different forms of abuse within the family can all be explained by the same theory has not been tested. Phillips concludes that for these and other reasons the situational model may be inappropriate.

Social exchange theory
Social exchange theory is 'based on the idea that social interaction involves the exchange of rewards and punishments between at least

two people and that all people seek to maximise rewards and minimize punishments in their interaction with others' (Phillips, 1986: 202). Phillips suggests that, conceptually, social exchange theory can easily be used to explain elder abuse, assuming that abused older people 'are more powerless, dependent and vulnerable than their caregivers and have fewer alternatives to continued interaction' (1986: 204). Deriving empirical support for this stance, however, has been far less simple. For instance, researchers have failed to produce unequivocal evidence that abused elders are more dependent than non-abused elders, thus 'violating the essential assumption that abused elders are more powerless, and as a result, caregivers have little to lose by their actions' (1986: 205). Phillips concludes that social exchange theory does not afford a complete explanation for elder abuse. It does not enable us to predict who will use violence and who will not. However, further testing of social exchange theory is likely to be productive.

Symbolic interactionism
A third theoretical perspective which has been advanced for elder abuse is 'symbolic interactionism'. 'Social interaction is a process between at least two individuals that (1) occurs over time; (2) consists of identifiable phases that are recurring, interrelated, and loosely sequenced; and (3) requires constant negotiation and renegotiation to establish a "working consensus" . . . about the symbolic meaning of the encounter.' (Phillips, 1986: 207). This is about cognitive processes, the adoption and improvization of roles, the imputation of roles, role support, reciprocity and compatibility. When there is a mismatch, then there is the probability of conflict and termination of the interaction. In such a context, elder abuse can be conceptualized as an inadequate or inappropriate role enactment. Phillips (1986) obtained data from abusive and non-abusive caregivers and found that 'an important part of formulating personal images of the other person concerns reconciling the image of who this person was conceived to be in the past and the image of who this person is now conceived to be' (1986: 209). An obvious example of this situation is the case of someone suffering from dementia. Conflict can be particularly acute for 'adult children and elders who had not had a continuous live-in relationship throughout the years and among spouses where one spouse had sustained a personality-altering illness' (Phillips, 1986: 210). After using this model in rigorous test conditions, Phillips believes that there are some advantages, as well as disadvantages, in using symbolic interactionism as an explanatory base for elder abuse. These three perspectives are not mutually

exclusive, 'nor do they include all the explanations that have been advanced in the literature for elder abuse' (Phillips, 1986: 214).

Abusers and victims

There are numbers of studies which have focused on the abuse of children by their parents and the abuse of women by men. In recent years, Pillemer has been developing a theoretical approach towards elder abuse which is based on the literature about child abuse and spouse abuse. He matched abused older people against non-abused older people and identified five areas:

1 Intra-individual dynamics (the psychopathology of the abuser).
2 Inter-generational transmission (the cycle of violence).
3 Dependency and exchange relations between abuser and abused.
4 External stress.
5 Social isolation.
   (Pillemer, 1986; Godkin et al., 1989; Wolf and Pillemer, 1989)

The study showed that abusers were more likely to have mental and emotional problems, to abuse alcohol and to have been in hospital for psychiatric reasons. The study did not indicate that the perpetrator had been a victim of child abuse. Abused elders were not found to be more ill or functionally disabled than the control group. However, the abusers were likely to be dependent on their elderly victims. External events did not significantly differ between the two groups. The perpetrators had fewer overall contacts. This tended to isolate the victim.

There was general support for theories of elder abuse that related abuse to the problems of the abuser and the relationship between the abuser and the victim. The early family lives of the perpetrators were not unusually violent. Chronic economic stress and stressful life events played only a small part. Wolf and Pillemer (1989: 146) have reflected that 'the characteristics of the abuser, rather than those of the old person, may be strongly associated with violence against the elderly'. As a result of this model, the authors believe that they are nearing a consensus model. More research is required to see if the findings can be replicated. They are singular in that they run counter to the usually accepted view which depicts the victim as very dependent and the perpetrator as an overburdened caregiver.

The role of the physician

The progress that has occurred over the past ten years in bringing the problem of elder abuse and neglect to the attention of the public, professionals and politicians has taken place, by and large, without the involvement of the medical profession. (Wolf, 1988: 761)

The role of the GP . . . is of the utmost importance. (Eastman, 1984b: 75)

In Britain, remarkably little has been written about the physician and elder abuse; McCreadie (1991) does not mention the physician. Nor is it clear why this is the case: is it simply that the average physician is not interested in the ageing patient? There is plenty of anecdotal evidence for that. Or is it that public policy is still tentative? Horrocks (1988) revealed that in Britain the Department of Health possessed a procedural instrument for cases of elder abuse which had never been used.

A handful of essays from America has attempted to draw the attention of physicians to the increasing visibility of the abuse and neglect of elderly people. Solomon (1983: 151–2), in describing the way in which physical complaints frequently mask underlying psychological or psychiatric problems, stresses that 'physicians are frequently unable to identify the results of victimization and abuse of the elderly.' Hooyman (1983: 382) went further and maintained that physicians encounter abused elderly people, 'but do not take any action'. O'Brien (1986: 620) reported that 'most physicians felt abuse was difficult or very difficult to detect' and in a survey that he conducted in 1984, he found that 70 per cent of physicians in Michigan and North Carolina were unaware of mandatory reporting and in consequence under-reported.

Taler and Ansello (1985), like Solomon, suggested that victims of elder abuse usually present to their physicians with complaints of a medical problem. They listed physical indicators as:

> bruises or welts on the shoulder, back, chest or arms in various stages of healing; rope burns around the wrists or ankles; hemorrhaging beneath the scalp and multiple fractures of the long bones or ribs are all signs of purposeful injury. On the other hand, pallor, dehydration and weight loss may not be evidence of willful neglect . . . These findings are common in confused and immobile patients. Bedsores should also be evaluated in context and may not represent neglect. (Taler and Ansello, 1985: 111)

They wrote also of behavioural indicators such as generalized fear on the part of the victim. Hostility, excessive concern, improbable explanations of symptoms or a harping on the burdens of caregiving may be behavioural clues to an abusing caregiver. Locks and barriers, the position of the elderly person's bedroom, lack of assistive devices for moving about, absence of a bedside commode, when the need for one seems appropriate, the existence of unrepor-ted drugs for sedation might all be relevant as environmental indicators.

Taler and Ansello (1985) also comment on counselling the patient and caregiver. The caregiver should not be present during a discussion about potential abuse or neglect with the victim. If allegations or suspicions are aroused about the behaviour of the caregiver, unless immediate counselling and follow-up can be offered, it is wise not to discuss the matter with the caregiver at all at this stage. If the matter needs immediate attention then 'pejorative or accusatory language should be avoided' and follow-up and counselling arranged immediately (1985: 111).

The Council on Scientific Affairs of the American Medical Association (AMA) published a report on abuse and neglect in 1987. In recognizing the complexity of the problem, it strongly recommended that intervention and management of abuse cases should be multidisciplinary. A typical team would be a primary care physician, a nurse, a social worker, a psychiatrist, a psychologist, a lawyer, a police officer and a case data coordinator. The need for harmonious relations between the agencies was emphasized by Wolf and Pillemer in 1989.

Writing in the *Illinois Medical Journal*, Cochran and Petrone (1987) provided an introduction to the identification and treatment of abuse cases. They included a classification table of types of abuse, quoted from the 1987 AMA report and provided a list of some 30 indicators. They suggest that if a physician suspects abuse, there are three points to be borne in mind. First, identification and treatment are complicated because of embarrassment or reluctance to admit the abuse. Secondly, victims have probably been traumatized over a long period of time and may therefore exhibit passivity, low self-esteem and indecision. Thirdly, the abused elder must make his or her own decisions. Cochran and Petrone (1987: 246) stress the need for:

privacy when interviewing;
the need to listen before beginning the physical assessment;
document the history of the injury;
observe the emotional status of the patient;
discuss the relevant services which would be required for an adequate package of care;
and make arrangements for follow-up.

Wolf (1988) has maintained that physicians must be able to recognize the potential risk factors and symptoms of abuse. They should become familiar with elder abuse laws and, as members of a multidisciplinary team, they can both educate other professional groups about the physical problems of old age and act as a link with the health service or medical care system. Wolf (1988: 761) believes also that:

Physicians have an obligation to make known their opinions about the laws, especially regarding some of the controversial aspects that affect medical practice, such as mandatory reporting, competency, professional judgement, patient self-determination, immunity and liability.

Bloom et al. contributed a paper for physicians which also stressed the importance of documentation. This, they emphasized, was an essential first step towards necessary involvement. 'Physicians . . . have a special responsibility to promote [a] greater awareness [of elder abuse] and effective interventions' (1989: 44).

In Britain, Hocking (1988) pointed out that, in cases of non-accidental injury (NAI), everyone in the household is at risk. The physician as coordinator of the primary care team has a central role in preventing the existence of NAI. The case notes of people in stressed households should be marked to facilitate a regular (monthly) review.

Legislative developments in America

It may be helpful to conclude this overview with a brief consideration of the principal legislative developments in the USA, bearing in mind that in Britain there is no legal requirement to report cases of abuse. In the USA, 43 states, by 1989, had passed mandatory reporting laws since the federal elder abuse legislation of 1981 (McCreadie, 1991). Much of this legislation was based on child abuse legislation and most of it was applicable to all adults, although it had been designed for and primarily used in relation to elder abuse. Much of the early legislation was drafted quickly and without recourse to expert advice. Because of this there is a lack of standardization in terminology; abuse and neglect may be used interchangeably.

Definitions of 'elderly' are not always helpful, particularly where, as in the case of Florida, ageing is a form of disability. Their statute defines an aged person as one 'suffering from the infirmities of aging as manifested by organic brain damage, advanced age, or other physical, mental or emotional dysfunctioning' (Crystal, 1986: 339).

Definitions of elder abuse are not clear in the legislation either. (Salend et al. (1984) and Fulmer and O'Malley (1987) among others have drawn attention to this.) Distinctions between different types of abuse are frequently not included. The majority of states failed to make provision for a central database of reports. Some required only physicians to report. Some required some professionals and not other professionals to report. Some required both professionals and lay persons to report. Some provided immunity. Some included provisions about confidentiality. All required names and addresses of victims and perpetrators. Not all laws included penalties for mistreatment or failure to report. Some specified penalties for one and not for the other. The work of identification and prevention has been under-resourced.

Some practice issues
Nevertheless, in some states teams of workers have been appointed as Adult Protective Agencies. Assessment tools have been developed. In most cases, if there is suspicion of abuse, the law requires investigation as soon as possible (within, say, 24 to 72 hours), with a service plan elaborated immediately if the case is proved (Bennett, 1990e).

Kosberg (1988) drew attention to the result of most of the legislation as it stands, namely that it focuses on abuse after it has occurred and necessitates both detection and reporting. This caused him to urge the development of assessment protocols for carers in order to prevent elder abuse.

Salend et al. (1984) urged the importance of immunity for those reporting cases and the necessity for assessment guidelines which could be used in a sensitive and informed way. They also raised the question of the rights and well-being of the alleged victim (as do Taler and Ansello, 1985; Mildenberger and Wessman, 1986) and the fundamental question of a thorough conceptualization of what should be reported and why.

Daniels et al. (1989) regard the mandatory reporting laws as merely symbolic. In their study of the operation of elder abuse laws in Alabama, they found considerable scepticism among physicians about the reporting procedures. In fact, they confirm O'Malley et al. (1979) and O'Brien (1986) in finding that physicians as a group tend to under-report cases of abuse. Crystal (1986) reported that a Syracuse study in 1983 found that only 2 per cent of reports came from physicians. Three-quarters were uncertain as to how to report cases. Most were uncertain about their own immunity in reporting cases. Eighty per cent felt that prompt action would not be taken by service agencies. Daniels et al. (1989) point out that most politicians in enacting this legislation assumed that service delivery would be accomplished with available resources. This they regard as a serious flaw in the elder abuse legislation, as do Crystal (1986) and Wolf and Pillemer (1989).

It is therefore not surprising that in 1990 the US House of Representatives issued a Select Committee on Aging report entitled: 'Elder Abuse: A Decade of Shame and Inaction' (US House of Representatives: Select Committee on Aging, Sub-committee on Health and Long Term Care, 1990). This led to five more states setting up adult protection services. The Committee found that in terms of funding their adult protection services, the states spent an average of $3.10 on each elderly resident compared with $45.03 for each child resident (McCreadie, 1991).

There is, however, evidence to show that amendments can be made to existing legislation. Foelker et al. (1990) describe how in Texas an amendment was passed in 1987 to sharpen the legislation at the point of caregiver responsibility and caregiver neglect. They also achieved an expansion in both staffing and financial resources.

Canada and Britain

The situation in Canada and Britain is very different. Sharpe (1988) and Gnaedinger (1989) list a variety of charges in relation to abuse and neglect that could be laid under the Canadian Criminal Code and the Power of Attorney Act (1979). Under Canadian law in 1988, there was still no legal protection for an endangered and mentally incapable adult (Sharpe, 1988: 64). There was the possibility of protective intervention under the Mental Health Act and the Mental Incompetency Act provided for guardianship of the person and the estate of a mentally incompetent adult.

Gnaedinger (1989: 11) has suggested that 'the primary hindrance to reporting cases of elder abuse is the reluctance of the victims to admit to their own abuse.' She has also described the basic difficulties of mandatory reporting: the violation of family privacy, the minimization of complaints because of lack of interest by elderly people, disbelief, fear of accusing the perpetrator, being sued and lack of awareness. She has also noted that, since 1988, the federal government has funded six federal departments to prepare a national approach to family violence. By 1989 special legislation concerned with adult abuse, including elder abuse, existed in Ontario, Nova Scotia, Prince Edward Island, New Brunswick and Alberta.

In Britain, when an elderly person is considered to be at risk or mentally incapacitated, the law in relation to decision-making on his or her behalf is fragmented and complex. Remarkably little has been written on the subject. The first text available in Britain on English law and elderly people was by Griffiths et al. in 1990. It is necessary to move towards positive legislative developments in this area of human vulnerability and this theme will be returned to later in the book.

Conclusion

This brief overview is intended as an introduction to the chapters that follow. In them, we will consider the clinical aspects of elder abuse and neglect, the implications for the reform of English law, the implications for social work, nursing, clinical psychology and general practice. We will consider the issues involved in assessment, the relationships between carers and dependants and the sociology of elder abuse. Finally, we will discuss the way forward to good practice. Kosberg (1988: 49) provides us with a summary:

> Elder abuse will continue as long as ageism and violence exist . . . Elder abuse results from the dynamic interaction between personal, family, social and cultural values, priorities and goals. Therefore, attention must be given to those factors which, although not causing abuse, contribute to its likelihood: poverty and unemployment, lack of community resources, intra-family cycles of abuse, and personal hedonism.

It is in the area of 'intra-family cycles of abuse' particularly that more information is required. Elder abuse has often been compared or related to child abuse (Rathbone-McCuan, 1980; Eastman, 1984b). This is because the relationship between the carer or care-taker and the elder (according to Finkelhor and Pillemer, 1988: 248) is often thought to have 'a parent–child character in the extreme dependency of the elder'. They have gone on to point out that in some states in the USA the same agencies handle both child and elder abuse cases. Both problems were first identified by professionals working with both populations. This differs from spouse abuse which was first identified by the women's movement through volunteers and private agencies. They also make the point that both child and elder abuse are social problems which have been 'medicalized' by health professionals, who have their own intervention strategies established within health care institutions. This is not the case with spouse abuse.

To press the parallel between child and elder abuse is dangerous. We have already noted earlier that much elder abuse is not committed by a carer against a dependent victim. In many cases, as Wolf and Pillemer have shown, it is the abuser who may be dependent. Furthermore, even if the elder is dependent, the relationship is different. Parents have a legal responsibility for children who are minors, but in most cases adult children do not have a legal responsibility for their parents.

> Older persons are considered to be independent, responsible individuals. Moreover, most [of the] elderly do not live with their children (fewer than 1 in 10 do so), and there is only a small and disappearing social expectation that they should do so . . . The elderly are in a very different structural relationship to their abusers than are children. (Finkelhor and Pillemer, 1988: 249)

They go on to reaffirm that elder abuse is often spouse abuse that has been going on for years, and they refer to their Boston study, which has already been mentioned. Even when the perpetrator and the victim are not husband and wife, the situation of elder abuse is more akin to spouse abuse than to child abuse. 'Both parties are independent adults; they are living with each other by choice; the elder is connected to the abuser by ties of emotional allegiance and perhaps economic dependence, but certainly has more social, psychological and economic independence than a child would have' (Finkelhor and Pillemer, 1988: 250). For this reason, Finkelhor and Pillemer (1988) – and Breckman and Adelman (1988) – are convinced that further studies in family violence are required.

Finally, Wolf and Pillemer (1989: 148–50) have recommended in relation to elder abuse victims and their families that:

1 A need exists for specific elder abuse programmes.
2 An elder abuse project should be located in, or affiliated to, a high profile community agency.
3 An elder abuse project should offer direct services.
4 Inter-agency coordination is critical for the success of the project.
5 The existence [in the USA] of a mandatory reporting statute, with insufficient financial appropriations, can hinder elder abuse intervention.

They also recommend direct interviews with abused elders and with perpetrators; and moving away from agency samples to population surveys, based on control-group designs. They regard it as necessary to focus in research on the consequences of abuse; the context of abusive acts; why abusive children come to live with their parents; the relation between physical abuse and parent–child relationships and child-rearing practices. They press for further definition of what is meant by 'case resolution' and 'neglect', and for further investigations into spouse abuse.

Wolf, Pillemer and their colleagues have arrived at these conclusions after a decade of rigorous fieldwork and research. In so doing, they have provided an agenda for action and research. Ideally, what is now required is a series of cross-national projects based on compatible designs, which can begin to create a database of international and meaningfully coherent proportions. In this context, we would undoubtedly further benefit in Britain from a rigorous examination of 'neglect' within the community, of abuse and neglect in institutions and of the prevalence of abuse and neglect. A great deal of the debate until now has centred on physical, psychological and material abuse within the domestic environment, but the delicate question of elder abuse and neglect in institutions requires rigorous study and resolution also. In terms of human vulnerability, it is unacceptable that investigations of this nature should apparently be discouraged. There have been so many official inquiries in Britain into alleged mistreatment in residential institutions, and so many adverse findings, that we now require a responsible and analytical commentary on the experience of elderly people in residential institutions in the statutory, voluntary and private sectors.

2
Clinical Presentation

Peter Decalmer

Disease is very old, and nothing about it has changed. It is we who change, as we learn to recognize what was formerly imperceptible.

> Jean Martin Charcot (French neurologist, 1825–93),
> *De l'expectation en medécine*

Elder abuse is a serious and much-neglected subject. In terms of recognition and debate it has followed the course of child abuse that occurred in the 1970s and the development of knowledge about family violence in the 1980s. The first published medical papers described cases of abuse of elderly patients who were being abused by relatives. They identified mental incompetence as an important factor, discussed carer stress and described the phenomena as 'Granny Battering' or 'Granny Bashing' (Baker, 1975; Burston, 1975): the reception from fellow professionals was one of dismay and disbelief. By the 1980s, Eastman, the British Geriatrics Society (BGS) and others in Britain, together with researchers in the USA and Canada, raised the profile of the abused elder person and the perpetrators. Unfortunately, but understandably, many made the mistake of comparing it to child abuse, with which it has very little in common. Our knowledge of various forms of elder abuse is rapidly expanding, but much of the information is confusing and contradictory. This chapter will attempt to clarify the important issues concerning various types of clinical presentation.

There is obvious under-reporting of old age abuse; the primary reasons for this are:

1 There is a failure to understand the size, severity and nature of the problem which is made impossible by the numerous and often all-embracing definitions.
2 The paucity of controlled studies, and a preponderance of case reporting which has been the most frequently used method of study, has produced difficulties in estimating the incidence and prevalence of the various forms of abuse and neglect.

It is interesting to note that 17 years have passed since Baker's first intervention and we still have no incidence or prevalence studies in the United Kingdom. In 1990, the US House of Representatives, as reported in Chapter 1, issued a Select Committee on Aging report entitled 'Elder Abuse: A Decade of Shame and Inaction'. They also made pertinent comments about the gross underfunding in this area.

The population

The size of the elderly population in Britain is going to rise very rapidly in the next 50 years. We know that the most significant rise will be among the over-75s, particularly those over 85 and they will have a number of important characteristics: mentally disordered, physically ill, lonely, poor people who are living alone (Jolley and Arie, 1978; Arie and Jolley, 1982). As a group they are socially isolated. The problem of the number of demented people, and the consequent demands on carers, is increasing dramatically because of demographic changes. In Britain, there will be a 16 per cent rise in the number of demented people by the year 2005 (see Table 2.1). The growing demands made on the carers are also increasing as a result of community care legislation and there will be a levelling out of the number of carers available to take up these responsibilities. This will compound many of the problems of caring for elderly people and make elder abuse and neglect far more likely (Jorm, 1990). The projected figures for the developed countries demonstrate this pattern (see Table 2.1 for the figures for Great Britain, USA and Canada). Another significant factor is the survival rates for demented people. These rates have risen steadily over the past 20 years (Table 2.2).

Table 2.1   *Projected increases in population and number of dementia cases in Great Britain, Canada and USA*

	Population (in thousands) 1980	% Increase over 1980 value				
		1985	1990	1995	2000	2005
Great Britain						
Total population	55,945	0.32	0.44	0.65	0.73	0.51
Population >60	11,271	3.21	3.09	1.77	1.65	3.06
Dementia cases	–	6.83	11.27	13.22	14.40	16.05
Canada						
Total population	24,090	5.55	11.03	15.89	20.08	23.84
Population >60	3,305	14.16	25.89	34.88	43.53	57.71
Dementia cases	–	15.51	32.27	48.71	64.02	79.39
USA						
Total population	227,738	4.52	9.09	13.57	17.78	21.71
Population >60	35,849	8.19	14.01	16.33	19.39	27.12
Dementia cases	–	7.59	16.91	25.74	33.47	40.03

Table 2.2 *Survival rates for dementia patients*

Age	Average survival rate (in years)
<65	8.3–8.7
65–75	6.2–8.4
75–84	4.5–5.9
86+	3.8–5.0

Source: Jorm (1990).

Note: Blessed and Wilson (1982) estimated survival rates for dementia patients at 18 months.

The role of the clinician

The physician's role, in the view of the British Geriatrics Society, is central in diagnosis and in the planning of programmes of care and prevention in relation to elder abuse, yet there are few details about this role and little published work defining it. McCreadie's (1991) review does not even mention the physician, yet general practitioners (GPs) and hospital doctors show great interest when the cases are identified and will become heavily involved when clinically or locally asked to do so.

The problem arises when the physician is asked to report cases of elder abuse. O'Malley et al. (1979) found under-reporting to be a real problem, only 2 per cent of cases in his sample being reported by physicians. Many were uncertain as to what to do, and concerned about their own medico-legal position (Crystal, 1986). Eighty per cent felt that prompt action would not be taken by service agencies. Many physicians felt that they need guidelines on how to act; where, and with whom, responsibility lies and strategies and advice on management for these cases. Social policy is still very tentative, even appearing at times to lack interest in elderly people. So the doctor's role in this area, other than a traditional caring one, is undefined. The medico-legal responsibilities and dilemmas include confidentiality of medical information, third-party responsibility, when and how to inform the police, and how best to work with non-health-related agencies, both statutory and voluntary, who are involved with the case. Clear guidance from the professional bodies is needed. These must, however, work in harmony with nationally and locally agreed guidelines for good practice in both health and social services. The doctor, of course, may well be responsible for the health of both the abused elder and the abuser. This presents the physician with a potential advantage or a conflict of interest.

Classification

Wolf and Pillemer are among the few workers who have attempted to approach this problem systematically. The classification that is used in this chapter is their classification of abuse and neglect, already referred to in Chapter 1 (Wolf and Pillemer, 1989).

1 *Physical abuse*: the infliction of physical harm, injury. Physical coercion, sexual molestation and physical restraint.
2 *Psychological abuse*: the infliction of mental anguish.
3 *Material abuse*: the illegal or improper exploitation and/or use of funds or resources.
4 *Active neglect*: the refusal or failure to undertake a caregiving obligation (including a conscious and intentional attempt to inflict physical or emotional distress on the elder).
5 *Passive neglect*: refusal or failure to fulfil a caretaking obligation (excluding a conscious and intentional attempt to inflict physical or emotional distress on the elder). (Wolf and Pillemer, 1989)

Attention needs to be paid to assessing the severity of the abuse. Fisk (1991) suggests parameters such as degrees of intimacy and levels of victim distress as possible ways of doing this. But there remains the issue of subjective assessment of the victim and assessor and much work needs to be done on this (see also Fulmer and O'Malley, 1987; Steinmetz, 1990).

A recent definition, which embraces the problems of distress and a subjective and detailed assessment, is described in Johnson (1991). She uses a holistic approach and defines what she calls 'elder mistreatment as self-or-other-imposed suffering, unnecessary to the maintenance of the quality of life of the older person by means of abuse and neglect caused by being overwhelmed' (1991: 4). It is used with a grid (Table 2.3) and is concerned with suffering, as a consequence of abuse, abuse and neglect as the means, and 'being overwhelmed' as the causal antecedent. This definition and the grid will be of use to clinicians when assessing cases individually and to managers who have to construct policy documents. As soon as the clinician starts to work with any of these classifications he/she will notice that many cases of abuse/neglect overlap.

When assessing a case of elder abuse for signs and symptoms, particularly if it is in a busy casualty department or ward, or when the person is inexperienced, a checklist of types of injuries/abuse can be very helpful. Just such a checklist, dealing with physical abuse, physical neglect, sexual abuse and emotional maltreatment, is given below. It is an *aide-mémoire* of signs and symptoms that can be used in conjunction with the assessment tool for nurses (see Chapter 5).

Table 2.3 *Indicators of possible elder mistreatment*

I PHYSICAL	II PSYCHOLOGICAL	III SOCIOLOGICAL	IV LEGAL
A Medication misuse	A Humiliation	A Isolation	A Material misuse
1 Absence	1 Shame	1 Involuntary withdrawal	1 Property mismanagement
2 Improper use	2 Blame	2 Voluntary withdrawal	2 Contract mismanagement
3 Adverse interaction	3 Ridicule	3 Inadequate supervision	3 Blocked access to property
4 Unnecessary use	4 Rejection	4 Improper supervision	4 Blocked access to contract
B Bodily impairment	B Harassment	B Role confusion	B Theft
1 Unmet medical needs	1 Insult	1 Competition	1 Stealing property
2 Poor hygiene	2 Intimidation	2 Overload	2 Stealing contracts
3 Ingestion problems	3 Fearfulness	3 Inversion	3 Extorting property
4 Rest disturbance	4 Agitation	4 Dissolution	4 Extorting contracts
C Bodily assaults	C Manipulation	C Misuse of living arrangements	C Misuse of rights
1 External injuries	1 Information withheld	1 Household disorganized	1 Denied contracting
2 Internal injuries	2 Information falsified	2 Lack of privacy	2 Involuntary servitude
3 Sexual assault	3 Unreasonable emotional deprivation	3 Unfit environment	3 Unnecessary guardianship
4 Suicidal/homicidal act	4 Interference with decisions	4 Abandonment	4 Misuse of professional authority

Source: Johnson (1991). Quoted with permission.

Note: See also Johnson (1991) for *Health Status Risk Assessment Evaluation Form, Glossary of Indicators of Elder Mistreatment* and *Evaluation Categories for the Health Status Risk Assessment.*

Checklist of possible physical indicators for types of physical abuse and neglect

Physical abuse
1 Unexplained bruises and welts:
   (a) on face, lips, mouth, on torso, back, buttocks, thighs
   (b) human bite marks in various stages of healing (it is advisable to note site of bruising)
   (c) clustered, e.g. forming regular patterns
   (d) reflection of shape of article used to inflict abuse, (e.g. electric cord, belt buckle)
   (e) different surface areas noted
   (f) regular appearance after absence weekend or vacation

2 Unexplained burns:
   (a) cigar, cigarette burns, especially on soles, palms, back or buttocks
   (b) immersion burns (sock-like, glove-like, doughnut-shaped, on buttocks or genitalia)
   (c) patterned like electric burner, iron etc.
   (d) rope burns on arms, legs, neck or torso

3 Unexplained fractures:
   (a) to skull, nose, ear (cauliflower ear), facial structure
   (b) in various stages of healing
   (c) multiple or spiral fractures

4 Unexplained lacerations or abrasions:
   (a) to mouth, lips, gums, eyes, ears
   (b) to external genitalia

5 Unexplained hair loss:
   (a) haemorrhaging beneath scalp
   (b) possible hair pulling, self or other
   (c) possible evidence of underlying severe head injury (subdural haematoma)

6 Evidence of past injuries:
   (a) Deformities – skull, nose and ears, cauliflower ear, hands (twisting reflex)
   (b) Contractures resulting from restraint and delay in seeking treatment
   (c) Dislocation, pain, tenderness and swelling (n.b. dislocation may be due to incorrect lifting)

Physical neglect
1 Consistent hunger, poor hygiene, inappropriate dress, including soiled clothing, unexplained weight loss, dehydration.
2 Consistent lack of supervision, especially in dangerous activities or long periods.
3 Constant fatigue or listlessness, unexplained or increasing confusion.
4 Unattended physical problems or medical needs, including urine burns or pressure sores.
5 Lost or non-functioning aids, e.g. glasses, dentures, hearing aids, walking aids and wheelchairs.
6 Over/under-medication.
7 Abandonment, immobility, hypothermia/indicating possible isolation.

Sexual abuse
1 Difficulty in walking or sitting.
2 Torn, stained or bloody underclothing.
3 Pain or itching in genital area.
4 Bruises or bleeding in external genitalia, vaginal or anal areas.
5 Unexpected and unreported reluctance to cooperate with toileting and physical examination of genitalia.

Emotional mistreatment
1 Habit disorder (sucking, biting, rocking etc.).
2 Conduct disorders (anti-social, destructive, self and others).
3 Neurotic traits (sleep disorders, speech disorders, inhibition of play).
4 Psychoneurotic reaction (hysteria, obsession, compulsion, phobias, hypochondria).

Note: It is necessary to assess whether symptoms and signs disappear in hospital or residential care over a period of time.
Source: Adapted from United States Department of Health and Human Services (1980) and Hocking (1988).

Physical abuse

When considering physical abuse it is useful to consider the victims as well as the abusers or perpetrators. It is important to try to identify certain characteristics in these two groups. We need to be aware of the common presentations that would alert professionals to the possibility of physical abuse. Hocking (1988) found that many of the patients presented with certain clues in the type of behaviour and injuries they sustained. We also have found in our studies (Decalmer et al., in preparation) similar characteristics.

Facial injuries
These include periodical bruising and bruising around the jaw caused by slapping; thumping marks to the ear causing haemorrhaging to the cartilage from twisting. Bruises can be roughly dated by colour as follows:

0–2 days:	swollen, tender
0–5 days:	red–blue
5–7 days:	green
7–10 days:	yellow
10–14 days:	brown
2–4 weeks:	clear

Case example
An 80-year-old married woman had had a 50-year close relationship with her husband, who was a very rigid man with marked obsessional traits. He was a life-long worrier who allowed her to make all the decisions. Four years ago she started to dement; this affected her speech, dressing and concentration. Her husband took over all aspects of her existence; she started to become resistive, and as the services which were provided – a home help, bath nurse, district nurse, social worker and community psychiatric nurse – were slowly dissipated, he started to hit her across the face and around her hands, arms and shoulders, and as well there were kick marks. He accepted that he was hitting her and was found to be clinically depressed. Her resistance continues today, even in continuing care, and she will hit out whenever attempts are made to bath or toilet her.

Thumb and finger marks
These are most commonly found on the shoulders, sternum and arm, due to restraining the patient, preventing him or her from wandering and trying to dress a resistive patient.

Case example
A 76 and 74-year-old couple were devoted to each other for 40 years; eight years ago she started to dement, and had problems with language, poor short-term memory and distractibility. He became ill with cancer; it was noticed that when she came to the day hospital she was extremely distressed and started to cower. Periodical and facial bruising was noted as well as haemorrhage on hands and arms from holding down. Fingers were dislocated from forcing and twisting, similarly with bruising around the ears from twisting. She was admitted for observation. His reasons were that he lost his temper when she wandered off while he dressed her, or during feeding times, or waiting for the ambulance to take her to the day hospital.

Urine rash
A urine rash is very common and this leads to pressure sores which develop around the umbilicus, front of abdomen and groin region, as well as the buttocks. Other areas include the internal malleus of the leg and heel. Arthritis of legs, particularly the knee joint, is common, due to forced restraint or inactivity. Incontinence at home may well be a sign of neglect or physical restraint.

Case example

A 74-year-old woman, living in her own home with her family, suffered from dementia and arthritis. She was cared for in a spartan back room and never had any encouragement to walk, becoming more immobile daily. Tablets were only given intermittently and, because of the harsh way in which she was spoken to, she would refuse medication as an act of defiance. No attempt was made to ensure continence and she was locked in the room during the day. As a result, when she was referred with 'behavioural problems' severe pressure sores were found all over her lower abdomen. The family ultimately rejected her and she was placed in residential care. Involvement with her family ceased, but they had acquired her home.

Kick marks and fractures

Kick marks on the legs are very common and we have found that in many of our cases of physical abuse, injuries to fingers and thumbs from twisting and fractures of the ribs are not uncommon.

Case example

A 74-year-old man developed vague paranoid ideas while he was in hospital just as he was about to return home. He seemed very frightened, but would not discuss why. His wife seemed quite an aggressive personality; both seemed to consume alcohol moderately heavily. On physical examination suspicious bruising was noted on his body; on chest X-ray fractured ribs were noted, both old and new. It was his 94-year-old mother who eventually revealed that she would counsel her son-in-law when his wife beat him up in one of her rages; this occurred at monthly intervals. It was found that she beat him when they were drunk and the case only came to light on routine physical examination.

Psychological effects

With physical injuries come psychological consequences; often the patient is extremely distressed or resistive. Cowering when approached is a common feature. The faces may be expressionless; the reasons for this include dementia, dysphasia from a variety of causes, or just giving up in the face of emotional or physical trauma. Some extreme examples include severe injury or torture.

Case example

A 76-year-old widow was living alone with a moderate degree of dementia and heart failure and was housebound. She would invite local children to enter her home to run errands for her, such as shopping for cigarettes. Money and personal possessions initially went missing. Then a particularly vicious gang of youths became involved. They tortured this woman to extract money, particularly with savings. The method used was to burn her legs with the electric fire. She was admitted to hospital with severe burns and later admitted to an aged person's home for her own protection. The culprits were never caught.

Severe physical abuse

This combines physical and psychological abuse with horrifying consequences. As well as torture, we have seen several cases of kidnap which again included severe physical and psychological abuse; and professionals can easily find themselves coerced into either cooperating or turning a blind eye.

Case example

A 72-year-old widower was living at home alone with a moderate degree of dementia. His main hobby was breeding budgerigars. His short-term memory deteriorated markedly when he was put in situations of anxiety. His family were very ambivalent about him going home alone, despite considerable support and his wish to manage alone. One weekend on a routine invitation he stayed at their home for a break. Instead of letting him go home he was placed in a private rest home and abandoned. When he became aggressive demanding to leave, he was sectioned under the Mental Health Act in another district and not transferred back to his hospital of origin. Very soon after admission he was transferred to a long-stay Elderly Severely Mentally Infirm (ESMI) ward where he stayed permanently. The family immediately disposed of the flat.

Signs of neglect

Other clues include signs of neglect, e.g. evidence of dehydration, unused, dirty food, stained glasses, hearing aids that do not work. Rooms in which these patients live are stark and cold, they may have locks and be sparsely furnished, with inadequate bedding and no toilet facilities. What is most noticeable is that the room is out of keeping with the rest of the household.

Case example

A 68-year-old man was suffering from moderate Alzheimer's disease and had a very poor short-term memory, nominal aphasia, and incontinence. His wife refused to accept the irreversibility of the condition and spent most of her energies taking him to other specialists both medical and non-medical. Some of the non-medical treatments were highly dubious, such as ointment to rub into his scalp to cure dementia. When she finally realized the course of his illness, she requested that he be locked up in a ward to ensure that no harm would happen to him. This was clinically inappropriate and illegal. The family refused all other offers of help and eventually found a nursing home with locked facilities. He was even tied into a Buxton chair to prevent him from wandering. This satisfied his family. He died within two months of his admission.

Sexual abuse

A number of cases come to light each year of adult children, usually male, who are having an incestuous relationship with their elder, usually a mother. As the elder starts to dement, the consent is less obvious and often physical injury described above is observed. One of the dilemmas facing the professionals is who is the original abuser. Many of these cases started out as child abuse cases, and now there is a role reversal.

Case examples
A 69-year-old woman attending a day centre was becoming increasingly forgetful and frail. When washing her she would talk about her son having sex with her and she was noted to have perineal bruising. The sleeping arrangements, one bedroom only, suggested a long-standing relationship. She became more damaged in physical terms and had a high dependency need on her son. Emotionally she had difficulty in coping. Sensitive counselling has led to a more normal relationship and no further abuse has been observed.

A 74-year-old widow who suffered from alcohol problems was found by her 70-year-old brother, who moved in with her. He used alcohol to bribe his way into her bed and resume an earlier incestuous relationship. She became so distressed by this that her alcoholism deteriorated to such an extent that she was admitted. This solved the problem. Alcohol abuse is found to be a very common factor which accompanies sexual abuse.

It is useful to bear in mind that sexual assault needs to be considered; evidence of bruising on the perineum, pain on micturition, vaginal bleeding and discharge are ominous clues. Unusual presentations must not be forgotten. These include referral to a haematologist with unexplained bruising, families going to their GP with vague symptoms, requesting tranquillizers or placement in residential care.

Case example
A 74-year-old woman was referred with increasing confusion and dementia. On physical examination, a vaginal discharge was noted and bleeding of the perineum. Her husband was found to be forcing her to have sexual intercourse because this was the only expression of love he had left. She no longer understood what was happening and was being physically hurt. The emotional trauma was excessive as well.

The patients themselves may try to indicate the problem with frequent presentations to GPs of vague aches and pains. However, the elder may be labelled as neurotic or senile, even paranoid, if they make accusations of abuse against the alleged perpetrator.

Psychological abuse

The lack of interest in elder abuse by psychologists is apparent in the literature. Life-span developmental psychologists have so far not found it significant to address themselves to the issue of elder abuse. This is understandable if their primary consideration is for the psychological development of older people themselves. Nevertheless, the clinical recognition of psychological signs and symptoms of elder abuse needs to be investigated in both the victim and the perpetrator. The victim feels deprived of emotional support, lonely, fearful, roleless, living at home with an adult child (Tomlin, 1989). There is often much more generalized fear on the part of the victim (Taler and Ansello, 1985), with 'cowering when approached' as an extreme example.

Case example
Mr and Mrs A were 76 and 74 respectively. They had been married for over 40 years and were totally devoted to each other. When young, they decided not to have children, in order to devote their time to each other. He was a scientist and she was a housewife. About eight years ago she started to develop senile dementia; she was scatter-brained, would not concentrate on anything, i.e. cooking, housework and dressing, and her husband had to take over these tasks. Holidays were a favourite part of their marriage, but gradually this became more difficult because Mrs A would wander out and become lost. Four years ago, Mr A developed cancer of the bowel and had successful surgery. Whilst convalescing, the first suspicions of trouble in

management appeared. Mrs A went into Part III accommodation as a paying guest. She became very frightened and was disruptive. He was hypercritical of the home. She returned to their home and started to attend the ESMI day hospital.

About three years ago we noticed a change in her behaviour. She became very agitated, cowered and cried a great deal. We noticed bruising on her face and body and at the same time her behaviour became more distressed. She was admitted for assessment. Mr A was becoming frailer and denied any abuse other than having to hold her when dressing. Even on the ward he would spend the day and most of the evening visiting her. We counselled both of them and shared the care.

Many of these patients are found to be immobile, incontinent, aphasic and dementing (Horrocks, 1988). Rathbone-McCuan (1980) found these victims to be female, functionally dependent with a history of psychiatric illness, alcoholism and abusive behaviour by the abused person, often with marked retardation in movements. There was evidence of intra- and inter-generational conflict, as well as a background of intra-family conflict. The victim was often living with the abuser (Gesino et al., 1982).

Pillemer and Wolf (1986) found a very interesting feature in their study that men outnumbered women in the violence perpetrated between couples. This often represented long-standing, intra-marital conflict where male violence and psychological abuse was a frequent occurrence early in the marriage. This role was reversed later in the relationship, especially where there was concomitant physical disability, a strong element of control and even revenge and poor communication between the parties (Homer and Gilleard, 1990a).

Case example

A 76-year-old man lived with his wife. He suffered from alcoholic dementia and below-knee amputation of his right leg. His wife worked; she was 65 and refused to give up her job. It was noticed that he was very frightened of her, which was very 'out of character' and would cower when she approached. She bragged that he had been free with his fists, especially on a Saturday night, at the beginning of the marriage, and now it was her turn. It was the language he understood. She subjected him to screaming and yelling outbursts, and eventually rejected him totally in order to live her own life.

The victim can have the feeling that he or she is less than human, subjected to infantilization: 'I feel as if I am just another child my daughter looks after, but with her it is just a duty.' There is a strong feeling of deprivation and loss among victims, especially those having to give up their homes to live with members of the family. There is a loss of independence, space and ownership. This is replaced by feelings of being a burden, loss of role, even competition for affection. If this situation deteriorates further, the victim feels that his or her place within the family lessens, leading to isolation, removal of choice or even exclusion from decision-making, with the sense that 'they no longer count' and the family 'knows best'. If the elder is demented, the family comment frequently becomes 'they don't know what's going on anyway, so why bother worrying them with making decisions?' This leads to intense feelings of worthlessness, depression and, in some cases, aggression.

The psychological abuse may go one step further where victims are imprisoned in their home, locked in the house or a room. Examples abound where the room has been found to be locked on the outside, poorly heated, with no furniture, poor amenities, dirty and with no toilet or washing facilities. The person is often locked in this room at night and becomes incontinent. During the day the locked door becomes a form of punishment. When elderly people treated this way are allowed into the family circle, they are virtually mute and remain on the periphery. They will be surprised if addressed and remain withdrawn, silent or depressed.

Case examples

An 82-year-old woman who suffered from a moderate degree of dementia was moved precipitously after discharge from hospital to the family home, where she lived in a back room, with no heating, carpet or furniture other than a bed. She was locked in her room for up to six hours a day. When she was brought on show, the family would talk about her as if she was not there, discussing in front of the grandchildren their grandmother's supposed incontinence. These grandchildren treated her with indifference just as her children did and would just ignore her, treating her as if she was a piece of furniture. The lady was mute, withdrawn and hopeless when she went to an ESMI Day Hospital and eventually to a rest home. Here this lady became transformed; she smiled and talked to her friends.

An 84-year-old woman was found in casualty with a head injury; a nurse noticed the address. She was living in a well-known violent household and had been hit and pushed to the floor during a family dispute. She fast got in the way. Her money was also being used to support the family alcohol abuse.

An 84-year-old widow living in sheltered housing suffered from severe dementia. The warden refused to supply medication for her heart failure. The GP asked her to go into an aged persons' home, which she refused. The GP then tried to have her admitted to hospital to confuse her further so she would be unaware of a placement in an aged persons' home. The Consultant refused, arranged regular medication and day care which successfully allowed this lady to remain where she wanted to be – at home.

When considering the psychological pressures which are suffered by perpetrators, it soon becomes evident that they are often under severe stress also (Hickey and Douglass, 1981a,b; O'Malley et al., 1983). Hirst and Miller (1986) found strong evidence of poor coping mechanisms, marital conflict and drug and alcohol problems, particularly in daughters.

Case example
A 72-year-old woman who suffered from moderate dementia, lived with her alcoholic daughter who was a nurse. This daughter became very frustrated with her mother's behaviour (which was to criticize her, especially for her alcohol and drug abuse). The daughter confined her mother to bed, refused her food and drink, until she weighed four stones. This occurred on three occasions when urgent hospitalization was required to save the woman's life because of malnutrition. She now has carer support and day hospital care. Even now she will eat little and has become an elderly anorexic.

There appear to be severe psychological pressures in relationships such as parent–child hostilities (Hickey and Douglass, 1981a,b). Some suggest that violence and psychological abuse occur because of learned behaviour. Some perpetrators are products of domestic violence or even, in certain cases, they are pathologically violent (O'Malley et al., 1983). Psychiatric illness in the formal sense was found among perpetrators by Horrocks (1988), depression being the commonest, together with anxiety neurosis. Lesser forms of stress were identified by Podnieks (1989), including a sense of hopelessness, rage and frustration, with verbal abuse more likely to occur in married elders who were living with an adult child (Rathbone-McCuan, 1980).

Two fascinating features emerge from such studies (for example, Shell, 1982), namely that abuse occurred when families had lived together for about ten years and that it was passed from one generation to another. This would suggest that the factors for psychological and physical abuse are complex and perhaps we are often dealing with the consequences of insidious breakdowns of relationships. Carers of elders who lose independence, interests, space and a feeling of self-worth as they become more frail physically and mentally, also lose their independence, interests, space and self-worth. They clash in these circumstances. If these issues are not identified and dealt with, abuse is extremely likely.

Material abuse

Breckman and Adelman (1988) suggest the following indications of financial abuse:

1 Sudden inability to pay bills.
2 Sudden or unexplained withdrawal of money from elderly person's account.
3 A disparity between the elder's assets and living conditions.
4 An unusual interest by family members in the elder's assets.

Case examples

A 76-year-old widower who suffered from dementia found that his ability to pay his bills, or manage his affairs, was becoming more difficult. He set up an Enduring Power of Attorney before he was found incompetent. However, as his dementia progressed and he found he was less able to organize his life (his bills remained unpaid, gas and electricity were disconnected), the family were reluctant to help him. Only the threat of legal action by social services allowed this man's financial situation to stabilize.

A 72-year-old widower was admitted as an emergency to an aged persons' home because of increasing wandering, physical deterioration and distress. On admission his aggression became severe as he had to go to the bank to collect £80 to give to his carers, otherwise he would be 'punished'. It transpired that this happened every day. It was impossible to know how long this embezzlement had been going on, but it was estimated for over a year. This case is currently being dealt with and the police have become involved. The man has been taken into care, with a Court of Protection Order. It was later found that his pension and attendance allowance were all used to support the carers; the money was not used for his benefit. He was poorly dressed, under-nourished and emotionally very frightened and disturbed.

A 68-year-old widow with severe chronic relapsing manic depressive psychosis was reliant on her son for her independence. She was quite wealthy and owned her own home. He moved in and then, by psychological pressure, such as threats to leave her or withdrawal of psychological support, he got her to sign over money and property. He eventually arranged to leave her, resulting in her admission to hospital and the loss of her home which he had sold; she then had to move into council housing. He withdrew, leaving her with no assets. She obstructed attempts to save her estate because of family loyalty; no action could be taken against him. She now lives alone penniless, needing carer support.

A 79-year-old woman with a moderate degree of senile dementia allowed her family to move into her house to look after her. They rented out their own home, took over her house, even moving in their children without the mother's permission and eventually gained control of all her assets. She felt her home was no longer her own. The situation deteriorated further when the family kept admitting her to hospital with a variety of vague symptoms, in order to obtain respite care and remove her from her home. They tried to force her into a long-stay bed (which they would not have to pay for).

The withholding of basic life resources and not providing care to the physically dependent is not uncommon (Sengstock and Liang, 1982) and often leads to institutional or 24-hour custodial care.

Eastman (1984b) found active abandonment to be common. A more subtle form is the removal of the choice of care available to the elder in order to ensure the cheapest option. This is very common where long-stay or continuing care beds are freely available. Tomlin (1989) found that the failure of a caretaker to withhold vital equipment (such as glasses, hearing aids, dentures or clothing), the ensuing involuntary isolation or sensory confinement, and the subsequent deterioration of the elder's mental state, are not uncommon in long-stay wards. This leads to a withdrawal of civil liberties (Hudson and Johnson, 1986). It is a common, neglected area in Britain, but has been addressed in some states in the USA and in some provinces in Canada. In the UK, the most flagrant abuses have been observed in residential care.

Case example

A 74-year-old woman, with a manic depressive illness, became mildly hypomanic and over-active and slightly disruptive. She had a lot of energy and would sleep only three or four hours at night. She was criticized by the other residents who were told that she would go berserk. The officers-in-charge wanted her admitted to hospital and removed from their home. They exaggerated her symptoms which distressed the family who were worried because the night staff complained because of their lack of sleep!

She was advised by the medical officer that admission would help. She refused treatment in her home. The rest of the home staff were not happy and the woman was removed to the nearest casualty department. A junior doctor was pressured into admitting her over the weekend. Much to her consultant's surprise, they met on the ward round. She accepted treatment (which she never refused), and she and her family found another more caring home for her where she lives happily. The original home have never understood, or cared, why she wanted to move.

These examples give the reader an outline of cases which are included under the category of material abuse. Many of these situations, however, go hand-in-hand with physical and psychological abuse, leading not infrequently to the older person losing his or her freedom and independence.

Active neglect

Active neglect is defined as the refusal or failure to undertake caregiving obligations, and includes a conscious and intentional attempt to inflict physical or emotional distress on elderly people (Wolf and Pillemer, 1989). This is very common in clinical practice but, although the multidisciplinary team is well aware of situations of neglect in which victims find themselves, it is very difficult to prove, legally or practically, in the case of financial abuse, or to do anything in terms of active intervention.

Little has been written about this type of abuse, often because of a lack of clarity over definitions. O'Malley et al. stated that active neglect is 'the deprivation by a caretaker of services, which are necessary for the elderly person to maintain their mental and physical health' (1979: 2). This does not highlight the active element which is so important in the definition we are using. Hall (1989) found numerous types of abuse in his study, but emphasized some important principles:

1 The failure to care for the person in the immediate living area.
2 Not seeking medical attention.
3 Failure to provide patient's maintenance, including hygiene, clothing and food.
4 Theft of personal resources.
1 and 2 constituted 30 per cent of cases.

Hall (1989) suggested that there was a core deterioration in the victim which made abuse more likely. We found in our study (Decalmer et al., in preparation) that more than 80 per cent of abused elderly people had been ill for more than one year. The core deterioration, especially in cases of dementia and depression, was well advanced, especially in terms of poor functioning and behavioural problems. One explanation is the way in which care services only refer when there is significant deterioration and early referral will need massive re-education, together with an alteration in treatment practices among GPs.

Medical abuse, such as withholding drugs to precipitate physical or psychiatric illness, either to engineer admission to hospital or to make the person more compliant when they are ill, is not uncommon. Medication may also be abused, especially when it is unsupervised or carelessly administered (Block and Sinnott, 1979).

Case example

A 72-year-old Polish man lived with his wife and physically disabled son. He suffered from dementia, depression, severe Parkinson's disease and chronic heart failure. Every time he was assessed, he was found isolated in a bedroom at the back of the house, with no medication and little food. He was admitted several times to hospital, immobile, in heart failure and in a severely neglected and under-nourished state. He always recovered and became mobile, only to return home and quickly revert to his previous desperate state. On closer investigation, it was found that his wife deliberately deprived him of food and medication in order to continue an incestuous relationship with her son, unimpeded.

Passive neglect

Passive neglect is defined as 'the refusal or failure to fulfil a caretaking obligation (excluding a conscious and intentional attempt to inflict physical or emotional distress on the elder)' (Wolf and Pillemer, 1989). This is far more common than was originally thought and little has been written about it.

The problem often arises insidiously, especially when the person develops an illness, such as dementia or chronic paranoid schizophrenia. Often coupled with it is a personality disorder which leads to the person being isolated or the illness itself leaves the client with a damaged personality. Thus, the families or carers may well attempt to help, but goodwill soon becomes exhausted. This will lead to abandonment, non-provision of food, or health-related services, because of inadequate knowledge, laziness, infirmity or disputing the value of prescribed services, leading to the kind of passive neglect which is shown in the following two case examples.

Case examples

A 74-year-old single man with multi-infarct dementia was referred after a stroke, with behavioural problems and a nominal aphasia. All that was known about him was his name, and that he worked on the fish-market. He had suffered from paranoid schizophrenia. No one ever bothered with him; he was mute and very depressed when we interviewed him. He had no family except people who were working in the home and they cared little, only wanting him away because he would not cooperate. He died from a further stroke on the ward. No further information was ever obtained about his history.

A 72-year-old single Irish man suffered from a multi-infarct dementia and frontal lobe damage. He was always a difficult man, but started to become violent and aggressive which was found to be due to neglect by the staff of the residential home. When we saw him he had not had a bath or change of clothes for six months. On examination, he was found to have pressure sores on his front and back below the umbilicus and both ankles, as well as carcinoma of his penis. His aggression was due to pain from his pressure sores and disappeared with treatment. He went to another home where he eventually died from his carcinoma, peacefully enjoying the last two years of life being eccentric.

Early warning signs of another type of neglect come when a person is living alone, with a family who are not committed to the care of the elder, other than in a perfunctory fashion, or when the family dynamics change, for example through illness to the key carer, and the old person becomes exposed.

Case example

A 78-year-old widow, who was always described as a difficult personality suffered from dementia and was partially sighted. She would only accept help from a daughter who was subnormal and from two carers. She was a fire risk due to excessive cigarette smoking. She was neglected by her daughter. Her GP wanted only to place her in hospital and never be visited. She had repeated episodes of hyperthermia because her daughter failed to buy fuel for her central heating boiler. She was under-nourished because her daughter failed to feed her. Eventually she developed a paranoid psychosis and was admitted on a section of the Mental Health Act, as she refused all offers of help because her daughter failed her. On admission she deteriorated and was admitted to long-stay.

The elderly person is often unknown to the GP or social services. The clinical and social picture is far from complete. It is not uncommon for the carer to be in dispute with the statutory agencies (such as home care or meals-on-wheels) as to who should administer medication or who should be the person responsible for the elder's care (O'Malley et al., 1984).

Case examples

A 72-year-old widow (Mrs S), living alone and suffering from paranoid schizophrenia, thought her husband's gravestone was used to build the house. Each night she chipped away the plaster trying to find the memorial. Each day the family papered over the cracks. The daughter provided her with food such as bread and biscuits, little else. No one else went into the house. Eighteen months before, she had gone to stay with a relative on holiday, and destroyed her bedroom in the same way. She was unknown to the GP or social services. The case came to light when her daughter became ill, suffering from a stroke, and was admitted to hospital. Mrs S's grandson became involved and could not even be bothered to bring her in food. The neighbours eventually contacted Mrs S's sister who alerted the psychogeriatric services. The severity of Mrs S's situation only appeared when she was admitted to hospital, where she eventually died after developing a carcinoma which required surgery.

A 94-year-old woman with a moderate degree of dementia was married to a 96-year-old man, who worked each day. He fed her on cat-food sandwiches and as a result she became very anaemic and had chronic diarrhoea. She was physically abused by a young lodger. On admission to hospital, she had a life-threatening anaemia due solely to a poor diet. On recovery from this she was still demented. She went home with carers monitoring her and placement in a day centre where she leads a full and contented life. The young lodger was charged with assault and theft but, although this form of abuse was dealt with, her husband began to assault her physically, and we have had to reassess the new presentation and set up a new clinical management plan based on the day hospital and rotational care.

Abuse of medication can take all forms: patients themselves often neglect to take tablets, or incorrectly take prescribed drugs, leading to disastrous results. Carers can often find medication an enormous trial and end up either not giving it or administering tablets inappropriately. The elder often becomes suspicious and disillusioned when he or she realizes that there is intra-family conflict and tends to isolate further, by becoming paranoid and refusing all offers of help. This often leads to total breakdown, precipitating hasty decisions by both family and statutory agencies.

Case examples

A 63-year-old recently married woman started to dement and had a poor short-term memory, some anxiety and a nominal aphasia. She developed paranoid ideas that she was being poisoned. The GP had advised her husband to mix a sedative in her food, resulting in some stew having a bitter taste, and she became unconscious. She never trusted her husband again and became very agitated and paranoid, requiring hospital admission.

A 74-year-old widow, living in warden-controlled flats, suffered from chronic paranoid schizophrenia and early dementia. For many years she had coped with her illness, even doing her shopping on a bicycle. She was a senile recluse. Over a two-year period she deteriorated and was very passively supported by an elderly sister, who went once a week to do her shopping over this period. Social Services became involved, but she found them too intrusive and a rumour was started that she was dangerous, and had a knife (a kitchen knife). Services were withheld. After complaints by neighbours, the GP alerted the psychogeriatric services. She was found in such a deteriorated state that faeces covered the floor and walls. The flat was over-run by vermin, including over 2,000 flies. She was admitted to hospital, treated for schizophrenia. She accepted full support and lived independently until her death five years later.

Institutional abuse

A person is often admitted as an 'urgency' to hospital or residential care and this may become a permanent placement, with the elder person never returning home. If the person is so physically or mentally frail that they require 24-hour care, this action may be inevitable. Where admission is a result of incomplete social or medical information, this is potentially very harmful. At present, this course of action is seen as the most expedient, and elderly people are forced into institutional care far too early, with the elder person feeling abandoned, cheated, and often abused, as no one has bothered to ask them what they want. Many feel that their wishes have been ignored. They are often victims of moral blackmail. It is to be hoped that the community care legislation will reduce the likelihood of this happening by allowing the older person to choose, putting the emphasis on staying at home and using the case management system, allowing the professional responsible to follow up the client.

Chapter 1 demonstrated clearly the lack of systematic research on abuse in institutions. Lau and Kosberg (1979) quoted a figure of 9.6 per cent who were abused in some way. Most of this group were severely physically and mentally impaired; many clients in institutions were deprived of their rights (Doty and Sullivan, 1983), and many have been found to be subject to financial abuse. In Britain, documented evidence is rare unless it reaches the point of official inquiry.

Case example

Two women were admitted to private nursing homes, both suffering from dementia, with a particular problem of wandering. Although Buxton chairs were not used, chairs were tilted back on blocks against a wall, so that the patient sat back at an angle and was unable to leave the chair, resulting in great distress. It was also noted that the last meal of the day was at 4.30pm, just sandwiches and a cup of tea. They were put to bed at 6–7pm. The diet was noted to be very bland, and there was no choice. On inspection of the kitchens, one tin of rice pudding and a giant size packet of fish fingers were found to be the stock items, together with one-third of a pint of milk for twelve residents. The excuse was that all food was obtained fresh from the corner shop. This was not confirmed. The issue of the chair blocks was only resolved when the Registration Board threatened to close the home.

There may be an attempt to place patients in institutions against their will, which is a violation of their liberty.

Case example

A 74-year-old woman was living in warden-controlled flats. The GP was coerced into trying to get her into a home against her will because she was dementing and was thought to be at risk if there was a fire in the building, but in fact this was not the whole truth. The wardens did not want the responsibility of a woman with a deteriorating dementia. It was proposed that she should be admitted to hospital to confuse her further and sedate her. It was proposed that on discharge she would be so confused that she would not realize she had moved to a private rest home. This course of action was refused and she willingly cooperated with ESMI day care and rotational care as she needed it, eventually requiring 24-hour residential care when she decided the time was right for her.

Misuse of financial resources and property takes place more often than one might expect in hospitals or residential and nursing homes.

The abuser may be a relative or relatives, or a member of staff. This is one example of many of these cases.

Case example

A 76-year-old patient, with terminal dementia was admitted to a continuing care ward. She was refused access to pocket money by the members of the family responsible for her monies. A family member was using it personally, giving the excuse of needing it for bus fares. This meant that the patient could not go out for a meal, or have her own toiletries, unless the ward subsidized her. It also meant that the person was unable to go on holiday.

It is difficult to assess how the changing patterns of continuing care in Britain will affect the plight of elderly people. The early findings are not encouraging. What is evident is the need for vigilant standard setting and the necessary legal powers to ensure that the elderly person is treated fairly.

Case example

A 78-year-old widow had severe dementia and behavioural problems, which included constantly asking for cigarettes up to 20 times per hour. She became more insistent and intrusive. A trained nurse who had worked on the ward for many years was observed on more than one occasion to shout and scream at this patient. Despite counselling on coping strategies, such as walking away, or time out for the patient or the nurse, the nurse ignored this and eventually was observed brutally hitting the patient. The nurse was dismissed. The patient and staff, with the aid of the multidisciplinary team, worked out a strategy of care. The patient's behaviour improved and the staff on the ward warmed to this lady. No further incidents have occurred.

Constant monitoring is needed, with particular attention being paid to unusual forms of restraint, feeding times and an inadequate diet of poor quality with lack of choice. Lack of privacy and loss of personal dignity must be avoided. Personal identity may quickly become lost when the regime itself becomes abusive.

Case example

A 76-year-old clergyman lived in a nursing home. It was standard practice to wash each person down leaving the door to the public corridor open. The nursing assistants were young and female. The embarrassment of the clergyman was great, but it was assumed by the institution that he was too far gone to notice. The clergyman used to visit his old parishioners regularly and even eat with them, behaving normally out of the institution.

A key factor is the need for regular training of all staff, paying particular attention to good caring and nursing practice, new techniques of behavioural management and the identification of situations likely to lead to abuse. Legislation is needed not only to be able to monitor standards, but to allow staff to report cases of abuse, without fear of victimization.

Abuse of the individual in institutions is common, but the commonest abuse of all is institutional abuse, where the environment, practices and rules become abusive in themselves. Historically, the work-house was a prime example of this type of situation, which must be met with constant vigilance. Institutional abuse does not depend on the size of the institution (Townsend, 1962).

False signs of abuse

It must be borne in mind that certain injuries sustained by patients are not signs of abuse, but are a part of their illness. Examples of this include cigarette burns in such diseases as Huntington's chorea and dementia.

Case example
A 56-year-old widow was suffering from Huntington's chorea. She lived with her son who was totally devoted to her. Despite a very high level of care, small circular ulcerated lesions were found on her buttocks and stomach. It was obviously caused by cigarette burns and concern of assault was expressed by the nurses. On careful investigation, including sensitive interviewing of her son, family and patient, it was found to be self-inflicted. Steps were taken to supervise her cigarette smoking.

These patients can have multiple burns and often falls or bruises due to movements. This does not mean that they have been subjected to active abuse. Care must be taken, nevertheless, that abuse is not occurring by passive neglect, and that the necessary prophylactic measures to prevent or reduce these incidents are being introduced and monitored.

Even cases involving alleged or suspected sexual abuse have to be very carefully assessed. Misleading or incomplete evidence may have tragic consequences and destroy, or severely damage, relationships.

Case example
An 82-year-old married woman was living in a private home. She was dysphasic and would just repeat words. Her husband visited

her every day and was very affectionate towards her; they had a very close relationship. Whenever he left she would become severely distressed. The staff became suspicious about sexual abuse because he would comment about her incontinence. This, coupled with her undue distress, made them suspect sexual interference. On careful assessment, no evidence of abuse was found. She was found to have a post-stroke depression. With treatment her mood lifted; she stopped crying. The couple's relationship deepened and the staff's anxiety was lifted when reassured.

Bed sores (Taler and Ansello, 1985) should also be evaluated in the same context, as they may or may not represent neglect.

Conclusion

Taking into account all these case examples and the classification of clinical abuse, it is obvious that a profile for the abused person and the abuser can be built up. During the 1980s, the characteristics of both victim and perpetrator began to emerge. The following represents a kind of consensus reached by 1988:

Profile of the abused person
 1 Female
 2 Over 75 years old
 3 Physically impaired, often chair or bedridden
 4 Mentally impaired, with child-like behaviour
 5 Socially isolated
 6 Depressed, with normalization and hypercritical attitude
 7 Ready to adopt the sick role
 8 Have thwarted many attempts for help in the past
 9 An abusing parent in the past
10 Too poor to live independently
11 Stubborn – last attempt to have some independence

Profile of the abuser
 1 Relatives who have looked after an elderly person for many years. Average length of care nine and a half years; of that group, 10 per cent have looked after an elderly person for more than 20 years.
 2 75 per cent live with victim
 3 Type of relative: 40 per cent spouse; 50 per cent children or grandchildren; daughter: marital conflict, ineffective coping mechanisms, alcohol and drug abuse patterns.
 4 75 per cent: 50 years-old; 20 per cent: 70 years-old

5 Relatives overburdened by stress; 48 per cent need victim's money; 50 per cent need victim's home
6 Socially isolated, having given up work
7 History of arrest/violence to property
8 Financial problems
9 Mental health: often a history of recent decline, depression, hostility, anger; 91 per cent clinically depressed; 63 per cent alcoholism, drug addiction
10 Poor communication between parties
11 Parent–child hostilities in early life
12 Whites are more common than blacks.

Sources: Shell (1982); Taler and Ansello (1985); Mildenberger and Wessman (1986); Pillemer (1986); Wolf (1988).

However, it is fairly clear that the most useful practical definition at present is that of Wolf and Pillemer (1989) as it provides a practical working point which does not bias the assessment either in favour of the abuser or the abused person, and allows scope for professionals to classify their cases of abuse, both practically and theoretically. It allows the clinician to plan case management of victims as well as allowing managers to set up the appropriate protocols and management structures for these cases, within the setting of social services and health strategies. It also provides a theoretical framework within which to carry out further research and investigations which will enable us to understand incidence and prevalence rates, as well as to determine more sensitive indicators of the types of abuse that occur among elderly people. Above all, it is now essential to conduct a number of controlled studies in the UK.

3
Elder Abuse and the Law

Aled Griffiths , Gwyneth Roberts and John Williams

There now exists a considerable body of evidence indicating that many elderly people suffer, or are vulnerable to, certain forms of abuse, often from those who care for them. Yet it seems that little use is made of legal and/or quasi-legal processes as a means of protection and redress. This gives rise to a number of key questions. Why are legal procedures so little used? Would more use of such procedures be a positive step forward? If so, how could existing procedures be better used, or better shaped, to protect elderly people from abuse?

There are several possible explanations for the existing situation. These include the reluctance of many victims to instigate and become involved in legal processes; the attitudes of professional workers towards elder abuse (Sutton, 1992); and the way in which elder abuse has been interpreted and defined. An additional factor is that a proportion of the elderly population suffers, to a greater or lesser degree, from mental incapacity. Where such individuals are subjected to abuse, particularly complex problems are likely to arise. Unfortunately, the law, in this respect, is 'fragmented, complex and in many respects out of date' (Law Commission, 1991: 5). It is impossible, for example, to provide a neat definition of legal capacity, and English law contains only a series of separate and quite discrete procedures which operate in different ways in different circumstances, depending upon whether an issue relates to the property and finance of the incapacitated person, or to his/her personal care and treatment. As a result, an elderly person may be deprived of autonomy and self-determination when he/she is capable of exercising them; or may be left without proper protection in situations where he/she is most vulnerable, such as, residential care. A study by the Royal College of Nursing, reported in *The Independent* on 27 April 1992, points to sub-standard nursing care in some residential homes for the elderly. A survey of more than 230 nursing managers and community nurses found that half of them thought that elderly people were wrongly placed in residential care and should have been nursed either in their own homes or in a nursing home (Royal College of Nursing, 1992).

Evidence suggests that some elderly victims of abuse refuse to take legal action against an alleged perpetrator because they fear retaliation at some future date, or because they wish to protect the abuser against punishment or liability (Powell and Berg, 1987). These findings may be given too much weight, however. Not long ago, similar reasons were routinely given by the police, and other law enforcement agencies, in order to justify their non-intervention in cases of domestic violence (Griffiths, 1980). Since then, attitudes have changed and evidence suggests that many victims of domestic abuse are only too willing to cooperate in the criminal process (Pahl, 1985).

It has also been suggested that certain legal procedures, particularly criminal prosecutions, are inappropriate in many cases of elder abuse, because the perpetrators of the abuse are themselves victims of the situation. There may be factors in the situation which cause considerable stress to the abuser (Costa, 1984), who is often the elderly person's carer and, usually, a son or daughter (Powell and Berg, 1987) for whom there is little by way of support in the community (Millard, 1984). It could equally be argued that many of those professionally employed as carers in the residential sector can be described as victims of the situation, in that their terms of employment have many of the features of other low status occupations, including stressful working conditions, low pay, limited career prospects, few opportunities for training, and minimal support from management (Donovan and Wynne-Harley, 1986; Downey, 1991; Mitchell, 1991).

Other possible reasons for the under-use of legal procedures may lie in the attitudes and/or level of expertise of professionals in this field, such as lawyers and social workers. This, in part, reflects the education and training which members of these two professions receive in certain areas of the law. There is evidence, for example, that social work training courses – in the past, at least – have varied considerably in the attention paid to properly equipping students with a sound knowledge of the relevant legal rules which govern social work practice (Ball et al., 1988). There is evidence, too, of some indifference – and even antipathy – towards the law and lawyers among not only those who plan and provide residential care, but those also whose function is to regulate its quality (Carson, 1985).

Some social services and health authorities, for instance, have been found to be remiss in the way in which they have carried out their inspection functions in relation to residential care. According to a case reported by the Commission for Local Administration for England (Complaint 89/C 1320), a local authority failed to respond to the concerns of a relative about the mistreatment received by a resident at a private home. The inadequacy of the local authority's investigation was said to amount to serious maladministration. The Ombudsman's recommendation was for the authority to pay financial compensation, and formally apologize to the family, for the serious shortcomings in the way it had investigated the complaint.

Problems in this field are a result, also, of the highly technical rules which, in English law, govern the granting of administrative remedies. For example, the main legal remedy – that is, an order of mandamus to compel the performance of a public duty – is granted at the discretion of the court. Also, as Lord Scarman made clear in *R. v. Bristol Corp., ex parte Hendy* [1974] 1 W.L.R. 498, the courts will not make an order of mandamus requiring a local authority to do 'that which either it cannot do or which it can only do at the expense of other persons not before the court who may have equal rights with the applicant and some of whom would certainly have equal moral claims'. Local authorities can, thus, successfully argue that they have limited resources with which to provide a service. As a result of these technical rules, it has often proved difficult, if not impossible, to make public bodies accountable for the non-provision of services.

These problems are, perhaps, exacerbated by the fact that elder abuse is seldom conceptualized in legal terms. Thus, according to Eastman (1984b), 'granny bashing' can consist of physical assault, threats of physical assault, neglect, including locking a dependant in a bedroom; abandonment, either to residential or hospital care; exploitation, including appropriation of finance and property; sexual abuse; and psychological abuse. The result is a highly diffuse definition of elder abuse (Cloke, 1983). Also, according to Eastman (1984b), abuse by persons other than relatives caring for the elderly person should not be included within this analytical framework. To differentiate in this way, between caregiving relatives and other abusers, seems arbitrary and illogical, and makes little sense in terms of the law.

More recent attempts at categorizing abuse are, perhaps, more satisfactory in that they treat the question without having regard to whether or not the alleged abuser is also a carer. For example, the categories of abuse that have been developed in the USA, and which are referred to in detail in Chapter 1, distinguish between physical, psychological and financial abuse, the abuse of civil liberties and neglect. These definitions are much more easily transposable into legal concepts, such as crimes or torts (that is, actionable civil wrongs). To adopt a simple metaphor, the pieces of the jigsaw are almost all in place. They simply need to be rearranged and fitted together to provide the complete legal picture.

Assault, battery and false imprisonment

The first category of abuse, that is, physical (and/or sexual) abuse, could give rise to either a criminal prosecution or a civil action, usually based upon the tort of trespass to the person, or it could give rise to both. In general, it does not matter in what order the proceedings are brought, although, normally, a civil action will be stayed until the criminal proceedings have been completed (Williams and Hepple, 1984). Also, according to section 11 of the Civil Evidence Act 1968, a criminal conviction can be used as evidence in a subsequent civil action. There are some statutes, however, which provide that a criminal prosecution is a bar to a subsequent civil action. In this context, the most important example is section 45 of the Offences Against the Person Act 1861. Under that section, conviction, or acquittal, in a criminal action before the Magistrates' Court is a bar to the bringing of subsequent civil action. It can be avoided, however, by the simple expedient of bringing the civil action first.

It is the Crown Prosecution Service (CPS) which now decides whether or not to prosecute in relation to crimes such as assault and battery. If the CPS is reluctant to prosecute, there are two possible courses of action. First, the victim can bring a private prosecution. The cost need not be excessive, since, under section 39 of the Criminal Justice Act 1988, common assault and battery are classified as summary offences. As a result, the defendant cannot opt for trial by jury, which may be more costly and slower for the person bringing the action. Secondly, it may be possible for the action to be brought on behalf of the person against whom the alleged assault and/or battery has been committed by a third party. In *Pickering v. Willoughby* [1907] 2 K.B. 296, an elderly woman, who had suffered a number of strokes, was assaulted by her niece who had moved to live with her. It was held that a third party – a great nephew in this case – could initiate the proceedings on her behalf. This was because, although the victim was *compos mentis*, she was feeble, infirm and incapable of instituting proceedings. In addition, she was effectively under the control of the person who had committed the assault.

In many cases, however, the most useful solution will be a civil action in tort for damages, or for an injunction. For an assault to be established it is sufficient for the threatened person to have reasonable cause to fear that actual harm will be directed towards him/her. A battery, on the other hand, requires actual application of force to the person, that is, an act which directly and, either intentionally or negligently, causes some physical contact with the person of the plaintiff without his/her consent (Brazier, 1988). The essential test is not whether the defendant's action showed ill-will or malevolence, simply that it was hostile (*Wilson v. Pringle* [1987] Q.B. 237). Although neither motive nor malice is relevant in determining liability for battery, they could affect the amount of damages which might be awarded. In other words, the tort simply requires the defendant to do something to which the plaintiff objects, and it would seem from *Forde v. Skinner* [1830] 4 C.&P. 239, that the least touching of another person, such as an unwanted kiss, or cutting an individual's hair against that person's will, could be sufficient to satisfy the tort. As a result, the tort of battery protects against intrusion into another's right to physical privacy and personal autonomy, so that pushing an individual in a manner which was undignified and uncalled for, as reported in the Registered Homes Tribunal Case no. 97, might satisfy the essentials of the tort.

In Tribunal Case no. 95, it was revealed that drugs had been taken by residents for whom they had not been prescribed. It is, however, unclear whether, in English law, this is an example of trespass to the person since the judicial tradition is to insist upon a direct relationship between the wrongful action taken by the defendant and the harm caused to the plaintiff. (This requirement has been abandoned in the USA and Canada.) Some fairly liberal interpretations of directness have been accepted by the courts, however, as in *Scott v. Shepherd* (1773) 2 Wm B1. 892. It would appear from the above that the tort of trespass to the person could be developed to provide a check on the indiscriminate prescribing of psychotropic drugs. In any case, such conduct might also be actionable on the basis of a tort known as wrongful interference (Rogers, 1989), which is discussed below.

Other medical examinations and procedures undertaken without the person's consent could, equally, constitute battery. As the decision in *Chatterton v. Gerson* [1981] Q.B. 432 indicates, consent may be given expressly or by implication, but it must be 'real' (Hoggett, 1990). An individual who offered no resistance to the infliction of a medical procedure because of the threat of another sanction, such as eviction from a residential establishment, might not be giving 'real' consent.

English law does not, however, require individual patients to be fully informed of *all* the risks associated with a particular treatment. It is enough for individual patients to be informed *in broad terms* of the likely, and possible, consequences. Nevertheless, according to *Sidaway v. Board of Governors of the Bethlem Royal Hospital and the Maudsley Hospital* [1985] A.C. 871, where there is substantial risk of grave adverse consequences disclosure might be so obviously necessary to enable the patient to make a choice that a failure to do so would negate any apparent consent. As has been argued in a different context (Williams, 1983; Hoggett, 1990), the implication of the 'broad terms' explanation, as a requirement, is that a high proportion of otherwise vulnerable elderly people will have sufficient understanding to exercise the consent which is required in law, and to enable them to refuse treatment as well.

Unfortunately, the test set out in the Sidaway case is subject to the principle of therapeutic privilege. As a result, according to Lord Templeman: 'An obligation to give a patient all the information available to the doctor would often be inconsistent with the doctor's contractual obligation to have regard to the patient's best interest.' The legal test as to the disclosure of information is the one set out in the case of *Bolam v. Friern HMC* [1957] 2 All E.R. 118, that is, a doctor must 'exercise such care as accords with the standards of reasonably competent medical men at the time'. It might be tempting for doctors to use the concept of therapeutic privilege as an excuse for not giving patients all the necessary information. In the case of elderly patients, medical paternalism may mean that they are not fully informed because they 'only get confused' or they 'do not understand'.

Where an elderly person lacks the capacity to give real consent, what is the doctor to do? Failure to examine or treat may result in the patient's condition deteriorating or in death. The question was discussed by the House of Lords in the case of *Re F* [1990] 2 A.C. 1. The case concerned the proposed sterilization of an adult who lacked the capacity to consent to or refuse the operation. It applies, however, to all incapacitated adults, and to all forms of examination or treatment (other than treatment within Part IV of the Mental Health Act 1983). Lord Brandon in the House of Lords said: 'A doctor can lawfully operate on, or give treatment to, adult patients who are incapable of consenting . . . provided that the operation or treatment is in the best interest of such patients.' This test may ensure that people get necessary treatment and in this respect it is welcome. It does, however, reinforce the idea of medical paternalism. The notion that the doctor always knows best is very powerful, especially when dealing with a generation who are not accustomed to questioning professionals in the exercise of their judgement. What is disturbing is that the *Re F* approach does not provide sufficient safeguard for the patient. Little regard is had to the need to consult the patient and to take account of his/her view, no matter how confused he/she may be. Greater emphasis should also be given to the need to consult relatives, friends and others who may be acquainted with the patient. There needs to be a mechanism, other than the courts, which allows for greater involvement in the decision-making process. Unless decisions are taken on the basis of wide-ranging consultations, there is a danger that patient rights will be relegated or even ignored. A legal mechanism, similar to an Enduring Power of Attorney (which is discussed below), is available in certain American states in relation to health care decisions. It enables a competent adult to appoint a proxy empowered to make decisions on his/her behalf in relation to life-sustaining treatment should he/she become critically ill.

Another method of ensuring that an individual's wishes are respected is by means of a 'living will', that is, a document, formally made beforehand, in which a person declares his/her wishes that life-prolonging procedures should be withheld should he/she become mentally or physically ill to such an extent that recovery cannot be envisaged. Since there is no legislative provision for living wills in this country, the status of living wills is uncertain. Despite the real problems they present, there are good grounds for putting this concept on a sound legal footing.

Those who care for elderly people, particularly when they are in positions of authority, may, unwittingly, even if not deliberately, be committing the tort of false imprisonment. Indeed, in some cases, restraint of an extreme kind is exercised. For instance, it was alleged and acknowledged in Tribunal Case no. 131 that residents in one residential care home had been confined to their bedrooms by the insertion of a nail into the door frame, through a hole in the door. The nail acted as a bolt to secure the door from the outside. In Tribunal Case no. 87, an elderly resident was tied to a chair by means of a rope and a jubilee clip. The records revealed that she was restrained on no less than 18 occasions within one month. On nine occasions in one month, the restraint continued all night. Those who excuse such behaviour should be mindful of the fact that the conduct in question was instituted without medical advice, and without lawful authority since the residents were deemed to be there of their own volition. Evidence also suggests that the welfare and life expectancy of frail elderly people are enhanced and prolonged if they are allowed to take normal risks (Hibbs, 1991).

False imprisonment arises where a person's movement is restricted by another person without lawful authority. It cannot, therefore, arise where a person consents to a restriction, although agreement must not be implied simply because no resistance was shown. An individual may be lawfully restrained, however, in an emergency, so as to protect him/herself or others (Hibbs, 1991). According to *Shaper v. Robinson* [1987] (unreported, but noted in C.L.Y. 1987, at 87/755), proving the existence of a reasonable cause for restraint falls on the defendant, since restraint is prima facie a tort and requires justification. Similarly, where detention or restraint is initially lawful, it may, subsequently, become unlawful because circumstances have changed. For example, a crisis may have come to an end (*Middleweek v. Chief Constable of Merseyside* [1990] 3 W.L.R. 481).

Restraint need not be physical, and could include, for example, wrongfully using one's authority to dissuade a person from leaving a room, as in *Harnett v. Bond* [1925] A.C. 669. That is, restraint effected by the wrongful assertion of authority is enough to establish the tort. It also seems, from decided cases, that the plaintiff need not be conscious of imprisonment (*Murray v. Ministry of Defence* [1988] 1 W.L.R. 692).

Negligence

A characteristic of the torts discussed above – assault, battery and false imprisonment – is that physical harm must be directly threatened or inflicted upon the plaintiff. The courts have, therefore, recognized that such acts are actionable *per se*, that is, without any need of further proof that the act in question caused *actual* harm to the plaintiff. But, in cases where actual harm (whether physical or psychological) is caused to the plaintiff, it might also be possible to bring an action in the tort of negligence, which can be founded on either an act or an omission – referred to elsewhere in this volume as active and passive neglect. To succeed, however, it is necessary to establish that the defendant owes a duty of care to the plaintiff. Establishing the necessary duty of care might not be such a problem with respect to a professional carer (Griffiths et al., 1990), but there may be considerable, if not insurmountable, problems with regard to informal carers. In contrast to some other jurisdictions (Steinmetz, 1988), English law imposes no statutory or common law duty upon adult children to care for adult dependants, from which a duty of care in negligence might arise.

No cases in negligence relating to the abuse of elderly people have been reported, although there are numerous examples of circumstances in which important elements of the tort of negligence seem to have existed. The following allegation was made in evidence to the Wagner Committee:

> There must be up to thirty residents and always at least four staff. However, after their dinner at about midday, the staff are not seen until afternoon tea . . . then the staff aren't seen again until the evening meal at 6pm . . . anyone could have fallen, died, haemorrhaged, wet themselves and the staff wouldn't know. (National Institute of Social Work, 1988)

It should be noted that the concept of vicarious liability can be important in the context of elder abuse. That is, where it is alleged that a tort has been committed by an employee, it may be possible to bring the action against the employer as well as, or as an alternative to, suing the employee.

Examples of possible negligence can also be found in relation to informal carers. In the report published by the Birmingham (England) branch of the British Association for Service to the Elderly (BASE) (1991) on elder abuse in the West Midlands, an example is given of Mr C, a 75-year-old, who lived with his daughter in a house which he owned. He suffered from Parkinson's disease, but was determined to remain at home, although his daughter wished him to go into residential care. His medical condition caused him to be unsteady on his feet. On her own admission, his daughter would frequently leave him stranded on the floor – 'to teach him a lesson'. For the same reason, it was also alleged that she would often place his meals just out of reach on the dining table.

Wrongful interference

A more fruitful area of law in relation to establishing the legal liability of informal and formal carers – and which is particularly important in relation to the category of psychological abuse – may be in the tort of wrongful interference, established in the case of *Wilkinson v. Downton* [1897] 2 Q.B. 57. The tort is not well developed, and its scope is a matter of academic debate, with some commentators suggesting it has enormous potential (Williams, 1982), but with others being more inclined to favour a narrower interpretation of the circumstances in which it might apply (Brazier, 1988). Nevertheless, *Wilkinson v. Downton* establishes that liability can arise where physical or psychological harm has been indirectly caused to the plaintiff by an intentional act of the defendant. The case itself concerned a woman who became ill as a result of a foolhardy and cynical practical joke.

It may not, however, be necessary to show a *deliberate* intention to cause the plaintiff the harm which resulted, if it can be shown that the defendant acted recklessly. It might, therefore, apply to a situation in which an individual suffered psychological damage as a result of being tricked into entering residential care by unscrupulous relatives or those working in the so-called caring professions (Brearley, 1982).

The tort of wrongful interference might also be relevant in the kind of circumstances described in the West Midlands report on elder abuse referred to above (BASE, 1991). In another case from the West Midlands survey, Mr A, a 69-year-old stroke victim, suffered extensive psychological abuse from his wife. She was overheard telling him that he had terminal cancer, which was a blatant lie. Mr A became totally despondent and withdrawn.

A legal principle, similar to the tort of wrongful interference, has been developed in the USA. Liability can arise as the result of extreme and outrageous conduct, which intentionally, or recklessly, causes severe emotional distress. It appears that the resulting distress need not amount to a recognizable psychiatric illness. What is extreme and outrageous is to be determined in each individual case. In the leading case of *Nickerson v. Hodge* [1920] 84 50 37, damages were awarded to a mentally infirm elderly woman who had been subjected to unsolicited ridicule. The case illustrates the American concern with the development of 'dignity law', a development which is long overdue in the British context.

Although verbal abuse leading to psychological suffering may not, in the absence of gesticulation, give rise to an action for trespass to person, an alternative action might be based on the tort of defamation. It would be necessary to show that the effect of the wrong was to subject the victim to hatred, contempt or ridicule; in other words, that they had the effect of lowering the plaintiff's good name or image in the estimation of ordinary sensible people (*Parmiter v. Coupland* [1840] 6 M.&W. 105; *Sim v. Stretch* [1936] 2 All E.R. 1237). The tort might well have been established, for instance in Tribunal Case no. 23, where the proprietor of a registered residential care home for elderly people was overheard to say to a resident 'I do hate you; your family hate you, that's why you are here.'

Financial abuse

Another category of elder abuse to which the West Midlands report refers is financial abuse (BASE, 1991). Research suggests that this is the most common form (Sengstock and Barrett, 1986; Powell and Berg, 1987). Legal intervention is particularly appropriate in such cases since it is unlikely that social workers, and those in allied professions, will be competent to deal effectively with this form of abuse. As with physical and psychological abuse, a range of remedies is available, including, possibly, the rescission of a contract (because undue influence had been exercised by one party in relation to the other party to the contract); an action for damages for trespass to goods, or for conversion; or, where a dishonest motive can be established, in the tort of deceit. Prosecution for theft or fraud may also be possible. A discussion of the technical legal rules is, however, beyond the scope of this chapter.

Contracts and wills can be set aside if undue influence can be shown (*Lloyds Bank v. Bundy* [1975] Q.B. 326; *Re Craig deceased* [1971] Ch. 95). For trespass to goods to be established, it is probably necessary for the act to have been committed with intent. Conversion is the wrongful interference with a plaintiff's right to possession of his/her goods. It could include, for instance, destroying or misusing goods, or refusing to return them on demand. If the tort of deceit is established, the plaintiff may be entitled to aggravated, that is, additional, damages for injury to his/her feelings (Brazier, 1988).

A contract entered into by a person 'who was so insane at the time that he did not know what he was doing' will be valid if the other party reasonably believed that a person had the necessary capacity (*Imperial Loan Co. v. Stone* [1892] 1 Q.B. 599). The test for incapacity is whether the person was capable of understanding the general nature of what he/she was doing. A contract made during a lucid interval will be binding regardless of whether the other person knew of previous incapacities (*Hall v. Warren* [1804] 9 Ves. 605). The use of terms such as 'insane' indicates how out of date the law has become in relation to this crucial issue. The test is vague: what is meant by 'understanding the general nature of what he/she is doing'? In its consultation paper, the Law Commission has argued that the rule has, probably, to do more with protecting one party who had no reason to suspect that the other party to the contract lacked capacity (Law Commission, 1991). An exception to this rule applies only to contracts for necessaries where a reasonable price must be paid regardless of whether the supplier was aware of the incapacity. Under the Sale of Goods Act 1979, section 3, necessaries are defined as 'goods suitable to the condition of life [of the person] . . . and to his actual requirements at the time of sale and delivery'.

To make a valid will a person must have testamentary capacity which has been defined as a 'sound disposing mind and memory' (see Cockburn, C.J. in *Banks v. Goodfellow* [1870] L.R. 5 Q.B. 549). This is another example of the vagueness of the test of capacity, although the judges have provided some guidelines for determining what is a sound and disposing mind. The person making the will must be capable of understanding the nature of the business in which he/she is engaged. Thus the person must appreciate that it is a will and not a gift or a contract. He/she must have a recollection of the property to be disposed of and be aware of the manner in which he/she wishes to dispose of that property. In order to revoke a valid will, the person must have testamentary capacity (see *Re Sabatini* [1969] 114 S.J. 35). This can cause difficulties if a person makes a valid will and then becomes incapacitated.

If a person has testamentary capacity, he/she is free to dispose of the estate in whatever manner he/she wishes, subject to the provisions of the Inheritance (Provision for Family and Dependants)

Act 1975. As Wigram, V.C. said in *Bird v. Luckie* [1880] 8 Hare 301, '[No] man is bound to make a will in such a manner as to deserve approbation from the prudent, the wise or the good.'

Among the examples of financial abuse quoted by an American study were instances of elderly people whose family members had removed money from their bank accounts without permission (Breckman and Adelman, 1988). Considerable sums were often involved. Other victims had had their homes or other property put into another person's name, without their permission. Several victims had had personal belongings, such as jewellery or furniture, taken from their homes by relatives or by landlords. The research concluded that the threat of legal intervention was often sufficient to rectify the abuse (Sengstock and Barrett, 1986).

One method by which an individual can protect him/herself against the possibility of financial abuse in old age is to create an Enduring Power of Attorney in anticipation of loss of capacity to conduct his/her own affairs. A person in the early stages of dementia may realize that he/she faces a disruption of mental processes and will eventually be unable to administer his/her affairs. An Enduring Power of Attorney allows the donor to plan for that loss of capacity. He/she can appoint a chosen person to administer his/her affairs upon incapacity, and give general or specific instructions as to the manner in which it is to be done. The Court of Protection exercises a supervisory jurisdiction over Enduring Powers of Attorney. The ability to plan ahead in this way is a welcome innovation. It ensures that, so far as practicable, the donor has maximum control over the conduct of his/her affairs following incapacity. His/her views, expressed during a period of capacity, must be respected and will be binding on the Attorney.

Another means of protecting a person who lacks mental capacity is the Court of Protection, which under the Mental Health Act 1983, section 93(2), exists for the 'protection and management of the property and affairs of a person under a disability'. In the words of Ungoed-Thomas, J. in *Re W.* [1970] 2 All E.R. 502, it 'has exclusive jurisdiction over all the property and affairs of the patient in all their aspects; but not the management or care of the patient's person'. Before it can exercise its jurisdiction the Court must be satisfied that the person is, by reason of mental disorder, incapable of managing his/her property and affairs. The definition of mental disorder is found in section 1 of the Mental Health Act 1983 as 'mental illness, arrested or incomplete development of mind, psychopathic disorder and other disorder or disability of mind'.

However, the nature of the medical evidence needed to satisfy the Court is not specified. This is unfortunate, given the vagueness of the definition of mental disorder. Some confused elderly people may be placed under the Court's jurisdiction without proper consideration of their mental state. Nevertheless, it is also necessary to show that he/she is incapable of administering his/her affairs by reason of the mental disorder. When under the Court's jurisdiction, the patient loses control of all his/her property and affairs. There is no flexibility at present in this 'all or nothing approach'.

Abuse of civil liberties

In relation to the final category of elder abuse, involving transgression of an individual's civil liberties and rights, the British legal system is not well developed. There are statutory rules only in relation to matters of race, sex or marital status. However, in relation to the issue of discrimination on the grounds of age, a complaint to the European Court of Human Rights might, possibly, succeed. Although Article 14 of the European Convention on Human Rights makes no specific reference to discrimination on the grounds of age, as such, it does refer to discrimination which relates to 'birth or other status'. Discrimination on grounds of age might fall within the 'other status' category. Article 8, too, provides limited protection for a person's private and family life, his home and his correspondence. The primary object of the provision is to protect the individual from arbitrary interference by public authorities but, according to a Dutch case (*X and Y v. Netherlands* [1986] 8 E.H.R.R. 235), it seems that a complaint could succeed on the basis of a state's failure to protect an individual's privacy against interference by another private individual. The case concerned the sexual abuse, in a private residential home, of a 16-year-old young woman with learning difficulty. The complaint succeeded because it was established that the Dutch civil and criminal codes provided insufficient legal protection.

Insufficient legal protection also exists in the United Kingdom. The common law (as was recently confirmed by the Court of Appeal in *Kaye v. Robertson* [1991] F.S.R. 62) gives no specific right of action for breaches of privacy. However, proceedings before the European Court are slow, sometimes taking five years or more. In any case, the primary function of the Court is not to offer a remedy for individual victims, but to bring to light any violations by an individual state of inter-state conventions (Bailey et al., 1991).

Change in attitude

Nevertheless, some of the worst cases of elder abuse could be more effectively dealt with now, without any need to change our existing legislative or constitutional framework. What is mainly needed is a change in professional attitudes. After all, assault is assault, fraud is fraud, theft is theft, and false imprisonment is false imprisonment, whatever the age of either the victim or the abuser (BASE, 1991).

One frequently offered excuse for inaction in this field is said to be the difficulty associated with producing and presenting satisfactory evidence. Here again, the problems may have been exaggerated. A statement by a vulnerable witness, which is then transposed into documentary form by a police officer, a social worker, or even by the person him/herself, is already admissible under existing law, as evidence of the facts stated. This might relieve the witness from the ordeal of appearing before the court (J. McEwan, 1989).

There are, however, particular problems in relation to mentally incapacitated people who may only give evidence if they understand the duty to tell the truth as well as the nature and consequences of an oath (*R. v. Dunning* [1965] Crim. L.R. 372). As the Law Commission points out, there is difficulty 'in drawing the line between normality and abnormality in areas, where conditions fluctuate and cannot easily be measured' (Law Commission, 1991).

The Law Commission has recently set out the possible aims for a general reform of the law on mental incapacity. These include enabling and encouraging people to take decisions for themselves which they are able to take; but where intervention is necessary in their own interests, or for the protection of others, that intervention should be as limited as possible and aim at achieving what the individual would have wanted; and that proper safeguards are provided against exploitation, neglect, and physical, sexual or psychological abuse. It sets out a number of possible options which include advanced directives; designated decision-making procedures; the reform of existing procedures such as guardianship under the Mental Health Act 1983; advocacy; or a new statutory institution possibly providing one single adjudicative body with jurisdiction over all mental health matters. Undoubtedly, radical changes in the law are necessary to meet a growing need.

If the hallmark of full citizenship is the exercise of rights, then many elderly people, it seems, experience only incomplete citizenship. Nowhere is this more clearly seen than in the context of elder abuse.

4

Abuse of Older People: Sociological Perspectives

Chris Phillipson

Mistreatment of older people, within the community and inside institutions, has been an enduring feature of our social history. At worst, this has taken the form of outright persecution of those who, lacking resources of any kind, were thrown upon the mercy of their fellow citizens. Keith Thomas (1978), for example, notes that tensions arising from the dependent status of older women played a significant role in the witchcraft craze that swept through many parts of Western society from the sixteenth to the later seventeenth centuries. At another level, mistreatment has been expressed through inter-generational conflicts of various kinds: through the elders control over property and the blockage of the aspirations of younger kin (Stearns, 1986); through the pressures faced by an unmarried daughter left to care for her parents (Bardwell, 1926); or through the crisis generated through economic recession, as families struggled with the contradictions of meeting the care needs of both older and younger generations (Murphy, 1931).

But the meanings attached to, and the concerns expressed about, mistreatment of the old, have varied greatly from generation to generation. It is in the past two decades (as we saw in Chapter 1) that we have attempted to translate a generalized concern about the suffering of the old into a more precisely defined concept of abuse. But the transition has been a difficult one, raising complex problems about how we define social relationships in later life and the reasons we give for focusing on some problems to the exclusion of others. The purpose of this chapter is, first, to clarify some of the sociological issues which surround the concept of elder abuse; secondly, to examine some of the issues it raises for understanding the lives of older people; thirdly, to identify some principles for those involved in working in the field of elder abuse.

Domestic violence

The concern with elder abuse reflects a more general focus on the issue of family violence. This is reflected in the language of the debate – for example, the early description of abuse in terms of 'granny battering' (Eastman, 1984b) – and in the anxiety about the changing pattern of family life and its effects on groups such as older people. In his classic study, *The Family Life of Older People*, Peter Townsend defined the centrality of family relationships in the following way:

> if many of the processes and problems of ageing are to be understood, old people must be studied as members of families (which usually means extended families of three generations); and if this is true, those concerned with health and social administration, must at every stage view old people as an inseparable part of a family group, which is more than just a residential unit. They are not simply individuals, let alone 'cases' occupying beds or chairs. They are members of families and whether or not they are treated as such largely determines their security, their health, and their happiness. (Townsend, 1963: 227)

Yet the anxiety of the 1980s was precisely that the family was in some sense moving away from being concerned with the plight of its elderly members. Despite the extensive literature dealing with the vital role of informal carers, by the end of the decade there was renewed emphasis, expressed in the debate around intergenerational conflict, about the divergent interests as regards financial and social support for the care of the old (Callaghan, 1987; Johnson et al., 1989). Running alongside this debate was growing evidence about the way in which families could inflict damage on their most vulnerable and weakest members. Dobash and Dobash (1992), in a major comparative survey of family violence, note that: 'It is . . . known that the family is filled with many different forms of violence and oppression, including physical, sexual and emotional, and that violence is perpetrated on young and old alike' (Dobash and Dobash, 1992: 2; see also Gelles, 1987).

For older people, there are considerable implications (and contradictions) in such observations. On the one side, changes in community care are moving older people back towards support from the informal care system (Phillipson, 1992a). On the other side, there seems to be evidence that it is precisely this system that can produce damage to the lives of older people, and especially the very old (Department of Health, 1992). At the same time, it might be argued that locating elder abuse within the spectrum of family violence raises more difficulties than it solves: is family violence the most significant form of oppression experienced by older people? What evidence do we have for mistreatment outside domestic settings? To what extent do theoretical perspectives support a broader perspective on the problems faced by older people? In dealing with these issues, we shall first look at the question of how family violence is defined before proceeding to examine its occurrence in the lives of older people.

The scope of family violence

Linda George (1989), in a major review of the politics of domestic violence, has challenged the view that the current problems in this area are more significant (or unprecedented in scale) in comparison with the past. She suggests that there has been an ebb-and-flow pattern of concern about violence over the past century, and that its incidence has changed much less than its visibility (see also Filinson and Ingman, 1989). George goes on to argue that:

> Concern with family violence has been a weathervane identifying the prevailing winds of anxiety about family life in general. The periods of silence about family life are as significant as the periods of concern. Both reveal the longing for peaceful family life, the strength of the image of home life as a harmonious, loving, and supportive environment. One response to this longing has been a tendency to deny, even suppress, the evidence that families are not always like that. Denying the problem serves to punish the victims of family violence doubly by forcing them to hide their problems and to blame themselves. Even the aggressors in family violence suffer from denial, since isolation and the feeling that they are unique make it difficult to ask for the help they want. (George, 1989: 2)

George goes on to argue that it is possible to see family violence as historically and politically constructed. This, she suggests, can be seen in two senses:

> First, the very definition of what constitutes acceptable domestic violence, and appropriate responses to it, developed and then varied according to political moods and the force of certain political movements. Second, violence among family members arises from family conflicts which are not only historically influenced but political in themselves, in the sense of that word having to do with power relations. Family violence usually arises out of power struggles in which individuals are contesting real resources and benefits. These contests arise not only from personal aspirations but also from changing norms and conditions. (George, 1989: 3)

The framework provided by George offers some important insights into the current debate about elder abuse. First, it is clear that the discussion has run parallel with, and has itself been influenced by, the wider debate about the resourcing of an ageing population. Thus, rather than the growth in the number of very elderly people being a key factor in the apparent 'increase' in abuse, a more substantive issue has been the support to be provided to older people and the relationships between the different groups providing this help. Following this argument, the key issue in the concern with elder abuse is the selective way in which the problem has been framed. Over the past ten years, the focus has been on the physical abuse of older people by their informal carers (Block and Sinnott, 1979; Department of Health, 1992). Yet actual research findings based on properly conducted surveys (as opposed to studies of the experiences of self-selected professionals) give no grounds for believing that physical abuse is the most significant form of abuse experienced by older people (Ogg and Bennett, 1992b). Stephen Crystal (1986) argues that the impression given by research is of substantial numbers of older people being beaten up by their children. This, he suggests, is 'palpably wrong'. He comments: 'Carefully read . . . studies typically reflect much lower rates of actual direct abuse; indeed, one of the problems in the research has been the difficulty in identifying sufficient numbers of truly abused victims to study' (Crystal, 1986: 333).

The argument here is not that the abuse of older people does not take place (after all, as Sprey and Matthews (1989) maintain, even *one* case is socially unacceptable) but that recognition should be given to the fact that there are a number of forms of harm or endangerment which affect the lives of older people. Crystal, reviewing the American experience, makes the important point that:

> [Elder] abuse . . . while dramatic . . . is not necessarily the most severe [problem facing the old] . . . Experience with a broad range of programs designed to respond to harm and endangerment – adult protection services programs in particular – suggest that abuse is only one of a variety of problems encountered by impaired adults . . . that it is not necessarily the most common or most severe form of harm or endangerment requiring protective intervention; and that where abuse does appear to be manifest, it is usually encountered as part of a complex set of problems, often revolving around an unmet or poorly met care need and/or an abuser who is himself or herself functionally compromised. (Crystal, 1986: 333–4)

This argument raises the issue of why abuse, and particularly domestic abuse, has appeared on the agenda of local and central government. Set beside the problems associated with the deprivation of key services to older people, the problems resulting from the decline in housing during the 1980s and the more generalized problem of age discrimination, the focus on abuse appears somewhat selective. This does not undermine the case for attempting to understand family violence as it affects older people (to repeat, even *one* case is unacceptable), but it does suggest that issues about the incidence and prevalence of domestic abuse should be placed in a wider context of the growing marginalization of certain groups of older people (Bornat et al., 1985; E. McEwan, 1989; Allen et al., 1992).

Elder abuse and kinship obligations

The second issue raised by Linda George concerns the question of family violence being rooted in the changing norms and conditions surrounding family care. This point may be especially relevant to understanding the emergence in the 1970s and 1980s of abuse as a social problem. In this context it is important to relate the debate about strains within family relationships to changes in attitudes towards the giving and receiving of family care. The evidence from a number of research studies is that older people are moving away from wanting any dependence on children, especially that which implies a long-term commitment arising out of a chronic illness (Lee, 1985) or the need to provide personal care (Ungerson, 1987). Such arguments about changes in preferences for care are highlighted by research on changing patterns of kinship obligations. Janet Finch (1989), in a major review of work in this area, has highlighted the complex set of rules determining the provision of family care. She notes that kin relationships do not operate on the basis of a ready-made set of moral rules, clearly laid out for older people and their carers to follow. In particular, the 'sense of obligation' which marks the distinctive character of kin relations does not follow a reliable and consistent path in terms of social practice. Finch writes:

> It is actually much less reliable than that. It is nurtured and grows over time between some individuals more strongly than others, and its practical consequences are highly variable. It does have a binding quality, but that derives from commitments built up between real people over many years, not from an abstract set of moral values. (Finch, 1989: 242)

This argument is important because it cuts across a central thrust of current policy on community care, namely, that families act as though there are cultural and moral scripts which they follow in supporting older people in times of crisis or dependency. Moreover, the argument is taken a stage further by some researchers with the assertion that older people themselves follow this path, with an almost instinctive tendency to move towards the family rather than bureaucratic agencies. According to Wenger (1984: 14): 'Research from a wider section of developed countries demonstrates that not only does most care come from the family . . . but that most people think that this is where the responsibility should lie.' But this argument relies upon a historical perspective which may no longer be acceptable as an accurate portrayal of the kind of care which people want. Families are variable in their response to requests for help and, in any event, as Janet Finch points out, the care given is always negotiated within a social and biographical context. In this regard, it is possible to see the debate about abuse reflecting a wider discussion about the nature of family care: who should provide it and under what conditions? Abuse, in fact, though a lived experience for some older people, may also be a metaphor for the way in which families and older people are changing in terms of care preferences (Phillipson, 1992a). Care for older people is *not* defined by any clear social norms (in contrast to care for children). It thus follows that our definition of abuse is equally uncertain. But the reasons are not just that older people are adults and hence supposedly in control of their lives, but also that issues of who should provide care and under what terms are in a state of flux. The idea of abuse may be an expression of this uncertainty as much as it represents the real experiences of older people. To repeat, this does not minimize the importance of abuse at an individual level; it does, however, indicate the complexity of abuse as a social issue.

Power and the family
A final set of issues arising from Linda George's work is where older people stand in terms of different forms of family violence. Here, it seems important to distinguish carefully elder abuse from other forms of domestic abuse. It is misleading to argue that: 'Elder abuse is clearly only part of a spectrum of domestic violence which affects all ages' (Department of Health, 1992). Elder abuse is similar but also very different. Unlike other types of domestic violence, there may not be a clear victim or perpetrator. Because most elderly adults are legally (and actually) autonomous human beings, responsibility for the abuse may be difficult to determine. This leads, as Linda Phillips has pointed out, to difficult questions for professionals working in the field:

> Is it the responsibility of an adult child to enforce rules of cleanliness on a legally competent elder when the elder does not want to be clean? What is the effect of geographic distance or filial distance on legal and moral responsibilities? Who is the victim and who is the perpetrator in situations where a legally competent elder refuses to act in his or her own best interests? And perhaps even more basic than any of these is the question of how can responsibility be assigned in a society that has yet to establish clear criteria regarding the minimum material and emotional rights to which every individual in society is entitled? (Phillips, 1989: 89)

Phillips' argument highlights the complex issues facing professionals working in the field of elder abuse. Contrary to the impression given in much of the elder abuse literature, direct cases of abuse will be the exception. The rule will be a far murkier area, where acts of omission and commission intermingle, and where elders may themselves be partly involved in the construction of abusive situations. In contrast, the problem with the debate on elder abuse is that it too often degenerates into a battle between 'innocent' elders and 'bad' families. On the one side, we have a stereotyped view of the old as relatively powerless, undemanding and invariably blameless in terms of the outcomes of family dynamics. On the other side, there are families for whom various 'risk factors' can be identified, these ranging from psychopathology on the part of the abuser to various forms of stress (Breckman and Adelman, 1988). This division has, of course, been challenged in more sophisticated studies, with researchers such as Pillemer (1986) showing the extent to which the *abuser* may be the dependent one in terms of his or her relations with an older person. But the tendency (especially in the British literature) has been to ignore such findings and to focus on the older person as a victim within a disturbed or highly stressed network of family relations (Eastman, 1984b). This presentation is, however, misleading in terms of how it presents the power relations running through families involved in the abuse of older people. Moreover, it is also important to acknowledge the extent to which abusive situations are themselves socially created, through low incomes, inadequate community care and ageism within society. Care, and family care in particular, is deeply influenced by this wider context of oppression affecting older people. The tendency has been to focus on the influence of 'family pathology' in creating certain types of abuse. But highlighting the role of individual families ignores wider issues about the labels placed upon older people and the resources available to them to resist maltreatment. Attention to these broader issues will be vital if progress is to be made in the debate on elder abuse.

Institutionalized abuse

The identification of elder abuse as a form of family violence has led to an additional problem: the failure, especially in the British context, to give proper weight to abuse in institutional settings. This must be considered surprising given the long history of mistreatment of the old within poor law institutions, elderly people's homes and long-stay hospitals (Townsend, 1962; Robb, 1967). Contemporary evidence of abuse is not hard to find. The first 96 cases of the Registered Homes Tribunal provide a number of examples of abuse and neglect.

Verbal aggression was characteristic of a number of the cases. For example, in *Mattarooa v. East Sussex County Council*:

> Concern from various sources had been expressed over a number of years focusing on the cold and regimented manner in which the residents were treated. It was clear that a number of persons involved in the placing of residents approached Mrs Mattarooa to try to improve the situation, but

the regime of strict control, concentration on the minutiae of table manners, humiliation of residents and lack of development of their emotional needs continued. Neighbours who gave evidence reported hearing shouting and abuse and use of such terms as 'idiot', 'stupid' and even 'animal' to the residents. One resident was observed at a day centre with a bruised face and bleeding nose. The police became involved but no charges were brought and the tribunal accepted Mrs Mattarooa's story that she had not struck the woman and that her face had become bruised when she accidently bumped it. (Harman and Harman, 1989: 21)

A combination of *physical abuse* and *verbal aggression* is contained in the following case involving *Scorer and Akhtar v. Cambridgeshire County Council*:

There was mental cruelty in that some residents had their hair rinsed with cold water, and that some residents were sent up to their rooms by way of punishment, and that some were abused and insulted by being called names to their faces and humiliated by being shamed in front of other residents. They were physically abused in that some residents were roughly handled, pushed and pulled unnecessarily, frog-marched, slapped; that some had their clothes yanked off; that two residents were roughly treated when certain medical processes were taking place . . . There was verbal abuse in that Mrs Scorer shouted at residents; insulted and humiliated them by calling them names (fat old pig, stupid, dirty, smelly, filthy), so that residents were frightened. All these matters constituted a serious risk to the residents' well-being. (Harman and Harman, 1989: 66)

Abuse may also occur where homes deny basic standards of privacy to residents. This was an area explored in the report *Not Such Private Places* (Counsel and Care, 1991), a survey of private and voluntary residential and nursing homes in Greater London. The study found that 70 per cent of all types of homes expect older people to use commodes within hearing of their room-mate. A large proportion of homes (24 per cent) expected residents to use commodes in shared rooms where no privacy curtains were available. The report also found a high proportion of nursing homes failing to ensure that residents could lock their rooms both on the inside and the outside (73 per cent). Finally, a high proportion (one-third) of homes did not provide any specific lockable storage space for residents. The report commented:

The observations of our visiting caseworkers produced some sad anecdotes of individual homes' lack of respect for privacy of their residents, particularly when caseworkers were shown round the homes . . . All too often residents' doors are not knocked on and the officer-in-charge simply entered a room without explaining the reason for the intrusion. This can result in embarrassing situations for the visitor but much more importantly for the residents themselves. Bursting in on a resident on a commode is an all too common occurrence. (Counsel and Care, 1991: 18–19)

Negative attitudes to older people may be more visible in long-term care facilities because of the greater concentration of older people in a single location. Kayser-Jones (cited in Monk, 1990: 7), has grouped the most frequently reported complaints of staff abuse into four categories:

1 *Infantilization* – treating the patient as an irresponsible, undependable child;
2 *Depersonalization* – providing services in an assembly line fashion, disregarding the patient's individual needs;
3 *Dehumanization* – not only ignoring elderly persons but stripping them of privacy and of their capacity to assume responsibility for their own lives;
4 *Victimization* – attacking the older person's physical and moral integrity through verbal abuse, threats, intimidation, theft, blackmail, or corporal punishments.

The categories identified by Kayser-Jones directly correspond to those developed in the area of domestic abuse. It now seems important to accept the view that there is a broad spectrum of mistreatment of the old, ranging from the interiors of private to those of public settings. It is invidious to select any one for particular emphasis (unless this is part of a clearly defined research strategy), and we should clearly look for an approach which sees abuse as an issue which is not tied to any one context or relationship.

Theoretical perspectives

One way of widening the debate on elder abuse is through a clearer integration of social theory and observation about abuse of older people. Two contrasting theoretical perspectives may illustrate this point: interactionist theory and the political economy perspective. These approaches are used to identify the complex issues underpinning the debate about elder abuse, the former raising questions about the relationship of older people to workers and carers; the latter posing questions about the social construction of dependent relationships in later life.

Interactionist theory, following Herbert Blumer (1969) and McCall and Simmons (1966), suggests that the way social life is organized arises from within society itself and out of the processes of interaction between its members. In this approach, abuse and neglect are viewed as a consequence of the interaction either within families or within institutions. More specifically, the theory predicts that processes arising from social and biological ageing might change role definitions in the social groups within which the older person is interacting. Such alterations might challenge hitherto stable identities, causing stress within social relationships. This could be resolved by the negotiation of new self-validating identities. Alternatively, forms of psychological abuse (such as infantalization) could emerge, possibly leading to other forms of abuse and neglect.

The implication of an interactionist perspective is that our understanding of abuse should acknowledge the way in which ageing processes affect workers and carers at a personal level. Contact with older people may be difficult (or may be avoided) because it is seen as unrewarding or reminds carers of their own ageing. This is partly because they have no direct experience of old age and therefore have to rely on social stereotypes. As these are predominantly negative, they affect perceptions of our own future old age as a time of dependency, poor health, poverty and vulnerability, even though this may bear little relationship to the lived experience of many older people or the old age which we may expect.

The likelihood is, however, that those most vulnerable to abuse may well experience some of the chronic conditions associated with old age. Age is particularly associated with changes to the physical appearance and functioning of the human body. This is both the most obvious visible way of identifying old age as well as being a disconcerting link which workers and carers can see with themselves. Physical decline is often seen to the exclusion of more positive attributes. Ageist attitudes and abusive behaviour may arise from the way in which older people come to be seen as failures as a result of the effects of chronic illness. The prevalence of disability increases from 12 per cent at age 65–69 to over 80 per cent above the age of 85. Arthritis and rheumatism affects 58 per cent of those 75 and over; poor eyesight 42 per cent; swelling of feet and legs 33 per cent, and giddiness 31 per cent (Victor, 1991).

These physical changes raise important issues in terms of how older people view themselves and how they are viewed by society. People are given full accreditation as human beings only when they have reached a relatively high level of cognitive, emotional and biological development. This aspect of how human development is perceived has major implications for older people. Featherstone and Hepworth (1991: 376–7) suggest that:

> If the process of becoming an acceptable human being is dependent upon those developments, the loss of cognitive and other skills produces the danger of social unacceptability, unemployability and being labelled as less than fully human. Loss of bodily controls carries similar penalties of

stigmatisation and ultimately exclusion. Deep [or late] old age is person-ally and socially disturbing because it holds out the prospect of the loss of some or all of these controls. Degrees of loss impair the capacity to be counted as a competent adult. Indeed, the failure of bodily controls can point to a more general loss of self-image . . . The loss of bodily controls also impairs other interactional skills, and the loss of real power through decline in these competencies may induce others to feel confident in treating the individual as a less than full adult. Carers may, for example, feel secure in the belief that the person 'inside' will not be able to return to wreak any vengeance on them whatever their former social status or class background.

Changes to the human body may, therefore, be a crucial agent in creating the conditions for abuse and neglect and for disturbing social interaction between older people and other family members. This has important implications for the prevention of abuse which we will turn to in the final section of this chapter.

Interactionist perspectives focus on the question of how individ-uals adapt and respond to old age. Critical or political economy perspectives, in contrast, examine the impact of society on the lives of older people, both within and beyond domestic settings. Critical perspectives adopt the view that old age is a *social* as well as a *biologically* constructed status. In this context, many of the experi-ences affecting older people can be seen as the product of a particular division of labour and structure of inequality rather than a natural product of the ageing process.

Alan Walker (1980) encapsulated this perspective with the notion of the 'social creation of dependency in old age' and Peter Townsend (1981) used a similar term when he described the 'structured dependency' of older people. This dependency is seen to be the consequence of the forced exclusion of older people from work, the experience of poverty, institutionalization and restricted domestic and community roles. Finally, Carroll Estes (1979: 2) has used the term 'the aging enterprise': 'to call particular attention to how the aged are often processed and treated as a commodity and to the fact that the age-segregated policies that fuel the ageing enterprise are socially-divisive "solutions" that single-out, stigmatize, and isolate the aged from the rest of society.'

The value of the political economy approach is that it places the struggles of carers and older people within a framework of social and political resources and ideologies. The implication of this approach is that abuse may arise from the way in which older people come to be marginalized by society (and by the services which they receive). If people are predisposed to abuse the old because of their biological dependency, the likelihood is increased through social forces which discriminate both against the old as well as those involved in their care (Bornat et al., 1985; E. McEwan, 1989). Such a perspective would suggest that the challenge to abuse must be seen as an issue of both social policy as well as problems to do with dysfunctional families (Department of Health, 1992).

Principles for tackling abuse

None of the above is to suggest that abuse and neglect should not be 'confronted' (and, it is to be hoped, understood) in day-to-day social work. But some basic principles need to be observed as a guide for action. In conclusion, the following points are offered for discussion:

1 Workers should be encouraged to be vigilant about the possibility of abuse/neglect while being aware of the fact that there are no clear criteria for identifying abused elders and no good interventions that are totally acceptable to all the parties involved.
2 Shared decision-making is essential. Sharing should be conducted by involving a range of professional workers in developing a strategy for tackling abuse and by ensuring that workers are supported in the decisions they make about protecting vulnerable elders.
3 Departments will need to develop policies which empower older people in situations where they are leading marginal lives. Policies for tackling abuse must therefore be concerned with advocacy and strengthening self-care abilities in old age.
4 The emphasis in work with all older people, in private households and residential settings, should be how to develop lives free of mistreatment. This means focusing on a variety of areas of which activities with informal carers, the primary focus of the Department of Health report, may be a relatively small part.

It seems clear that we are set for a major debate about the extent and nature of abuse of older people. The range of publications devoted to this topic is expanding, especially in areas such as training and research (McCreadie, 1991; Phillipson and Biggs, 1992; Pritchard, 1992). However, there will be a need to place the discussion within a critical perspective which acknowledges the social construction of abuse and the influence of this on dynamics within individual families and communities. So far, the debate has tended to focus on the risk factors which may be attributed to individual families. We must, however, pay attention to risks arising from ideologies about older people and the resources at their disposal. This dimension would seem an important next step for the debate on elder abuse in society.

5
Elder Abuse and Key Areas in Social Work

Jill Manthorpe

This chapter considers three areas of social work practice in elder abuse. First, it looks at the role of social workers in the identification process. This may be at the level of referral when skills in communication need to be finely tuned or at the level of reporting or suspicion. Secondly, the social work role in respect of intervention is considered, identifying what resources are available and how these may be mobilized. The care management approach and mandatory reporting will be discussed in this context. Finally, changes in perspective necessary at practitioner level are discussed, including the development of new skills and support as well as management implications that will determine whether or not individual practitioners feel empowered and confident in this area of work. Abuse is, of course, not new – it is the professional response that is changing.

Social workers may work with older people who live in the 'community' or in various forms of residential care. The division between the two is somewhat blurred (Higgins, 1989). Accordingly, each section of this chapter will consider community or home-based work and then work related to an institutional environment. Naturally, there are many inter-connections, particularly as one traditional response to allegations of self-neglect and abuse has been the removal of the individual to a residential facility (Age Concern, 1986). Eastman's survey (1984a) quotes figures to show that up to 80 per cent of suspected victims were admitted to residential care. We have little evidence, other than brief follow-ups of cases of compulsory removal under section 47 of the National Assistance Act 1948 (Forster and Tiplady, 1980), to illustrate intervention and its possible effects, but it is clear that removal from problematic home-based settings to institutional settings is no guarantee of improved quality of life.

Identification

The problems facing social workers in identifying abuse may be grouped together into three main areas: the referral, the initial collection of information and the investigation.

The referral

According to Bennett (1990c: 50) (a consultant physician) social services, the police and legal practitioners are rarely the first to be involved in cases of elder abuse or neglect; instead, it is more likely to be the general practitioner, district nurse, health visitor or casualty officer who picks up suggestions of abuse. However, this may simply be the result of researchers' concentration on physical abuse/neglect or the fact that much UK evidence so far has come from medical sources (e.g. Homer and Gilleard, 1990a).

Referrals then to social services departments (SSDs) may come from a variety of sources, but as Hildrew (1991a,b) points out, only a minority of SSDs have published guidelines on procedure. In her survey of SSDs in England and Wales, she notes that those authorities which have published guidelines (11 out of 115 in 1991) have clearly followed the Kent model. Kent SSD issued practice guidelines in 1987, updating them in 1989.

It is worth examining the Kent guidelines to consider one procedural model. Kent clearly underlines the importance of elder abuse which has implications for departmental resources and staff work: 'Every reported incident of elder abuse must be treated with the same urgency as that accorded to incidents of child abuse' (Kent Social Services Department, 1989, para. 3.1a). The guidelines note the information that should be collected on referral, including basic details of alleged victim's name, address, gender, age and contact information (first language, address, telephone). It may also be relevant to ask the informant if there is any disability or impairment that may affect communication so that, for example, a visit could be made by someone who was able to use sign language. Naturally, the status of the informant may determine whether it is appropriate to ask such questions and whether to rely on the evidence. Information at the initial referral stage may also be asked about relevant contacts with other services and agencies, together with any knowledge about significant family members or other individuals. Many authorities will have their own referral forms which may be adapted for this purpose.

It can be much more difficult to elicit information about alleged abuse in evidential terms and skill may be needed in helping the informant to spell out suspicions and concern. Kent clearly warns informants who give their name that their evidence may be needed if they have reported what may turn out to have been criminal activity. Referrals, though, may be made anonymously and it may be appropriate for social workers to share skills with staff working on child protection issues about encouraging anonymous callers to discuss their concerns about identification and possible recrimination. There should obviously be a consistent pattern in response to allegations between community-based workers and those inspecting the residential or institutional sectors and staff may wish to liaise with local Benefit Agency Officers about their local practice when allegations of financial abuse are made.

Finally, in order to avoid duplication, confusion or inaction, the initial referral, if made by another agency, needs to clarify the roles of each agency. A district nurse, for example, may be asked to confirm that he or she will continue visiting daily, or asked if he or she has informed the general practitioner, or informed that a visit will be made to the person concerned within a specific period. It is vital that the nurse knows the outcome of the referral, otherwise he or she may feel ignored, taken for granted or demeaned in status. Good future working relationships may be jeopardized by failure to communicate.

Initial collection of information
Bennett (1992a) outlines the features that should alert a doctor to the possibility of inadequate care, and these physical manifestations are considered in Chapters 2 and 6. Their relevance to social work is that, although detailed physical examinations are not undertaken by social workers, it is possible to note bruises, welts, lacerations, abrasions and burns, particularly around the face, lips, mouth and hands.

It is possible for social workers to note carefully the explanation offered in a manner which is both accurate and helpful to other professionals. Several methods of collecting physical data have been suggested, ranging from sophisticated elder assessment instruments (Fulmer, 1984) and summarized by Bennett (1990c) and health status risk assessment (Johnson, 1991) to the taking of detailed case histories and developing the use of body maps for adults. However, screening instruments are in their infancy in the UK in all professions.

Little attention is given in social work training to physical aspects of ageing. This lack of knowledge can exacerbate difficulties of differentiating between suspicious factors and 'normal' processes. This is particularly the case with bruising, broken bones and broken skin where knowledge of skin and tissue changes might help to clarify accidental damage.

Pritchard (1989), a practising British social worker, notes that of 11 cases of elder abuse in her area office in one year all the older people had suffered physical harm in some form:

> However, social workers' descriptions of the injuries were often vague, possibly because the majority of them had not seen the injuries themselves. When dealing with child abuse cases, social workers are much more

specific about injuries, aware that they must be able to describe the injuries and their location on the body. (1989: 12)

None the less, social work training equips the practitioner with many skills to assist in the collection of a holistic picture. These include the building of trust and rapport with the older person. Mixson (1991) notes the importance of these in cases of self-neglect where perhaps just one individual is involved. It is even more important to understand the ambiguity and meaning of help in situations of possible abuse. Johnson (1991) writing of the US experience summarizes this possible conflict between the view of the 'helper' and the individual:

> Adult protective services (APS) workers are often called as a last resort. They are authorised by the legal-political system to enter the private lives of individuals whether those whom they serve wish their intervention or not. Consequently, their roles as helping strangers may be viewed as invasive and adversarial. (Johnson, 1991: xi)

Investigation

In the event of a referral suggesting an immediate danger, either life-threatening or serious harm, then it is necessary to inform emergency services such as the police or ambulance service. It may be necessary to follow up this action in the event of the emergency services not clarifying what has happened. In such cases there may be a multiplicity of professionals or agencies involved and it is by no means certain that they will view the social worker or department as having a key role or any responsibility. Equally, with pressure from other work, it may be appropriate to establish who is to be the 'key worker' or 'link person' for the individual and to reduce involvement, particularly if there is an advocate working for the person concerned, for example, or the person concerned is able to exercise choice and make decisions.

However, in some circumstances there will be a need for an investigation to be made and principles of direct social work with individuals remains to the fore. These include developing communication, building a relationship and the exercise of negotiating, bargaining and advocacy skills. Froggatt (1990) outlines some of the key elements of purposeful interviewing along such lines with an emphasis on developing relationships. Some authors have begun to consider the methods of interviewing older people in the context of alleged or suspected abuse. Ramsey-Klawsnik (1991), for example, in discussing elder sexual abuse, notes that interviewing requires training and supervised practice. The Kent guidelines (1989) suggest the following preliminaries:

- visiting with another worker
- explaining the purpose of the visit
- interviewing the dependent elder alone
- interviewing the caregiver separately afterwards
- arranging appropriate interpreting services if required

It is also appropriate to consider the manner of the interview. General good practice appears to draw out the following as important:

- a conversational style
- a relaxed atmosphere
- avoiding leading questions
- looking as well as listening
- being non-judgemental
- assessing mental capacity to some extent

Warnings are also given about premature diagnosis and making promises or raising expectations.

Time and sensitivity are particularly relevant where there are communication disorders. Jones (1992) discusses the difficulties of communicating with people who have dementia of the Alzheimer type. She gives guidelines for helping to compensate partially and temporarily for some of the memory and other deficits common in this group which include:

- optimizing the environment: good lighting, little noise, close seating positions
- personal presentation: eye contact, body contact (touch)
- validating the feeling behind an apparent inappropriate comment
- re-orientation when required
- giving time, repeating when necessary
- following the 'thread' of a conversation

In such interviews, the difficulties may be such that it is inappropriate for a social worker to continue an assessment. It will then be vital to liaise with individuals or services who may better know the person or condition, for example, a community psychiatric nurse or day services worker.

Mandatory reporting

Ethical dilemmas are common to social work. Gilbert (1986) explores these issues in a consideration of the ethics of mandatory reporting of elder abuse in the US. Laudable objectives, such as removing people from harm, preventing harm and providing benefits, may be in conflict with other principles of obtaining consent, maintaining confidentiality and inflicting no harm. Gilbert's work is a salutary reminder that there is evidence that laws based on one ethical principle may in practice conflict with other principles.

In the UK context the issue of 'at risk registers' for elder abuse cases raises such dilemmas and is highly relevant to the debate over published guidelines and procedures. Gloucestershire Social Services (1991) guidelines, for example, include the development of an adult at risk register. Their model is likely to be highly influential as it considers all adults and so may be perceived as non-ageist. Many community care reorganizations in the 1990s are also to be based on children/adult organizational divisions. Finally, Gloucestershire is likely to be influential because its guidelines were developed from a response to a well-publicized case of adult neglect, that of Beverley Lewis (Fennel, 1989). However, research evidence on the effectiveness of adult at risk registers is lacking and so it may be appropriate for those making policy to build in evaluation before committing resources to this expensive and unproven procedure.

In the area of residential and nursing home care where, arguably, residents are highly vulnerable and there is political and professional pressure to minimize scandals, mandatory reporting of suspected abuse may form part of developments in quality assurance and inspection. In part of Canada, Leroux and Petrunik (1990) explain that mandatory reporting is required for all suspected cases of abuse within nursing homes (1990) under amendments to the Ontario Nursing Home Act 1987. In the UK, the Kent guidelines (1989) are slightly different for private residential care homes (suspected abuse should be notified to the registration officer) than for the local authority's establishment (report immediately to a manager and investigation to be done by a senior manager from another area, with a maximum time limit for this investigation of 48 hours). However, procedures for equal treatment between sectors are likely to converge in the UK as the inspection process moves to assess quality in all services. The position of nursing homes, however, is less clear and varies geographically.

Institutional abuse

Few studies have considered the social work response to institutional abuse or neglect. As indicated earlier, institutional care may be seen as the solution to domestic abuse. Intervention may be clouded by relationships between agencies, professions and personalities, but clearly the response to allegations or suspicions of abuse needs to prioritize the apparent needs and safety of the alleged victim.

A minority of social services departments make specific reference to abuse within institutions or non-domestic settings either in published guidelines or draft guidelines. In such areas it may be a matter of local managerial or even individual professional discretion whether to follow guidance on domestic abuse and apply it appropriately or whether to follow an alternative model of complaint.

The general response to abuse within for-profit or voluntary sector establishments (the independent sector) has been to refer matters to the local authority's inspection officer or nursing home inspectorate based within the local district health authority. *Caring for People* (Department of Health, 1989), with its development of arm's length inspection units (5.18) continues such monitoring procedures and legal safeguards.

Naturally, these are fine in principle but we have little knowledge yet about the inter-play between inspection and the detection of abuse, its prevention or its cessation. We do know that individual social worker's contact with residents of private residential care homes is often minimal (Phillips, 1990) at the point of entry and thereafter. We do not know how or even if residents of a home where there have been allegations of abuse are supported and counselled during investigations. Neither do we have much UK research to help residential care workers who may be expected to work with and care for people who have left one injurious residential setting for a new establishment. There is great scope for local practitioners from all client groups to explore such practices sensitively, with staff from all sectors. Support for staff who wish to raise questions about practices in their own establishments may be one result of such personal networking.

Ideally, complaints procedures should assist individuals and their representatives in improving the quality of services offered by all sectors. Many social services departments have restructured their procedures in the light of new community care legislation (Department of Health, 1989). North Yorkshire Social Services Department (1992), for example, make a three-stage process:

- complaint to staff member
- written complaint to complaints officer asking for an investigation
- attendance or representation at a complaints panel

In the residential care sector as a whole complaints may also be made to the registration officers about the conduct of establishments. Such rights are important but there are obvious difficulties for vulnerable people in making and sustaining allegations of poor quality or abusive treatment.

Individual social workers will need guidance about the procedures adopted by their employers in respect of complaints relating to care provided in all sectors. The Kent guidelines (1989) referred to earlier notes that: 'Any case of suspected abuse occurring in a K.C.C. establishment must be reported immediately to the local Area Manager, and investigated by a Senior Manager (Elderly) from a Sub-Area other than that in which the alleged incident occurred.' This attempts to give both confidence to the complainant and relative independence for the investigator. Evaluation of quality assurance mechanisms are in their infancy (Pfeffer and Coote, 1991); it will be important for public confidence and accountability to assess whether complaints are responded to sensitively, fairly and quickly.

For the social work professional, institutional abuse may then appear to be at a remove as many have no responsibility for the person concerned after admission. The introduction of care management, however, may alter this perspective as it appears that some care managers may continue to hold a monitoring role in respect of people for whom they have made financial arrangements for residential services. Equally, the emotional involvement of a care manager with a client may well be greater as he or she may have had a relationship for some time or of some intensity. It will be interesting to see whether quality assurance issues are able to link in with safeguards against abuse and it may be that the issue of neglect becomes more important in terms of institutional care.

None the less, social workers have equal though perhaps different difficulties in working with people at risk of abuse or neglect in institutional settings. On a basic level, few social workers now have experience of residential work in training. Some courses may attempt to offer observational placements but most reflect the dichotomy of the world of employment where residential care and community care are divided. There is also the perennial problem of acting as a 'whistle-blower' and being viewed as a trouble-maker by both one's employer or an agency with which one would like to maintain good working relationships. Here again, though, the importance of procedures may be a safeguard for the individual worker as well as the allegedly abused individual.

Winkler (1990) adds another concern to the problems of dealing with suspicions of institutional abuse. She notes that the United States has witnessed an early growth in voluntary organizations becoming care providers which may have compromised their watch-dog role. The US long-term care ombudsperson, established under the Older Americans Act, provides support to training programmes for volunteers who act as citizen advocates in the City of New York. This programme, separate from the inspection service, sees itself as an independent advocate. Winkler reports that its volunteers are trained to look for abuse.

Such a programme may be one meaningful way of reducing or preventing institutional abuse and neglect. If such work was to be developed in the UK, the social work task would appear to be both educational and supportive; educational in the sense of helping with the training of such advocates and supportive in giving advocates confidence that their concerns will be acted on in a sensitive and equitable manner, in line with agreed procedures and interventions. It may also be appropriate to remember that schemes of voluntary visiting have a long history in the UK and it may not be necessary to invent new programmes, simply to value and consider work that is already happening outside mainstream social work.

Norman (1987b), for instance, argues that the social watchdog role of volunteers is invaluable, particularly for residents of homes who lack family members or communication skills. Social workers involved in community activity or voluntary groups may wish to consider how both informal and formal advocacy can help reduce the opportunity for abuse to go unchallenged. Norman also notes that isolated residents, perhaps because of cultural or ethnic factors, may benefit from such independent and non-professional relationships.

Working together

When investigating abuse, the relationships between social worker and almost all concerned may be complex, inhibiting, stressful and problematic. Dalley's (1989) points about the divide between the health and social services are relevant in this context. Her interviews suggested difficulties in inter-professional working in both organizational and practical terms as well as matters of orientation, culture and attitudes which governed professionals' political and moral perspectives.

Moreover, it would appear that issues of collaboration or coordination may also be affected by the perceptions of the individuals involved. Lucas (1991) examined the relationship between the attitudes towards older people held by professionals and their recognition of abuse. She found that those who held positive attitudes towards older people tended to recognize patterns of abuse earlier and also felt able to make appropriate interventions. This suggests that the problems of working together effectively will have a number of dimensions. Although a 'case conference' or 'case meeting' may be the official or semi-official forum for inter-agency contact and collaboration, it is only one of a range of opportunities for social workers to inform, liaise, discuss, question and make decisions.

There is no set national procedure for deciding when a case

conference in respect of adults, or whatever name is chosen locally, should be called. Neither does any agency have the duty to do so nor the right to compel others to attend. Some guidelines, therefore, develop different models of the case conference, either basing them on child protection conferences or informal, advisory meetings in which the emphasis is on information sharing. We have no research to judge the efficiency of these approaches for adults deemed to be at risk in the UK.

One consequence of developing the case conference as a forum for discussion is the development of time limits and trigger mechanisms. One set of draft guidelines (Humberside Social Services, 1992) suggests that a case conference or discussion must be called in the following circumstances:

1 If access is denied in cases of serious or consistent suspected abuse within seven working days. All involved agencies should be invited to attend.
2 If after investigation an individual is considered to be at risk, a case conference has to be arranged within 72 hours and held within five working days. All agencies should be invited, together with the allegedly abused person and the carer if possible.
3 A case discussion is to be called within seven working days (all agencies invited) if an individual is deemed not to be at risk following investigation.

While these are only draft guidelines, they illustrate some common themes such as information exchange, the identification of risk factors, the clarification of roles, the legal context and ensuing action. Record-keeping and minute-taking are seen as important in terms of accountability and data collection. The role of the conference chair may be prescribed or otherwise. The Kent guidelines (1989) note that the chairperson of the six-monthly review should not have line management responsibility for day-to-day case management, while the Humberside draft guidelines limit the chair to people from health or social services management.

Hildrew (1991a) reports that few of the authorities she surveyed in England and Wales had at risk registers for adults and elderly people and suggests that this method of monitoring risk and coordinating care is falling from favour. However, case registers do have their proponents, especially among the medical and health professions. It may be useful to consider Sayce's points (1991) about safeguards and good practice to balance rights against risks. She advocates:

● specific criteria to determine entry on a register
● legal safeguards for individuals

- allocation of key workers to clients
- data protection
- clarity about confidentiality and ownership of material

While the UK legal position is such that there is no protective legislation specific to older people, many local authorities will continue to develop their own guidelines in the context of locally perceived need and concern. The Department of Health Social Services Inspectorate report (1992) argues that a more systematic approach is needed in the UK 'to alleviate the intolerable conditions suffered by abused elderly people'. However, its authors warn that public opinion may not be prepared for a more legalistic framework for intervention along the lines of many states within the US (Johnson, 1991).

Unfortunately, it may be that public opinion is swayed more by arguments based on scandals and scapegoating than by evidence and research. In order to develop procedures to assist vulnerable older people, joint guidelines for staff working with cases of suspected abuse may be a wise development by management in all relevant agencies. However, such guidelines need to be open to the continuing reconceptualization of the reality of elder abuse and need to link in closely with systems of mental health protection, criminal justice and the protection of other vulnerable adults.

Intervention

The Department of Health Social Services Inspectorate (SSI) report *Confronting Elder Abuse* (1992) gives useful information about social workers' responses to elder abuse in domestic settings. The SSI studied fieldwork in two London boroughs in 1990. Generally, they found that the primary goal of intervention was to maintain the abused person at home, with outside support or monitoring from statutory services. However, such support was limited by the options available in the locality. These findings confirm those of Pritchard in Sheffield (1990a,b).

The SSI report notes that the first response to allegations of abuse was for the person who received the information to discuss it with their line manager or a senior practitioner. It is not clear to what purpose these discussions were directed but one might expect that they were centred around the priority that should be given to the case, the reliability of the evidence, the mode of assessment and available resources. Despite this form of supervision, the SSI note that a significant number of cases were not assessed; in only half were care plans made and most cases were not regularly monitored or reviewed.

Such factors are also shown in another SSI report on services provided for disabled adults in Gloucestershire (Department of Health, 1991). Here, in a small sample of cases, the SSI found that assessment was ill defined and incomplete. The sample also revealed that care planning was mainly focused on the provision of support from a narrow range of existing services. Needs were not clearly identified, priorities were not made and objectives were unclear.

Both SSI reports indicate that interventions offered to disabled or vulnerable adults were in the form of traditional services, such as respite care, domiciliary care and meals services. Indeed, for many of the individuals concerned in the study of abuse (Department of Health, 1992) such services were already being provided; an allegation of abuse increased the amount or changed the pattern of service delivery. At the time of this research such services may have been available; however, changes in the pattern of provision and assessment may mean that this form of response is less common. For example, it is not clear what will be the effect of increased charges upon the recipients of services.

The less preferred strategy for intervention was to offer long-term residential care for the older person, that is, to remove them from potential or actual danger. Despite the philosophical change urged by the Wagner report (1988), this was seen by social workers to be an admission of failure.

Homer and Gilleard's (1990a: 1362) research challenges these attitudes. They question the value of increasing services input to relieve abuse:

> Few carers expressed the desire for increased home help or district nursing input, and it was not the physical or personal aspects of caring that caused the distress; distress was caused by the socially disruptive and abusive behaviour. When this behaviour has been present for many years it will be very resistant to change.

They suggest that behavioural techniques may be useful in respect of either or both the carer and older person. These may be offered individually through counselling or in a group setting. In a significant number of cases, advice on alcohol abuse or family therapy may be appropriate. However, they warn that long-term relationships of poor quality are difficult to change: 'Care in the community may not offer the best deal for everyone' (Homer and Gilleard, 1990a: 1362).

Significant risk factors identified by this study were alcohol consumption by the carer, a poor pre-morbid relationship and previous abuse over many years. The 'victims' often reciprocated in abuse and had difficulties in communicating. This study offers key indicators and also refers to the importance of the dynamic relationship between carer and older person, both in the past and present. The authors hold that separation between 'patient and carer' should be considered. In some cases, this should be done sensitively without the social worker viewing this as a failure on his or her part.

Social work intervention, therefore, needs to be built on principles of good assessment, care planning, monitoring and evaluation. Particular complications arise in the area of adult abuse; the SSI report (Department of Health, 1992) may be influential in urging social workers to develop a professional social work framework alongside a management strategy to develop guidelines, resources and inter-agency agreements.

Prevention

It may be the role of helping agencies, as well as other social groupings, to help prevent situations of abuse and neglect developing. We are given little idea from research of how, in particular, to 'help older adults help themselves' (Johnson, 1991: 7) but it may be worth considering the role of social work in preventing mistreatment. Such aspects may form a useful counter-balance to the stresses identified in working with older people at risk or casework generally.

Prevention of abuse is often perceived at a number of levels: the provision of resources generally, a change of attitudes towards ageing and older people, the development of safety nets, the ability to complain effectively and the development of monitoring systems to advocate for people who are incapacitated to some degree.

In the UK we have seen evidence of all these broad strands; in particular, at the domestic level where reducing carer stress through resource input has been most clearly argued by carers' lobbies (Pritchard, 1990b) and professional providers (see Tomlin, 1989). Within institutions, although resource levels have been less highlighted in respect of abuse (see Horrocks in Tomlin, 1989: 11), the focus has been on developing quality measures and inspectorate systems that enable residents or staff to voice complaints and concerns.

It may be worth summarizing the role that social workers can play in prevention at the macro-level. First, there is the role of public educator, particularly focusing on older people directly. Groups such as the University of the Third Age have a key role to play in developing older people's own interest in the subject and members are often in significant other networks. This should not be a one-way process as links with such groups often challenge preconceived notions about older people and their concerns.

Within health and social care agencies, social workers may also choose to extend and verify their knowledge by listening to the experience of other workers, particularly those with direct contact with vulnerable older people. Education about the limitations of social work powers may be an important feature here but prevention, in terms of understanding how care staff diffuse conflict or develop intervention strategies, is likely to broaden mutual understanding and respect. In the UK context, networking with general practitioners, community psychiatric nurses, district nurses and advocates may be the key to developing a fund of local experience and support.

The role of resources in preventing abuse is difficult to prove unless unmet needs are clearly identified and deficits of provision are systematically collected and reported. There has been much debate in other countries (see, for example, Podnieks (1989) on the Canadian perspective) about the ethical issues of raising expectations by pressing for action on abuse when services or resources are not available.

In conclusion, it may be useful to consider Johnson's (1991) prevention strategies for professionals and para-professionals. She develops a simple checklist which can be grouped into three main areas: the professional context, the client context and the personal context. On a professional level, she suggests that training and information are key tools to good practice. In the context of the client, working with older people and their families, she stresses that this should be creative, encouraging and assistive. Professionals should encourage people to ask questions, to look for alternatives and develop appropriate strategies. On a personal level, she advises workers to guard against ageism and, implicitly, against being 'overwhelmed' by their work. Interestingly, the strategies she develops for informal caregivers and older adults are very similar (1991: 184). One of the key issues in social work in the future may be how professionals work with clients in this area to acknowledge their individuality and adulthood when there is public pressure to protect and pity.

6

Recognizing Abuse: An Assessment Tool
for Nurses

Michael Davies

This chapter is intended principally, but not exclusively, for nurses, both hospital and community-based. It will explore the implications associated with elder abuse from this perspective. It will also incorporate the development of an assessment tool, which could help *all* health care professionals to recognize early signs and actual incidences of abuse in elderly people.

Specific reference to community psychiatric nurses and social workers will not be made, as strategies for their intervention are explored elsewhere in this volume. However, it is hoped that the possible outcomes highlighted could well be adapted for use by others in the field, including practice nurses, when carrying out their screening role of the over-75s, which now forms part of the new General Practitioners (GP) contract in Britain.

A cause for concern?

There is no doubt that the abuse of elderly people occurrs both in the community and in health care institutions. This chapter will look at the evidence regarding the prevalence of abuse in hospitals and elderly care units. In so doing, it is hoped that a measurement can be ascertained concerning the overall existence and identification of abuse in all areas of health care where nurses are involved.

Nurses, whether based in hospital or in the community, are in an ideal position to identify possible abuse. However, to be able to carry out this role, they will need specific education, training and guidance to heighten their awareness:

> The abuse of vulnerable elderly people is usually assumed to be either physical or psychological ill treatment by unpaid carers – most frequently by members of the victims family. However, it is not necessarily confined to those living at home, in the community. Deliberate ill treament may also involve paid staff. (Age Concern England, 1986: 35)

Perhaps the best-known exposé for nursing staff is the book '*Sans Everything': A Case to Answer* in which Robb (1967) exposed the frightening conditions endured by elderly patients in some state psychiatric institutions, in the hope of raising public and professional awareness of the need for reform. Robb concentrated on the conditions within the geriatric and psychogeriatric wards and, for a while, some improvements were perceived, but several inquiry reports have followed (see Chapter 1), often instigated by distraught relatives and occasionally by staff.

A King's Fund report (Glouberman, 1990) further compounds this evidence. Twelve monologues were selected from 60 interviews with workers from 27 different institutions, including prisons, long-stay hospitals, a long-stay geriatric unit, wards for mentally handicapped adults and so on. This should perhaps be compulsory reading material for policy-makers, particularly in the light of the impending community care reforms in Britain.

What is not so obvious, possibly due to the preoccupation with large pyschiatric establishments and their gradual reduction in size and eventual closure, is the amount of possible abuse occurring in those hospital wards caring for elderly patients, either in purpose-built units or in the large Victorian establishments scattered around the majority of health districts and National Health Service (NHS) Trusts. This does not, of course, preclude the need to question the possibility of abuse in other health care settings, specifically in the so-called acute care wards, and in medicine, surgery, orthopaedics etc.

> Old people today make greater use of hospitals than ever before. Roughly half of all occupied hospital beds are used by people aged 65 and over; nearly a third of such beds are occupied by people over 75. Departments of Geriatric Medicine and the Psychiatry of Old Age, contribute massively to the hospital care of older people, particularly those over 75, and have special knowledge of their needs. But to be able to look after older patients effectively is now a need in virtually every hospital ward and department. (Royal College of Nursing, 1987: 5)

There is, therefore, an urgent need to develop education/training programmes which may, in the long term, help to change a negative approach to nursing and/or caring for elderly people. 'Being a nurse or social worker, does not in itself create an immunity against being an abuser, neither does it prevent the possibility that, as we become older, and perhaps dependent on our own adult children, we too may become victims' (Eastman, 1988: 16).

Attitudes towards elderly people

The way that older people are perceived can be important indicators of caregiving.

There is a prevalence of ageist attitudes and inherent in such attitudes is the denigration of older people, where they are regarded as less than fully human and therefore not deserving of equal respect. This may be exacerbated by their mental frailty, by their neglected appearance, or by sensory defects, for example, deafness or some other impairment. (Stevenson, 1989: 23)

The vast majority of patients admitted for care into our hospitals and elderly care units are in a poor state of health, whether physically, psychologically or socially, but very often due to all three factors. The majority are especially prone to multiple loss, which is associated with the gradual process of ageing as Green (1985) describes. Loss of:

- income
- body function
- health
- independence and home
- sexual attraction
- company (spouse, friends, pets)
- life

and in addition, reduced mobility, physical handicap and often the living bereavement of dementia. Demographic trends indicate that the flow of these particular patients will probably increase. However, the quality of life that these people can expect is not guaranteed, and the provision for their care will still be, on the whole, hospital-based, as the services they require are not adequately provided for in the community.

The general attitude towards elderly people, particularly in the health care setting, is invariably a negative one. This view is held by staff working within such units, as well as by those outside. These negative attitudes are brought about by:

- perceived dead-end professional progression;
- low-level staffing and inappropriate skill mix, causing staff constantly to choose procedures of care, which are sometimes incompatible with the ideal of good practice or their Code of Professional Conduct;
- finances perceived as always going to the high tech areas, at the expense of elderly care;
- low sponsorship potential.

Student nurses have no more positive attitudes towards elderly people than secondary school pupils (Hope, 1992). General practitioners may present in a similar way:

Does your heart sink when the request comes in for a visit to an 80-year old patient with dizzy spells? On your way in the car do you have a mental picture of a confused, deaf, octogenarian with multiple pathology and chronic disease? Do your expectations make you ageist? (Grace, 1991: 11)

Grace goes on to say that, although one may dislike the word, it is clear that 'ageism' exists and that it has important consequences in health care, particularly in a world of finite medical resources. Dangers arise, however, when age assumes an inappropriate import- ance in decision-making, to the detriment of the patient and therapeutic options are withheld. This is a serious issue that will become increasingly apparent as the population ages, especially if the National Health Service continues to move in the direction of the market place. Hope (1992) argues that the negative attitudes of students are a prime factor in the delivery of sub-standard care and that society has allowed sub-standard services to become the norm for this client group. We are now reaping the consequences, having to deal with problems that should never have arisen.

Ageist attitudes, it is argued, are a contributory factor in cases of abuse.

As elderly people lose mental and physical capacities they are marginal- ized by society and by individuals and looked upon with contempt. They may come to accept this low evaluation of themselves and learn to be helpless. When people are considered to be of little value to society there will be less restraint on treating them with abuse and neglect. (Johnson et al., 1985, citing Block and Sinnott, 1979)

In hospital, in many instances the specialty of geriatrics, elderly care or elderly mentally infirm, still retains a poor image. 'Geriatric medicine is a second-rate speciality, looking after third rate patients, in fourth rate facilities' (Lye, 1982: 129). Although one might feel this to be an overstatement, and in several places to be outdated, there is little doubt that attitudes to nursing elderly people are still negative and are seen by many young, as well as mature, nursing staff as being less than glamorous and certainly not their first choice of elective placement.

The way forward

The importance of raising the profile of the care of elderly people cannot be over-emphasized; but professional education alone does not provide the panacea, changes in social attitudes are also required.

Patients' quality of life is closely associated with that of the staff who share with them the human need for recognition of worth and for self-esteem. All staff working with elderly people need to be skilled and confident and should be given every opportunity to initiate better methods of care and ways of working.

Supporting patients with their family and friends to come to terms with irreversible disability, or to accept death, can be rewarding. Staff need to understand and believe in what they are doing and above all to know that their contribution is valued. Staff also have a right to effective management and leadership, an efficient communication system, a meaningful working environment and continuing professional education opportunities.

Caring for elderly people, though rewarding, is nevertheless physically and emotionally demanding. Professional carers are under ever-increasing pressure in their daily work. At times, they all may feel anger, frustration and hostility. We should realize that this is a natural response to pressure.

> [But] What is totally unacceptable is to vent those feelings on those in our care. The dependent elderly in hospital are often, unpopular patients. They demand a lot of nursing time and attention: the skills required to care for them are not seen as important or specialised. (Williams, 1989: 23)

Podnieks (1985) identified key areas which contributed to possible neglect and abuse of elderly people by staff as: negative attitudes towards ageing, a lack of understanding of the ageing process, inadequate staff preparation and opportunity for professional growth.

The basic education/training of nurses in the Project 2000 programme has been under review and, it is to be hoped, will change radically in the next few years, as more programmes are designed and taught. But the Project has elected to keep elderly care nursing within the generic adult branch. Despite specific topics which must be addressed within the holistic approach to care of the individual, greater emphasis should be placed on the specialty of elderly care nursing.

Opportunities for qualified staff to attend English National Board post-basic courses on the care of elderly people must be made available. They are equally relevant to both specialist and generalist nurses. Care of elderly people demands skills which are of a very high standard. In all disciplines there is a continual need for further training, and it is vital for Health Authorities and NHS Trusts, to allow time and finance for staff to attend course and study days.

Each unit needs to explore what provisions are made for:

● newly appointed staff orientation programmes;
● continuous in-service education;
● post-basic course, leading to certificate, diploma and degree.

We need to ask:

● are all the multidisciplinary teams involved, including night staff?

- are opportunities available for staff to share knowledge and skills and express feelings and attitudes in their day-to-day work?
- are there adequate learning resources available?

(adapted from the Royal College of Nursing Project, 1987)

These educational innovations should involve all staff who have any dealings with elderly patients in any setting. Once implemented, they would begin to raise the profile of the nursing of elderly people.

Nurses are ideally placed to identify possible cases of elder abuse. However, to carry out this role they need training and guidance, as already said, particularly in interviewing and assessment skills. The approach should be multidisciplinary, involving social work, psychological, medical and nursing staff, both hospital and community-based. The involvement of other professions, such as occupational therapists and physiotherapists, could also be included. Together, they can form supportive teams to collaborate in producing a package of care for any elderly person who may be suspected of being at risk of abuse.

Assessment

The assessment tool will be primarily concerned with the identification of potential abuse of patients when they are admitted to hospital from their home or other residential setting, and how these indicators may be recognized by nursing staff.

Implications for nursing practice
The need to improve the detection and prevention of the abuse of elderly people has direct implications for nursing practice. Nurses need to be aware of the importance of a comprehensive nursing history. Meticulous attention, using the nursing process in identifying the elderly person's individual needs and problems, should be employed to help nurses identify the elderly at risk. There is clearly also a need to formulate and implement a valid and reliable tool which will assist practitioners to detect neglect and abuse. This should be the focus of a sound knowledge of 'high risk' indicators and an awareness of the available support systems that can be used in the case of intervention.

Perhaps the biggest problem in assessing the extent of abuse is that the abused person is reluctant to report the incident for fear of retaliation (Ross, 1985). This could also account for the reluctance on the part of health care workers to report cases where they have witnessed abuse of elderly clients by their colleagues. However, the United Kingdom Central Council for Nursing's Code of Professional

Conduct (1984) leaves us in no doubt of our responsibility to our clients. The Code states that nurses should 'act always in such a way as to promote and safeguard the well being and interests of patients/clients'. If nurses are to maintain their role as the patient's advocate, they must be willing to act to prevent abuse to one of the most vulnerable groups in our society.

Detection
Detection is often problematic because of the victim's reluctance to admit that abuse is taking place. This may be because of pride, shame, fear, bewilderment or confusion, or because of heavy dependence on the abuser, blaming themselves for the situation.

The nurse's assessment role in cases of physical abuse begins at the initial contact with the elderly person and continues with each subsequent interaction. During routine physical assessment, the nurse must be alert for clinical symptoms that are inconsistent with the information collected from the patient's history. This becomes difficult when the elderly individual has cognitive defects and exhibits confusion and disorientation. In such cases it is advisable to locate the primary carer or, where appropriate, other workers who have been involved in the care of the patient, to confirm details. Often neighbours and relatives have additional information that may clarify the nature of the injury and its cause.

The nurse's observational skills are paramount in all cases whether or not the patient's mental state is functional or organic. Indicators of abuse should be considered in clusters because, although while not proving the existence of abuse, they certainly indicate a risk (see Chapter 2). Part of the detection process is the importance of observing if the 'symptoms' disappear in hospital or residential care and reappear at home or in cases of 'respite admission', when the patient is re-admitted. It is therefore essential that close liaison exists between the multidisciplinary elderly support group.

Signs of physical abuse and neglect are often not evident, and therefore the psychological and material features of abuse are not so easy to detect and there may be very little overt evidence to raise suspicion. However, nurses should be aware of possible indicators which may denote the presence of such abuse. These include:

- undue anxiety or aggression displayed by the elderly person;
- depression, helplessness, hopelessness;
- fearfulness, 'what are you going to do to me?' or being left alone;
- ribbons in hair, toys, baby talk;
- cowering;
- expression of ambivalent feeling towards family;
- excessively tired, confused, experiencing insomnia, tearful;

- unusual interest being shown by others in the elderly person's possessions, especially money;
- necessities not being provided by carers, for example, money for soap, sweets, newspapers, despite holding the pension/bank books;
- patient being distressed by being 'forced' to sign unexplained documents etc.

In cases where these indicators are present, it would be advisable to involve other health care professionals, for example, district nurses, health visitors or social workers, where they have been involved in the care of the individual, as they will be in a better position to confirm any suspicions, having possibly observed relevant factors in the home/residential environment.

Carers

When nurses are carrying out their patients' assessment, they need to be aware of the vital part that carers play. In any case where there may be reason to believe that abuse has taken place, the assessment must involve the primary carer(s). This must be conducted with great sensitivity. In cases that 'appear' to indicate neglect, it is important to assess the carer's level of understanding, the resources that they have available to them and the elderly person's willingness to accept care. Older people have the right to self-determination and may knowingly refuse the care necessary to sustain health. Many carers themselves are elderly and nurses have an obligation to 'care for the carer', as well as those being cared for. Many carers find themselves in an overburdened situation with other family and employment commitments making considerable demands upon their time, energy and loyalties.

> It is important not to jump to conclusions that relatives are being cruel and heartless to frail old people. Old age abuse is a significant problem but it also includes the abuse of relatives by old people, perhaps using emotional blackmail and sometimes physical aggression effectively to keep the relative under control. Indeed we have come across probably more instances of the caring relative being attacked by the patient than vice-versa. (Matthews and Woods, 1980: 37)

Observing carers for signs of physical abuse will not be easy, as they too may well be reluctant to volunteer information, but nevertheless a carer assessment is important, if we are to be in a position of building up a complete picture, which could lead towards a resolution of the situation.

Perhaps the best indicator that all is not well with the carer will be signs of stress, but most carers will exhibit these signs, and the role of the nurse will be to attempt to measure the intensity of feeling associated with the common signals that might be expected. These could include:

- frequent requests for help (self or patient), which includes admission to care;
- aggression: frustration or despair often towards staff;
- obvious signs of physical or mental illness, exhaustion;
- non-visiting or telephone enquiry;
- non-participation in discharge planning;
- anxiety and worry, feeling isolated, lonely, low self-esteem, depression;
- indifferent relationship with patient;
- obvious alcohol/drug dependence;
- over-critical regarding aspects of care towards patient.

A carer will often express a lack of time for self, of not being able to see an end to the situation and no future – that all has gone beyond control. These signals are not necessarily an indicator that abuse is/has taken place. But assessment and recording of these indicators are important pointers towards collating the most appropriate package of care for both the patient and the carer and may well help to stop an abuse situation occurring.

Precise, informed detection skills on the part of nurses, and the completion of the necessary assessment protocols, though perceived as lengthy and time-consuming, will provide definitive information regarding suspected cases of abuse. This in itself may be sufficient to instigate action or at least to alert medical colleagues to the need for further investigation.

The assessment protocols (Appendix 6.1 and 6.2), one for use with patients and the other for use with carers, are designed to comp-lement the existing, history-taking documentation that exists within the nursing process procedure. Initially, both could be used in cases where abuse/neglect is suspected but, once adopted, they could in the long-term be incorporated within the documentation used during the 'normal' assessment of all elderly people admitted to hospital, thus performing universal screening mechanisms, including identification of possible abuse, as a matter of routine.

Training
Before attempting to implement these protocols, it will be essential for all staff to receive training and guidance in their use. This will ensure that staff are made aware of the specific terminology employed and that the assessment tools are used in a uniform and

objective way. A glossary of terms, particularly for use with Appendix 6.2 might be helpful.

Elder abuse assessment protocol (Appendix 6.1)

If a nurse suspects that the patient is a victim of abuse or neglect, this assessment tool may be employed. The process may take several days to complete and should involve both day and night staff. Many of the more obvious 'signals' which may alert a nurse to the possibility of physical abuse will be observed during routine admission procedures. Examples of these are:

- general appearance, nutritional state, mental attitude, awareness;
- condition of skin, ulcers, pressure sores, need for aids, dentures, hearing aid, glasses;
- activities of daily living, including mobility.

Cognizance can be taken of these general areas during the physical examination, while accompanying the admitting doctor. Further observations can be made during either bed or general baths. The patient may well be reluctant to answer direct questions. They are more likely to respond to indirect conversation. Too many questions will often deter compliance.

Other aspects, for example psychological abuse, will need to be handled very sensitively and again may need to be carried out in several stages, once the nurse has gained the patient's trust and confidence. Learner nurses may participate in this procedure, but they must be accompanied by a qualified practitioner, and the patient's consent to the observer should be sought prior to the assessment.

Carer's abuse assessment protocol (Appendix 6.2)

This is designed to be used to obtain indications of possible stress and its intensity. It could be used usefully to assess any carer where staff feel stress is apparent and need not only be used in cases of suspected abuse.

The assessment will need to be carried out in stages, in order to allow the carer to build up a sense of trust and confidence in the staff. The nurse's approach needs to be supportive and at all times sensitive and never judgmental.

Valid assessment

'People who ask questions must expect to be told lies', whether deliberately, inadvertently or unconsciously. Clients are often 'too close' to evaluate their own needs, and their ability to articulate may vary from day to day (Wilkin and Thompson, 1989).

Conclusion

It is reasonable to assume that elder abuse is a significant problem that nurses who work with old people can expect to encounter. They also face major problems when caring for the victims of elder abuse. As Ross (1985: 11) argues: 'Knowledge on the topic is limited and nurses cannot locate quality research to guide their practice.' Furthermore, since elder abuse has only recently been identified as a family and social problem, there are few established resources, services and treatment programmes available which can be used in an attempt to solve the problem. The data collection tools discussed here are intended to serve as a guide in the detection of neglect and abuse of elderly clients. But this can only be part of the process. However, they may alert nurses to a possible diagnosis of neglect and/or abuse.

Nurses should continue to make inroads towards becoming more sensitive and responsive to the issue of actual and potential abuse, by acknowledging that the problem does exist among elderly members of the population. They must be willing to ask difficult and sensitive questions surrounding the appearance of bruises, fractures or other untoward injuries to an elderly patient.

Appendix 6.1: Assessment Protocol for Elder Abuse (adapted from Fulmer, 1984; Ross, 1985)

Initial guidance for use

Before attempting to carry out the assessment, reference should be made to the section on 'detection' above.

The assessment is meant to serve as a screening procedure and to document cases of suspicion of abuse or neglect. You are not asked to 'rate' any particular section but rather to use your powers of observation, instinct and 'gut feeling'. Remember, seldom will you find isolated symptoms, but a 'cluster' of symptoms may give rise to suspicion, and should not be ignored. Any suspicion will need to be fully explained in the 'Assessor's summary and general opinion' section.

A tick (√) should be placed against the applicable description and, where appropriate, expanded upon in the summary section. For example, if you tick Physical Assessment 1. Bruising: shoulders √ left; colour: purple/yellow 2″, in the summary section, you will need to expand, for example: bruise left shoulder, approximately 2″ in diameter, purple in centre with yellow ringed edge.

In cases where the patient is not able to communicate or cooperate, this fact should be indicated in the summary.

ELDER ABUSE ASSESSMENT PROTOCOL

General Assessment

Clothing:	*Hygiene*	*Grooming:*	*Nutrition:*
Torn _____	Body odour _____	Unkempt hair _____	Pallor _____
Soiled _____	Unclean _____	Uncut nails:	Lips _____
Disarrayed _____		Finger _____	Mouth _____
		Feet _____	Hydration _____

Skin:
PAs: _____
sites _____

Ulcers: _____
sites _____

Urine burns: _____
sites _____

Excoriation: _____
sites _____

Physical assessment: Evidence of:

1 *Bruising:*

Site:	*Colour of bruise/size*
Shoulders	_____
Buttocks	_____
Thighs	_____
Forearm	_____
Lips	_____
Mouth	_____
Face	_____
Eyes	_____
Other	_____

Colour of bruise: Please indicate black/purple/yellow (this may give some indication of age of bruise)

2 *Abrasion/Laceration:*

Site:	*Colour/state*
Mouth	_____
Lips	_____
Gums	_____
Genitalia	_____
Buttocks	_____
Others	_____

Please state colour/state: e.g. red/pink/open/closed/scarred/scabbed/tenderness etc.

Please indicate site of bruising/abrasion/laceration on torso.
Colour code: Bruise (black biro)
Abrasion/laceration (red biro)

3 *Alopecia/haemorrhaging*
Comment:

6 *Cognitive/emotional assessment:*
(a) Worried/anxious
(b) Aggressive
(c) Depression:
      Sad
      Loss of interest
      Feeling hopeless
      Withdrawn
      Tearful
(d) Slurred speech
(e) Drowsiness
(f) Reduced
      responsiveness
(g) Cowering
(h) Irritable, easily upset
(i) Defensive
(j) Evasive
(k) Guarded
(l) Suspicious
(m) Confused
(n) Disorientated
(o) Sleep disturbances
(p) Evidence of
      infantilization

Comment:

4 *Obvious deformities*
Comment/site:

Contractions
Comment/site:

                                    Site
Pain
Tenderness
Swelling

7 *Relationship with carer:*
(a) Defensive
(b) Guarded
(c) Hostile
(d) Passive
(e) Afraid

Any change after carer has left?

Comment:

5 *Sexual abuse* (By observation not examination)
Genitalia: vaginal and anal area
Bruising
Bleeding
Pain
Redness
Itching
Scratch marks
Discharge
Marked embarrassment
evident
Comment:

8 *Personal possessions:*
Petty cash
Toiletries
Tissues
Newspaper
Writing material
Stamps
Confectionery
Cordials
Personal clothing

Assessor's summary and general opinion:

Signed: ....

Appendix 6.2: Assessment Protocol for Carer Abuse (adapted from Fulmer, 1984; Ross, 1985)

Before attempting to carry out the assessment, reference should be made to the section on 'carers' above (pp. 109–10).

The assessment is meant to identify indications of possible stress and its intensity.

Again, you are not being asked to 'rate' particular sections, but to use your powers of observation. A tick should be placed against the applicable description and the 'Assessor's summary and general opinion' area should be used to explain your observations. For example, in section 7, if you tick 'exhaustion', you will need to explain how this was displayed ('appears continually drained, tired, listless etc.').

Please now see p. 116.

CARER ABUSE ASSESSMENT PROTOCOL

1 *Relationship to patient:*
Relative
Other

2 *Age range:*
Under 21
21–39
40–59
60–75
75+

3 *Gender:*
Male/Female

4 *Marital status:*
Married
Single
Separated
Divorced
Widowed
Other

5 *Domestic arrangements:*
Alone
With patient
With spouse
With children
With others

6 *Evidence of:*
Alcohol dependence
Drug dependence
Physical illness
Mental illness
Mental retardation
Financial dependence
History of family
   violence
Other

7 *Evidence of stress:*
Frustration
Exhaustion
Anxiety
Low self-esteem
Lack of leisure time
Problems with children/marriage

8 *Knowledge of patient's situation:*

	Good	Poor
(a) *Physical/emotional health*		
(b) *Assistance with ADLs:*		
Bathing		
Dressing		
Eating		
Mobility		
Toiletting		
(c) *Any treatment regime:*		
Medication		
Nutrition		
Exercise		
Treatments		
Others		

9 *Attitude towards patient:*
(a) Angry
(b) Blaming
(c) Critical
(d) Over-concerned
(e) Resentful
(f) Non-concerned

10 *Attitudes towards staff:*
a. Defensive
b. Aggressive
c. Irritable
d. Suspicious

11 *Behaviour with patient during visiting:*
Demonstrates lack of:
Physical contact
Facial contact
Eye contact
Verbal contact

Assessor's summary and general opinion:

Signed: ....

7

The Multidisciplinary Assessment of Clients and Patients

Peter Decalmer and Alison Marriott
with contributions from
Dudley Ainsworth, Robert Bamlett and Jan Cowley

The main purpose of this chapter is to give some insight into how a multidisciplinary team approaches cases of elder abuse. The case examples that follow include the previously discussed elements of physical, sexual, psychological and material abuse, together with active and passive neglect. They demonstrate the complexity of this area of social, legal, medical, psychological and psychiatric concern. The chapter will explore the ways in which each professional involved, using their professional expertise, can find ways of providing strategies of care and intervention.

Using a team conference is a well-established method of drawing these strategies together and leads to a way forward of how best to manage these very complicated cases. A team conference provides a method of open discussion, reporting findings and formally formulating cases so that a written record can be drawn up. The record should consist of the information obtained from all the sources, including an account of the types of abuse from the victim and perpetrator, the assessment from the professional and an agreed strategy of care and intervention. An assessment of risk is essential (Phillipson and Biggs, 1992). Clear statements are necessary about whether it is a definite or probable case of elder abuse. The conclusion should declare methods of intervention, including who is to be responsible for this. A keyworker or coordinator is desirable, and arrangements in writing should be made for reviewing the cases at regular and stated intervals to ensure that strategies of intervention have worked, and to address new developments or facts of the case which have been overlooked or subsequently come to light. There is an urgent need to develop these strategies (Allen et al., 1992) in the light of the NHS and Community Care Act (1990) as many professionals are still uncomfortable working in this way, particularly with elderly people. However, Bebbington and Davies (1983) have shown that there was a marked improvement in efficient case management using horizontal target efficiency principles. Thus case management as defined in the White Paper, *Caring for People* (Department of Health, 1989), will provide an excellent model to help with elder abuse (Ferlie et al., 1989). It provides a coordinator who can mobilize resources and integrate service allocation with cost information (Goldberg and Huxley, 1980). Worsam (1991) looked at assessment and broke the process down into:

● purpose
● process
● method
● occasions for assessment
● outcome of assessment.

When deciding who to invite to a multidisciplinary team for an elder abuse case conference the following should be considered essential: the general practitioner, a consultant psychiatrist or geriatrician, a social worker, a specialist nurse or community psychiatric nurse, a clinical psychologist and either a legal advisor or the police.

The *general practitioner* is the physician with responsibility for primary care medical services. His/her duties include:

1 Confidential relationship between doctor and patient.
2 The determination of clinical needs of an individual patient which may include the victim and the perpetrator.
3 Provision of the best possible treatment within his/her experience.
4 The power to delegate authority (to diagnose or treat) but not responsibility.

The *consultant's* responsibilities include:

1 The ultimate medical authority within the hospital service for patients within his/her care.
2 The same duties as listed 1–3 above for the general practitioner.
3 A responsibility to describe deficiencies in the service, especially if they impede the satisfactory implementation of clinical and ethical duties to patients.
4 A special role as responsible medical officer, as defined within the Mental Health Act 1983.
5 Supervision and training of junior medical staff and other doctors in training.
6 Effective coordination of the contributions of the variety of disciplines involved in clinical care.

The *psychiatric nurse* possesses general skills in the assessment of nursing needs and in the planning and delivery of nursing care. In addition, he/she often has skills in:

- behavioural modification
- group work and leadership
- community psychiatric nursing
- family therapy and prevention
- individual counselling

He/she should establish a relationship when visiting the client at home:

1 to look at nursing needs;
2 to establish social and rehabilitation programmes;
3 to help the elder abused person regain lost skills and provide diversion;
4 to be able to monitor medication schedules and drugs safety policies, especially if there are problems with medication abuse;
5 to establish individual care plans.
6 The community psychiatric nurse should develop close links between the primary care teams and the psychiatric teams to assist both parties in difficult nursing problems.

He/she should follow up complex management problems when the patient is discharged from hospital and liaise with the multidisciplinary team.

The *social worker's* duties can be summarized under four headings:

1 Casework: a range of techniques employed by the social worker with the client to enhance the latter's personal functioning. This includes support and counselling.
2 Statutory powers, as defined by the Mental Health Act 1983.
3 Liaison and consultation between social services, other local authority departments and the health service.
4 In elder abuse, serious consideration may need to be given to the social worker carrying a central administrative role.

The *clinical psychologist* has responsibility for the following areas:

1 Planning and carrying out treatment, particularly on counselling or behavioural lines.
2 Psychological assessment, formulation of the patient's problems and capabilities in objective terms. (In elder abuse, capacity and understanding may be a vital issue.)
3 Education of other team members in the principles and findings of scientific psychology.

4 Contributing to the (social) psychological perspectives of abuse cases.
5 Undertaking research in relevant areas.

The *police and legal advisors* have duties:

1 To assist the group in legal matters, or if a crime has been committed.
2 To help with collecting evidence or to make clear the legal position, and subsequent courses of action in often very complex cases.
3 To advise the team on the correct course of action, especially if prosecution is advised, and to suggest the correct procedures with both parties.

Problems of a multidisciplinary team

These can only be summarized here as a full description would be beyond the remit of this book:

1 *Outside accountability*. The doctor is probably the only member of the team with clinical autonomy. Other representatives of the team have line managers to whom they are responsible. To overcome this, the other members have to negotiate autonomy within the group. The Community Care Act, using case management, will formalize this problem and lead to the provision of probable solutions.
2 *Failure to distinguish between specific and shared skills*. Each discipline is now developing its own professional identity in relation to their respective skills and this has the potential for considerable rivalry which can be divisive unless roles are agreed and the group is accountable to the team manager (Lomas, 1991).
3 *Clinical versus executive function*. This may lead certain members of the group to have to withdraw from the team (Bebbington and Hill, 1985; Bennett and Freeman, 1991) to ensure that their statutory responsibilities are met, especially if overruled by the group. This applies to medical officers and social workers in particular.

Once the multidisciplinary team has decided on a course of action with a case of abuse, a keyworker system is best employed. This person can act as a facilitator, coordinator and an integrator of the action to be taken (Mechanic, 1989), thus making sure that the case is properly managed and information is disseminated to all members of the group. The case can then be reviewed at regular intervals with the keyworker calling and organizing further case conferences. The cases described give some insight into the management of these complicated cases using the keyworker system.

Case example 1
Keyworker: Community Psychiatric Nurse (Although this case was managed by a community psychiatric nurse, it was later reviewed by the same nurse as a clinical nurse specialist.)

Mrs G, aged 70, was referred by her GP. She lived with her husband in a mobile home in Wales. She had a dementing illness, characterised by loss of short-term memory and was doubly incontinent. She was unable to cook or do any housework. Her husband, Mr G, had mobility problems due to a varicose ulcer, but no psychiatric history.

Mr G, who was 72, alleged that his son had removed £6,000 from the joint account of Mr and Mrs G without his permission. There was also evidence of threats of physical assault and actual bodily harm to Mr G by his son.

General comments

- realities of work in rural area
- risk to worker of violence and legal responsibilities
- code of practice: policy for health and social services workers
- Resettlement/Community Care Act: implications for problems when dealing with elder abuse cases
- use of assessments (psychiatry and psychology) in legal proceedings

Case Review 1

The initial assessment was performed by the community psychiatric nurse at the request of the GP. The patient and family were informed of the planned visit. The couple were found to live in an isolated, rural, mountainous part of Wales. They relied upon calor gas for heating and cooking, and bottled water for drinking, cooking and washing. The house was filthy, with faecal smearing on the bed and carpets; and a strong smell of urine pervaded the house. The kitchen revealed piles of unwashed crockery and mounds of rotting food. The couple had moved only recently from the Midlands and deeply regretted it because of lost friends and money. The son and daughter-in-law were the main carers and resided 200 yards away. Mr G accused his son of removing £6,000 from the account of Mr and Mrs G and of denying them access to their full pension. He also believed his son to be over-charging him for provisions which the son delivered to them.

When the community psychiatric nurse conducted an assessment visit to the son and daughter-in-law in their cottage they maintained a different perspective of the situation. Mr G's son felt that his father had a rigid personality and they agreed about little. The son also felt that his mother had always been dominated by his father and had never been allowed to manage her own affairs until they sold the house in the Midlands, whereupon the proceeds were divided between them. At this point the younger couple described how they were happy to continue to care for the elderly couple and dismissed Mr G's claim as being part of his difficult personality.

The community psychiatric nurse continued to visit the family on a weekly basis for the next two months to monitor the situation. At one point, the daughter-in-law phoned complaining that 'everything was dreadful'. She described how her husband and father-in-law had had a fight; the son was talking of killing his father and had indeed threatened him with a carving knife.

The senior nurse manager was informed of the situation. A visit to the family found the son in a very distressed state. He described an argument which had taken place between himself and his father after the father had accused him of stealing £6,000. The son acknowledged that he had accepted £6,000 from his mother as a 'loan', and expressed the view that this had nothing to do with his father. The whole situation escalated and threats had been made.

Mr G was found to be breathless and agitated; and Mrs G was tearful and tried to hide in the bedroom. While they were relating the incident, the door burst open and the son threw himself at his father, dragging him from his chair onto the floor and hitting him. They had to be separated and the younger man returned home. After ascertaining that no physical harm had been incurred, the discussion with the elderly couple continued and they expressed the view that continuing to live near the son was impossible and they wished to return to the Midlands. However, they had little money to facilitate this.

The community psychiatric nurse again visited the son and advised that the police would be informed as battery had been witnessed. No objection was raised to this by the son. The GP was informed about the incident. An urgent referral to the Department of Social Services was made requesting an assessment with a view to initially discussing the provision of an emergency relief placement in a residential home for the elderly couple.

Mr and Mrs G were seen by a social worker two days later and immediately offered, and accepted, a double room in an aged person's home in a nearby village. Initially, the offer was for a month's holiday relief, but the placement became permanent. An application was made to the Court of Protection to administer their finances.

Team Conference 1

The community psychiatric nurse was the keyworker in this case and the case illustrates the realities of working in a rural area, where a limited number of professional staff typically cover a large geographical area which is often sparsely populated. An immediate response to a crisis can result in a lone worker taking responsibility for responding to situations which may pose a risk. With hindsight, social services might have been involved at an earlier stage and joint work undertaken. The police would also have been involved, ideally at the point at which threats of violence within the family were suggested by the daughter-in-law's phone call. Codes of practice covering when and how to intervene exist in many areas for services involving children at risk, but rarely exist when an elderly adult is the service consumer. In this instance a code of practice was required that when there were threats of, and evidence of, assault and battery, they should be immediately reported to the police. This would afford greater protection for the community psychiatric nurse and the victim, but might compromise the relationship with the family.

A psychiatrist's opinion should be sought to ascertain Mrs G's capacity to decide how her money should be used. This should be supported by a neuropsychological assessment. A clinical psychologist, using standardized assessment procedures to suggest the severity and extent of the dementing illness, would be essential. It would be advisable for the assessments to be conducted as close to the time of the incident as possible in order to remove any doubts that may be raised about a possible deterioration in Mrs G's mental state, since her reported decision to allow her son access to the money. If any future legal action was taken by Mr G against his son, these reports would help the courts to clarify Mrs G's mental capacity.

The decision about a change of residence was determined by the discussions between the couple and the Social Services Department. Under the Community Care Act, resettlement of the couple back to the Midlands may have been a theoretically preferable option here, but *in practice* might have been difficult to achieve.

Case example 2

Keyworker: Community Psychiatric Nurse

Mrs B, aged 69, came to the renewed attention of the psychiatric services following an incident when she threatened her neighbour with a knife. She had a long history of psychiatric illness, characterized by auditory, somatic and gustatory hallucinations. Her behaviour was driven by voices which she heard emanating from the street, and led her to believe that her life was in danger. She believed that she was a victim of poisoning and widespread discrimination. Her well-developed delusional system was encapsulated within her home environment.

An examination by a consultant old age psychiatrist confirmed a psychotic illness, probably schizophrenia. A physical examination indicated physical injuries consistent with sexual abuse. She was fully orientated, showed no cognitive loss and exhibited no abnormality of mood. Her pre-morbid personality showed evidence of immature and inadequate traits.

General comments

● role of professional psychiatric treatment for the victim
● seeking help for the perpetrator
● involving the police/legal system
● use of rehabilitation in preventing further abuse
● primary care role of the GP

Case Review 2

This case, presented by the community psychiatric nurse, highlighted aetiological factors in her illness and personality. It is significant that since the age of ten years, when both parents died, she spent time in an orphanage and was often with foster parents. It is worth noting that her mother was a heavy drinker and that the children, it is said, were neglected.

In adult life, Mrs B entered into service and eventually started working in the confectionery trade. During this period of her life she had a number of cohabiting relationships which produced three children to three separate fathers. Eventually she married, but this relationship soon terminated. Following this, she was taken into hospital and diagnosed as suffering from a psychotic breakdown. As a result of the hospital admission Mrs B's three children were taken into care, with no further contact.

Her life in recent years has been characterized by a similar pattern of short-lived cohabiting relationships with men, who she says harass her. Mrs B describes herself as being shy, but others, she says, see this as snobbishness.

An assessment by a consultant psychiatrist found Mrs B to be psychotic and in need of treatment. A depot injection of a major tranquillizer was prescribed and given by the community psychiatric nurse. During the visit, Mrs B admitted to a relationship with a man which had been distressing her and sought advice.

The man was asking her for money, insisting that she cook and clean for him and was also raping her frequently. She was compelled

to acquiesce to his demands, resulting in physical injury, characterized by bruising around the inner thighs and vaginal bleeding,
confirmed on physical examination by a doctor.

Mrs B informed the perpetrator of her contact with the psychiatric
services. The man attempted to frighten Mrs B into believing that the
services were trying to return her to hospital and that the injection
would cause her harm.

Assessment of her case by the team took place over a three-week
period and agreed intervention strategies conducted by the community psychiatric nurse were as follows:

1 Regular visits to monitor the episodes of physical and sexual abuse.
2 To liaise with social workers, consultant psychiatrist and police.
3 To interview the perpetrator and challenge his behaviour.
4 To encourage Mrs B to be more assertive in her relationships with
  men and to make Mrs B more aware of the perpetrator's
  behaviour.
5 Regular administration of depot medication to control her
  psychosis.

Over the next few weeks, the perpetrator took her out regularly at
night and did not make any sexual demands of her. He tried to
persuade her to marry him, in an attempt to legitimize the sexual
relationship.

The community psychiatric nurse interviewed the perpetrator. The
interview took place at Mrs B's house. He became indignant, denying
allegations. During the interview it was obvious that he was suffering
from a paranoid illness, characterized by bizarre ideas about the
neighbourhood in which he lived and the nature of the injections
which Mrs B was receiving.

At a subsequent meeting, Mrs B with the help of the community
psychiatric nurse was enabled to express her feelings about the
perpetrator and terminate the relationship. The man agreed to have
no further contact with her. Following this, the community psychiatric nurse agreed with Mrs B to provide continued support with a
series of regular visits. Mrs B expressed a wish to have no legal action
taken against this man. Subsequently, she had no further contact with
him. Continuing work enabled her to become more assertive in her
relationships with others. She remains well, in the community.

Team Conference 2
Discussion within the multidisciplinary team concerning this case
centred upon a number of questions relating to the potential risk of
the man perpetrating further abuse, and the potential involvement of
the police in this case. It was felt that the community psychiatric

nurse's view that the perpetrator of the abuse may be himself mentally unwell necessitated an attempt to contact the man's GP and to offer assessment for him. This was felt to be particularly relevant as it was unclear to what extent the man's inappropriate sexual conduct related to his existent mental state and there was felt to be a risk that he might seek other victims when his relationship with Mrs B terminated.

It was also felt by the team that Mrs B should be more strongly counselled to inform the police of the sexual assault and the ensuing physical injuries. If she continued to refuse to do so, it could be argued that her mental state at the time of the assault and her difficulties in asserting herself would make it necessary for a mental health assessment to be carried out to establish whether there were sufficient grounds for her to be treated under the Mental Health Act. This course of action might be desirable in order to protect the patient and the (male) community psychiatric nurse from future counter claims by the man. There might be claims by the woman herself (if her mental state again deteriorated) that the community psychiatric nurse had become a part of her delusional system as the perpetrator of sexual abuse or poisoning through the depot injection.

Separate roles should be agreed by various members of the multidisciplinary team.

1 The community psychiatric nurse to administer medication and maintain supportive contact with the woman.
2 The social worker to take on the role of informing the police of the sexual assault.
3 The clinical psychologist to plan and implement a social skills and assertiveness programme.
4 The consultant psychiatrist to assess mental state and treat psychotic illness.
5 The GP to be kept regularly informed of the situation through the assessment and intervention phases.

Case example 3
Keyworker: Psychiatrist
Mrs W, aged 70, was suffering from severe dementia presenting with increased frailty, very poor short-term memory, a dressing apraxia, and failure to recognize her husband. She started to cower on approach, and on physical examination was noted to have bruising on her face, front of arms, chest and inner thighs. The bruises were like finger marks.

Her husband, aged 76, was depressed with a very dependent personality. He admitted hitting her and dressing her very roughly. This was not in character. They married as teenagers, and survived the trauma of Mr W being severely and permanently injured in the War. As Mrs W's dementia progressed, she would treat her husband as a stranger. He became jealous because of her lack of affection. He sexually abused her as a result. Mrs W was physically very hurt by this. She was admitted to a long-stay ward. Eventually Mr W became so hopeless that he planned a homicide/suicide as a lovers' pact.

General comments

- how to protect the victim after hospital admission
- how to support the carer/perpetrator
- how to assess consent concerning continued sexual relations between Mr and Mrs W
- role of family in advocacy for Mrs W
- how to monitor further abuse of the patient

Case Review 3

The clinical presentation of Mr and Mrs W showed that before the illness affected her they were emotionally very close. They were childhood sweethearts, choosing to have no children. They isolated themselves from their families. The war wound became a focus of their mutual dependency and Mrs W dressed the wound daily. She was the strong one in the relationship. When she developed her dementing illness he lost a wife, a confident lover and his only friend. Her physical coldness he found devastating and this led to sexual abuse. His physical abuse was a result of her changing role and increasing physical dependency.

As a clinician, the immediate problem after analysis of their problem was Mrs W's physical safety. This was achieved by short-term care and later continuing care to protect her from physical and sexual abuse. Mr W wanted to continue to look after her and applied to the courts for custody. His social worker persuaded him to look after the psychological needs of his wife while she remained an inpatient and to accept treatment for his depressive illness with medication and specialist help including individual psychotherapy.

Staff were faced with the problems of him wanting to take her home for one last time for what was felt to be a planned homicide/suicide. This was approached by not allowing her to be taken home and gradually working at them being together on the ward, as much as they wished; concentrating on the psychological support that he was still able to give to his wife. He presently spends a minimum of six hours a day with her. However, there are still verbally aggressive outbursts and occasional physical abuse. These are supervised and monitored by nursing staff. When she dies it is likely that he will become a suicidal risk.

Team Conference 3

The initial discussion centred around what constituted consent to a sexual relationship when Mrs W's dementing illness precluded the usual assent. Nursing staff felt that their observations of the interaction between the couple, namely Mr W's rough physical handling of his wife, and Mrs W's physical withdrawal and non-verbal signs of distress, precluded the freedom and privacy normally granted to couples visiting to participate in a sexual relationship on the ward. It was felt that Mr W's approaches to his wife, in full view of the ward, demonstrated disinhibited behaviour. A member of the ward staff could be appointed to ensure Mrs W's safety and to set agreed behavioural limits on Mr W. Mrs W's relatives, who had been alienated by Mr W's behaviour when the couple were at home, should be invited to a case conference and be encouraged to reinstate visits to Mrs W, to advocate her needs and provide a balance to the very extended visits of her husband.

The team discussed whether the anger displayed by Mr W to his wife and towards ward staff could be viewed in terms of a pathological grief reaction, relating to the loss of his wife as he had known her, because of her dementia. But it was felt that his dependent behaviour as evidenced by his angry responses to events had always been a feature of his personality, even prior to his wife's illness and precluded therapeutic intervention.

It was agreed that Mr W was likely to contemplate suicide in the event of his wife's death, and indeed much of his time was invested in visiting her and caring for her. It would be appropriate to consider a social worker being assigned to Mr W to attempt to help him to develop other interests and activities outside the hospital, but this would potentially be a difficult task in this case. The risk of Mr W becoming dependent upon the worker, particularly if female, needed to be recognized and positively utilized in assisting him. Indeed, it might be of benefit to him to encourage a long-term dependent relationship.

It is recognized that the abuse has continued on the ward, but is more supervised and monitored. The above therapeutic strategies will lessen the abuse, without resorting to legal action by the hospital against Mr W at this stage.

Case example 4

Keyworker: Clinical Psychologist

Mrs Z, aged 77 years, living with her husband aged 75, to whom she had been married for 49 years, was referred by her GP after her husband detailed a 12–18 month history of 'character change' and 'irresponsible behaviour'.

Psychological assessment concluded that Mrs Z's general intellectual, memory and visuospatial functioning were relatively unimpaired. Tests for frontal lobe impairment showed that she performed badly, characterized by garrulous and inappropriate familiar remarks with a lack of insight into her condition. Detailed neurological investigations and brain scan confirmed frontal lobe atrophy with a probable diagnosis of Pick's disease.

Further assessment of the couple showed Mrs Z was to be a victim of physical and verbal abuse by her husband. He was denying her access to food and cigarettes and attempting to prevent her leaving the house.

General comments

- ensuring civil liberties of the victim
- identifying and implementing appropriate help for the carer
- establishing workable behavioural regimes for the patient and the carer
- importance of keyworker having ready access to services
- information about forms of dementia, other than Alzheimer's disease

Case Review 4

The assessment was undertaken at the couple's home. The tension in their relationship became immediately apparent. Mr Z made a series of complaints about his wife's behaviour, namely that she was 'eating too much' and he had to 'take action' to prevent her from taking food from the fridge without his permission. She was 'biting and picking at her nails' which annoyed him. She was repeating his statements and 'pretending to cry when [he] told her off'. His main complaint, however, was that she was repeatedly asking him for cigarettes, when in his view she ought not to be smoking 'at her age'. He had been trying to prevent her smoking for some months, although she had smoked 20–30 cigarettes a day since the age of 23. He has responded to his wife's disinhibited attempts to seek cigarettes subsequently either from strangers, or smoking cigarette ends found in the street. He removed her outdoor shoes, demanding that she never left the house unaccompanied. He locked her in the house when he went out. When she did manage to leave the house barefoot, he became more angry. During the interview he verbally threatened his wife frequently with derogatory comments. He raised a rolled up newspaper to threaten her on a number of occasions when she tried to leave her chair without his permission.

Mr Z had retired at 75 from his full-time job as a barman/waiter, but continued to work part-time. The house was littered with bottles of beer which he received as part of his remuneration, but he was never found to be intoxicated or smelling of alcohol even on unannounced visits. He denied drinking to excess.

Mrs Z had worked as a shop assistant until she was 75 years of age. There had therefore been a change in the amount of time they spent together. Mr Z appeared to have little understanding of the possible causes for his wife's behavioural changes, which he regarded as purposeful and wilful. Mrs Z sometimes responded to his verbal threats by wailing in an exaggerated fashion without becoming tearful. This was a feature of her dementia. It also served to reinforce her husband's view that her behaviour was intentional. The couple had three sons, all professional people with families of their own. They visited once a fortnight and placed the responsibility for care firmly on to Mr Z.

Initial attempts by the statutory services to support the couple were dismissed by Mr Z. At the time of referral to the psychology service, Mrs Z was attending a social services day centre twice a week, but Mr Z complained bitterly that the centre did not control his wife enough and allowed her to 'wander out' (although, in fact, she was fully orientated to the area around the day centre and always returned unaided). He also refused to allow her to take cigarettes to the day centre which resulted in disagreements between himself and the staff, who found that Mrs Z would sit down and settle for quite long periods, either knitting or looking at magazines and books, if provided with an adequate supply of cigarettes. Otherwise she spent the day looking for cigarettes.

Mr Z demonstrated his ambivalent feelings to his wife, threatening to place her in an aged persons' home, but stated on the majority of occasions that he did not wish her to leave him or move out of the house. He was able to speak affectionately about their previous relationship and his wife's previous capacities as a working mother. He admitted that he would feel 'lost without her'. Mrs Z's distress when he threatened her with residential care seemed to diffuse his anger. Mrs Z's own strongly expressed wish was to remain at home with her husband. It seemed appropriate initially to attempt two ways of helping them:

1 to try to assist Mr Z to a greater understanding of the nature of his wife's illness, by shifting his perception that her behaviour was entirely wilful and upsetting him;

2 to attempt a behavioural approach aimed at Mr Z's reaction to her behavioural problems and at Mrs Z's wish that her husband be less aggressive. Mr Z's perceptions and cognitions of Mrs Z's behaviour would be important considerations here.

Superficially, Mr Z responded well to receiving information about the nature of his wife's dementing illness from the community psychiatric nurse and written information sheets and booklets about dementia supplied by voluntary organizations. However, although he was subsequently able to recount an impressive range of information about dementia and to relate this in abstract terms to his wife's behaviour, when faced directly with that behaviour, his emotional state appeared to prevent him from applying his newly acquired knowledge objectively.

Behavioural assessment using a simple A, B, C (antecedent/behaviour/consequences) model suggested that the couple were engaging in recurrent cycles of behaviour with predictable negative consequences. Their behaviour was driven by opposing and conflicting motives and this allowed the situation to escalate:

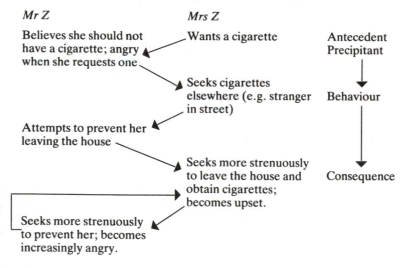

The couple had various ways of escaping this cycle of behaviour but none of these provided a solution. For example, Mr Z's efforts to restrain his wife succeeded only in abusing her rights and temporarily controlling her behaviour. Intervention was directed at the antecedent/precipitant stage before the cycle of abusive behaviour could be initiated. Mr Z was taught to respond in alternative ways to his wife's behaviour:

1 He was asked to keep a diary of his wife's 'demanding behaviour', outlining how her behaviour affected him. Regular meetings were arranged with the clinical psychologist to discuss the daily record. This diary was expanded to include Mrs Z's other 'positive' and 'negative' activities. This provided him with an alternative way of managing and diffusing his anger and delayed or prevented a more direct confrontational response to her behaviour.

2 He was taught a relaxation technique to reduce his level of anger and tension.

3 To reduce Mr Z's rigidity and control of his wife's smoking behaviour, it was suggested that Mrs Z should have a cigarette on request. This involved many weeks of work directed at his unrealistic idealism concerning his wife's smoking habits. Eventually, he compromised by allowing his wife an agreed number of cigarettes on request. The daily record was used to demonstrate his wife's positive and less negative demanding behaviour, as the number of cigarettes allowed each day rose from four.

Over a number of months Mr Z was able to accept further help gradually from support services, although he continued to complain regularly about them and blamed the staff for not curing his wife's dementia.

Six years from the original referral, Mrs Z's dementing illness has progressed. She requires and receives inpatient respite care, attends psychiatric day hospital, but continues to live at home with Mr Z. At times intensive work is still required when Mr Z is under stress.

Team Conference 4

Discussion of this case initially centred around Mr Z's needs, which included further domiciliary support and the advisability of a male confidant (community psychiatric nurse, social worker or GP). The clinical psychologist, consultant psychiatrist and the social worker who were responsible for his wife were all female. It was felt that he would nevertheless find it difficult to view himself, rather than his wife, as the person needing help and support. However, he should be encouraged to join a carer's group, which would give him the opportunity to share his own plight and positively use his considerable knowledge about dementia to help others.

The team discussed the problems of carers who have relatives with dementing illnesses other than Alzheimer's disease, where the information is sparse. This leads to relatives questioning the diagnosis and failing to understand and cope with abnormal behaviour.

The clinical psychologist being the nominated keyworker had instant access to inpatient respite care and day hospital. This was vital in order that services could be provided quickly and reliably when needed.

Case example 5
Keyworker: Social Worker
Mrs T, aged 77 and living with her husband, was suffering from a dementing illness. Mr T referred his wife to the GP with a request for medication and a referral to a psychiatrist as she had started to wander from the house over the past four months. Her husband was the sole carer. The social work assessment revealed that Mr T was regularly tying his wife to a chair and gagging her when he left the house to prevent her wandering.

General comments

● central role of GP
● care and restraint
● importance for carer of planned breaks
● developing coping strategies to avoid passive neglect

Case Review 5

Mr and Mrs T had been married for 56 years and had one son, who visited his parents each month and kept in touch by telephone each week. Mr T was aged 79 years, a retired civil servant and in good health. He was described by the GP as a loyal, caring, gentle man who seemed in control of the situation.

Mr and Mrs T attended for an outpatient psychiatric appointment after referral from the GP, and were seen by the social worker who became a keyworker. On assessment, Mr T initially reported no problems until three or four months prior to his visit to the GP, when he claimed that his wife's concentration was poor and that she appeared to be forgetful. He felt able to cope.

In the clinic Mrs T was diagnosed as suffering from early senile dementia. She appeared pleasant and uncommunicative. Mr T exhibited denial by saying that these had been lifelong characteristics.

Follow-up appointments were arranged and minor adjustments to medication were instituted. Home visits over the next two months by the community psychiatric nurse and the social worker dealt with queries about dementia and the use of medication. Mr T seemed able to cope.

However, on one occasion the social worker arrived early for an appointment to find Mr T returning from shopping. On entering the house, the social worker found Mrs T tied firmly to a chair and gagged. Mr T explained that this was his normal practice. It was his solution to her wandering. Mr T made it clear that he did not wish to discuss the incident further, even when pressed.

A psychiatric outpatient appointment for Mr and Mrs T was made by the social worker for the next day. The social worker was convinced that the bond between Mr and Mrs T was so strong that intentional harm was not the question. At outpatients, Mr T was able to talk about his situation. He challenged the knowledge of the team and it became apparent that Mrs T's illness began three years ago. He had disguised the presentation of the illness because he did not wish to alarm his son, who was recovering from a depressive illness, following his divorce.

Mr T had arranged for his son's visit to last only one or two hours each month, during which time he took him out for a drink. He claimed that his son did not realize the extent of Mrs T's dementing illness, nor that she was being restrained.

It was agreed that Mrs T should attend an ESMI day hospital and have respite care breaks on a planned basis. Mr T should receive counselling from the social worker and support from the GP, and organize his trips out of the house while Mrs T is at the day hospital. Mr T also began attending a carer support group. A community psychiatric nurse worked with the couple at home. The basis of work with Mr and Mrs T was to build in additional support to enable them to continue living together as a couple for as long as possible.

Team Conference 5

Discussion between members of the team highlighted the importance of being able to assist Mrs T with her husband's cooperation and in so doing to support him as well. It was felt to be important that Mr T be made aware of the potential risks he was taking in tying and gagging his wife in a locked house.

Further assessment of Mr T by the team could place appropriate emphasis upon *planned* care management, rather than responding to each *crisis* as it arose. Neuropsychological assessment by the clinical psychologist could identify areas of functional deterioration in Mrs T for which additional services could be provided. 'Aids to daily living' assessment (ADL) by an occupational therapist would indicate in which areas of daily care Mrs T required assistance. The team could then work with Mr T to assist him in developing further coping strategies with Mrs T's deficits.

The case highlights how many carers do not seek early help, but wait until a crisis has been reached. This will often lead to strategic intervention that could be viewed as abusive. It was not felt appropriate by the team to involve the legal system in this case because of the full cooperation of both parties and the very close emotional ties of the couple. However, if right of entry to the house had been refused, legal powers to gain entry could be acted upon by the social worker to ensure Mrs T's safety and to perform a further assessment.

Some concluding remarks

When the team conference has been held it often raises as many questions as it answers. Conclusions must be written down. The name of the person responsible for taking any action should be recorded in the minutes. A regular review date should be agreed at the team conference and also minuted. Managers who are responsible for resource implications should be contacted and informed of the decisions of the group.

Legal advice about the case should be investigated with respective legal departments in health and social services. Much more care needs to be taken with regard to the law and how it affects elderly people (Griffiths et al., 1992). Training of personnel should also be a priority and helpful manuals are now available, for example, Phillipson and Biggs (1992). Underpinning the whole assessment procedure is multidisciplinary teamwork with all its strengths and weaknesses (Lodge, 1991).

8

The General Practitioner and Elder Abuse

John F. Noone, Peter Decalmer and Frank Glendenning

How is a family doctor to know if one of his elderly patients is being abused, physically or otherwise? If such abuse is brought to his attention, perhaps by a neighbour or by a health professional who has stumbled onto this knowledge in the course of routine visiting, what is the general practitioner (GP) to do with this information?

The context of general practice

Over 40 local GPs from one area attended a meeting recently on elder abuse. Only a small minority volunteered knowledge of any such cases within their own practices. The majority expressed surprise and a few disbelief that this could be a serious problem in their district. Doctors, generally, have not been trained to recognize elder abuse. They have not been in the habit of screening for it and they may not be aware of high risk factors for elder abuse.

Before the introduction of their new contract in April 1990, GPs in the United Kingdom were not required to see their elderly patients on a regular basis. The majority of contacts were not doctor-initiated and were interventions at times of crisis. Since 1 April 1990, GPs have been required to offer all patients over the age of 75 years, an annual consultation and/or a home visit, to assess whether any personal medical services or social services are required (*Terms of Service for Doctors in General Practice*, Department of Health, November 1989). Assessment should cover:

- general health
- coping
- sensory functions
- mobility
- mental condition
- physical state, including social environment

Williams et al. (1972) offered a full screening to the 342 patients aged 75 and over in their practice. This process took about one hour per patient and included a full medical and social history, physical examination and blood and urine testing. Perhaps significantly, 41 patients (12 per cent) refused to participate. Four were in hospital and 297 (87 per cent) were included. Of these, 77 were assessed at home. A number of previously unknown medical conditions were detected and referred for appropriate treatment. Effective health was assessed and 60 per cent had normal mobility. Most of those who had a disease process were still cheerful and coping. Physical or other abuse was not specifically referred to.

In 1990–91 in one Manchester practice, 50 of 268 patients refused the offer of a home visit for assessment, although 16 of these were subsequently assessed at home fortuitously, after they had requested a home visit for an acute illness. Seventeen patients did not respond to the invitation and an attempt was made to visit these to carry out the assessment. After failing to gain access to the first six addresses in the computer-generated register, time constraints forced a halt to the exercise. In five of the six cases, neighbours reported that the patients appeared well and regularly went out without assistance, or drove their own motor car. In the sixth case, no neighbour information was forthcoming.

The morbidity register was inaccurate in that 11 of the 268 patients listed on 1 April 1990 were deceased, leaving a target population of 257 (10 per cent of the total practice list compared with the regional average of about 6 per cent). Of these, 240 (93.4 per cent) were assessed. Thirty-four assessments were carried out at the surgery only and 206 at home only, or both at home and at the surgery. The assessments were almost all done by the GP, with less than 10 per cent carried out by the practice nurse. They have added significantly to the workload of the GP and the secretarial staff, which has been overburdened by this and other aspects of the new GP contract, such as child health surveillance, the setting up of health promotion clinics and three-yearly check-ups for under-75s.

A number of recent surveys have shown GP morale to be low and GP vocational training schemes, which in 1988–90 were attracting 20–25 applicants per place are, in our experience, now down to a fraction of that level. Much of this malaise must be as a result of current governmental revisionism in the National Health Service, which has brought much opposition from the medical profession. It is within this context, then, that one needs to consider the two questions posed in the opening paragraph:

- How does a family doctor discover elder abuse?
- What should he/she do with the knowledge?

Screening

A number of authors have described conditions that may be manifestations of abuse or neglect or those associated with a high risk of abuse. O'Malley et al. (1983), for example, produced a checklist of conditions that may be associated with abuse and neglect and a lengthy checklist has been included in Chapter 2 of this volume. Either of these would make a useful appendix to the screening cards or sheets used by many United Kingdom GPs when carrying out their statutory annual assessments of their patients aged 75 and over. Many of the conditions referred to would be recognized as pointers to high risk without such a checklist, but the fact of assessing and recording each one on paper helps to ensure that the chances of overlooking or not following up such instances are reduced.

Ogg and Bennett (1992a) recommend a six-point elder abuse screening checklist of good practice for the GP and practice nurse. The list includes knowledge of high risk factors (present and future); involving family and carers (but interviewing them separately from the elderly person); being prepared to see the elderly person on more than one occasion, using procedural guidelines where they are available; working closely with other agencies; and introducing recording mechanisms to detect significant changes in the elderly person.

The question of the follow-up of elderly people who ignore or refuse the GP's invitation for a regular check-up is a difficult one. In many cases, an assessment can be made fortuitously when a home visit has been requested for some other coincidental medical problem. In other cases liaison with a home care worker, community nurse or relative may bring suspected abuse to the GP's attention. In cases where there is no evidence or even suspicion of abuse, it is very difficult not to respect the rights of elderly people and cater to their privacy.

Need for guidelines for action

Bennett (1992b) has pointed out that few social services departments and fewer health districts have drawn up guidelines and procedures for dealing with suspected cases of abuse and neglect (see also Chapters 1 and 10). He went on to press the need for a national information base or agency to detail current research. He urged the government to set up a working party to investigate the scale of the problem and emphasized the need for revised and new legislation, and for the allocation of new resources. Undoubtedly, working parties should be set up by social services and health authorities to involve representatives from the family health service authority, police and voluntary agencies, working in close liaison to produce local guidelines also.

It is precisely because of the lack of national and local guidelines that GPs are reluctant to act when they find evidence of elder abuse. If guidelines are available to the family doctor any referrals of suspected abuse can be reported to the local social services department. The case would then be investigated by a social worker or duty officer, a case conference would be called and proper follow-up and recording would be ensured. Continuing negotiations made with the elder and carer to deliver mutually acceptable levels of support and care would be agreed, thus removing much of the uncertainty and anxiety that has been generated by all parties.

The role of the family doctor

It is essential that the cooperation of the GP is sought at the earliest possible stage, and that his/her particular role in detecting and managing elder abuse is carefully considered. The involvement of the GP, with his or her unique position as physician, counsellor and sometimes arbiter in family health and related matters, is likely to be crucial in cases of elder abuse or neglect.

On the one hand, it might be thought that a conflict of interest would arise where both victim and perpetrator are patients of the same GP. On the other hand, the experienced GP is well used to managing situations where his professionalism is rigorously tested. Family doctors in the United Kingdom still enjoy a degree of influence and a status which enables them to mediate successfully in domestic crises, where others would not be in a position to do so. A negative effect of the family doctor's status may, however, manifest itself in that because of his/her professional detachment, he/she is less likely to be approached in the first place by the abused elder or a third party who suspects abuse.

The GP is well placed also to assess carer stress, and its impact on the elderly person, due to his/her long-term professional involvement with the family. 'The Cost of Care Index' by Kosberg and Cairl which is cited in Ogg and Bennett (1992a) is a possible screening instrument for avoiding future distress. This may not transfer well from the American situation. Robinson's 'Caregiver Strain Questionnaire', cited in the recent training manual by Phillipson and Biggs (1992) may prove to be more bland.

Case conferences

The case conference system should ensure that abused or neglected elderly people enjoy the same access to a caring professional team approach as do abused children. The difficulties of the situation and the potential conflicts involved are, if anything, greater in elder abuse than in child abuse. The abused child can be taken from the parents to a place of safety. The abused elder may choose to stay with the carer in spite of the abuse or inadequate care. The carer may decline help and support when it appears obvious to the professional that such help is essential.

It may well be that the continuing responsibility for the following up and monitoring of elder abuse or neglect is too much for a single keyworker. Perhaps a better option would be the formation of a sub-group from the case conference to follow up and monitor the progress of cases. One possible sub-group might be (elder, carer), key social worker, community nurse and GP. Brief meetings, held once a month between case conferences, would enable the group to compare notes and to modify tactics. It would be possible for this group to call (or bring forward) a case conference should changing circumstances warrant it. One member of the group, probably the key social worker, would be responsible for the recording of information at these meetings.

An important practical point for the GP is the timing of case conferences and the amount of notice given. GPs have, in the past, been criticized for their failure to attend case conferences when child, adult spouse or elder abuse has been suspected. However, these case conferences are often called at short notice and held at a time which clashes with a previously booked surgery. GPs in the United Kingdom have a contractual obligation to be available at their surgeries at fixed hours which are published in local directories. Many are single-handed and are not able to absent themselves from their patients without adequate notice and many do not make the effort because, rightly or wrongly, they believe inter-disciplinary case conferences to be a waste of time.

Case examples

Four cases of physical abuse encountered in one practice are now described. They represent the most obvious manifestations of elder abuse. Hidden cases of psychological, sexual, financial and other types of abuse present even more complex and difficult management implications.

Case example 1

A 73-year-old woman presented to the GP with early dementia characterized by a deterioration of her personal skills from an excellent home-maker and provider to a person who neglected herself and her household tasks. Her short-term memory deteriorated. She started to hide items in the house and failed to make decisions. Her husband, who was 74, was a professional man with marked obsessional traits who found his role changing as he was losing his wife's support, having to make decisions for her and take over household duties which previously he had not performed. The diagnosis was confirmed by a consultant psychiatrist with the help of a CT scan. The husband found it difficult to accept help but was supported by a community psychiatric nurse and day care. In less than a year the family were reporting to the GP physical (slapping) and psychological (shouting) abuse by the husband. A further psychiatric opinion revealed the patient's further deterioration in behaviour; her mood was labile, her behaviour unpredictable and she was not able or allowed to carry out the simplest of tasks. Her husband's obsessional coping mechanisms meant that he had to be in control and he was the only one who could provide the best care. Further assessment by a psychiatrist and a social worker provided him with more support and more successful coping mechanisms such as 'time out' for him to be away from the stress. Holiday relief and day care are still refused but they are coping together with only occasional episodes of shouting. Slowly more services are being accepted.

General comments

This case illustrates the following risk factors for and pointers to abuse:

- a degree of imposed isolation, elder and carer
- moderately severe cognitive impairment in the elder
- moderate degree of dependency on the carer
- carer's obsessional personality
- mention of physical violence by the carer
- refusal of outside services

Case review 1

This case demonstrates many of the difficulties in balancing caregiving with the risk of abuse. The predisposing factors of the abused person are that she is over 73, demented, physically frail, dependent on her husband, has lost her skills as a housewife and is no longer able to be independent. Her husband (the abuser) is obsessionally rigid, has difficulty in coping with change or interference and needs to feel that he is in control. When confronted by unreasonable or threatening behaviour he will decompensate, developing a paranoid reaction, often resulting in abuse.

The GP can be in an ideal position to help. He often has a long-standing relationship with them both and because he is trusted may be able to be more directive, giving practical instructions of how to help the abused and abuser, such as arranging specialist help, putting them in touch with supportive organizations such as the Alzheimer's Society, and allowing him to ventilate his frustrations. Social services can offer help with social support, day care, home care and financial advice, but always ensuring that he feels that he is in control and people are merely advising rather than controlling him. His wife needs medical and social work support to cope with her own emotional needs and frustration. Thus the GP is pivotal in making sure that this couple can stay together and be supported. A case conference is essential to ensure that each worker and the patient's family know their role and what they should do.

Case example 2

An 88-year-old woman suffered a long history of manic depressive illness and self-poisonings. She suffered from heart failure as well as looking after her husband who was diagnosed as having a dementing illness, chronic bronchitis and partial blindness. As a result of this, he had become physically and verbally abusive. The problems were identified by the community psychiatric nurse who noticed personal deterioration, a dressing apraxia, and increased confusion. The GP found the wife depressed, suicidal and not complying with her medication, as a result of carer stress. A further assessment by the consultant psychiatrist and social services identified the need for day care for the couple, home care and meals-on-wheels. The GP ensured compliance of antidepressant medication by supportive visits. Her mental state improved with resultant coping. The abuse ceased. A stepdaughter started to support her step-mother. Unfortunately, her husband became physically so frail that he was admitted to continuing care. His wife remains unhappy and lonely, but is slowly adapting to her new role.

General comments

This case illustrates the following risk factors for and pointers to abuse:

- elder's depression and fearfulness
- reversal of roles due to deterioration in the carer's mental state with cognitive impairment
- inadequate treatment of medical problems
- elder's financial dependency

Case review 2

This case illustrates how abuse can occur in someone who is dementing and losing their coping skills. The abused person may be the elderly carer who, because of a depressive illness, loses her coping skills. The community nurse was the alerting agent. The GP was able to identify clearly various key people to perform specific tasks. The consultant psychiatrist was able to assess both parties' mental states, suggest treatment, arrange day care and eventual continuing care; the social services provided practical help with home care, and meals-on-wheels; a step-daughter gave emotional support with weekly visits. Once again, the GP is pivotal here, providing monitoring of any change, a regular review of antidepressant medication, and support, all of which resulted in the abuse ceasing and the reduction of suicidal risk which is not uncommon in cases like this. The GP was able to help the wife to be positive with her outlook of her depression, to start to look after her husband and to cope with the emotional trauma of her husband going into continuing care. Suicidal and homicidal acts, often combined, are not uncommon in cases with this profile.

Case example 3

Mrs C is an 81-year-old widow of six years who lives with her 41-year-old unmarried son. She suffers from long-standing hypertension and severe deafness, requiring a hearing aid, and regularly attends the GP. Her son who suffers from severe migraine was known to have personality difficulties, being diagnosed as inadequate and immature by a consultant psychiatrist. He did not abuse alcohol or smoke. Her married daughter identified to the GP physical and emotional abuse from the son. She noted that her father exhibited similar abuse to her mother before his death. The son was seen by the GP about his migraine and sensitive questioning about his mother revealed the son's feelings of depression, failure and frustration. He admitted to losing his temper and abusing his mother. His worsening migraine and unemployment were significant precipitants. The GP achieved success by reviewing and successfully treating his migraine, referral to a stress management group and positive support of the son. The abuse ceased.

General comments

This case illustrates the following risk factors for and pointers to abuse:

- the elder's depression, fearfulness and deafness
- dependency, physical and social

- the carer's personality disorder and social and medical problems
- family history of violence

Case review 3

This case illustrates the problem of a competent elderly person who has chronic physical problems and sensory deficits. She has been subject to two abusers (husband and son), suggesting that the son's behaviour is a learned response. Her son, the main carer, has personality problems, is depressed and has migraine. He has a very negative cognitive set, reinforced by unemployment. He is not a substance abuser and cares deeply about his mother, which is very positive as he is quite prepared to discuss his problems with the GP. The daughter who identified the abuse remains peripheral and is quite accusatory and judgemental, but not prepared to get practically involved. This is not unusual and increases the carer's stress. The GP is the first and only contact. He is trusted by all parties. He identifies the stress factors of migraine which he treats, deals with the son's poor coping skills, using a stress management group, and supports the son. By helping him as a carer, he removes the guilt of unemployment. Thus a happy outcome.

Case example 4

Mrs D, a 78-year-old widow, presented to the GP with depression and fearfulness. She suffered a traumatic perforated ear drum in 1984 needing specialist treatment. In 1991, she developed breast cancer and also had a heart attack. She lives with her 41-year-old daughter who was diagnosed as an immature histrionic psychopath by many consultant psychiatrists. Her daughter was very unstable and the police requested the mother to press charges for assault when neighbours identified incidents. The mother was very protective towards her daughter insisting that she was ill. With community support and psychiatric treatment for the daughter, the abuse was lessened and the daughter's personality has matured. The relationship between mother and daughter has grown and they have stayed together.

General comments

This case illustrates the following risk factors for and pointers to abuse:

- the elder's recurring injuries
- and depressive fearfulness
- the carer's psychiatric condition

Case review 4

This case illustrates that sometimes it is necessary to work with potentially very dangerous situations and identify and accept the risks. The positive aspects of this case are (a) the strong mother/daughter relationship; (b) the daughter's continued cooperation with psychiatric and psychological treatment which lead to her eventual mental health improvement and maturing relationship with her mother; (c) the refusal of the mother to report episodes of violence, ensuring loyalty to the daughter. The mother also would have felt she had failed as a parent. The emotional stresses of this abuse may well have played a part in the mother's physical problems. The community and psychiatric services organized by the GP led to the eventual improvement of this chronic case, but careful monitoring by the GP was essential as non-compliance may well have been fatal.

Conclusion

In the four cases described, two were obvious to the GP in the course of consultations; one was brought to his notice by a concerned relative and one by a community psychiatric nurse. Important knowledge about patients of all ages is often received by the GP at second or third hand, passed on by other health professionals, by concerned relatives or from other sources.

It may be that the traditional aura of respect and authority that surrounds the GP precludes the disclosure of sensitive information directly in many cases. Women may report incontinence to a practice nurse when they are too embarrassed to mention it to the doctor. An elderly woman who has seen her GP a month before about her arthritis may disclose to a sympathetic home carer over a cup of tea that her husband has been shouting at her because she was too slow in reaching the toilet. The carer may not pass on the information for fear of the consequences. The clear implication is that there is a need for better communication. Informal carers need to know how they can get the help and support that they frequently require. Professional carers, social workers, community nurses, health visitors and voluntary workers need guidance and direction as well.

In addition, it must be recognized that GPs find themselves faced with distinct conflicts of interest (as we have already said) and, in the absence of nationally accepted guidelines, definite uncertainty about their legal position. As the law stands at the moment, the burden of responsibility for action and intervention is unclear and, while the management of both victim and perpetrator may be medically, psychologically and socially positive, the GP is by no means confident of his or her ground legally and ethically in relation to what further action may be advisable. This is a major reason why so many GPs do not wish to become involved.

One further issue may well be a result of the changing image of the GP and family doctor. Very many GPs need assistance to understand that in the contemporary world of care in the community, they may head the primary health care team, but they are still only representing one of a number of disciplines which contribute to the well-being of the patient. A refusal to admit to the possible existence of elder abuse, when recorded information is presented, amounts to a rejection of the findings of another professional from a para-medical or social work discipline, or risks ignoring information presented by an informal carer or relative. GPs must learn to share their knowledge and decision-making. Their traditional elitism can become a cloak for ignoring what they do not wish to hear.

The recent British Geriatrics Society's conference report (Tomlin, 1989) envisaged that the GP would play a key role in the detection of elder abuse. Such a key role must carry with it the implication that it is the GP who will need to coordinate the assessment of others, taking careful note of the nature and degree of physical or mental injury or material harm which has been reported and decide how to proceed in order to prevent as far as possible a recurrence, usually in consultation with the key professionals. The legal aspects of each case need to be borne in mind for, in the absence of effective legislation, it is necessary to protect the rights of vulnerable elderly people by maintaining confidentiality, but not avoiding accountability.

This has obvious resource implications. Unless GPs have support and guidance in this area they will not look for cases of elder abuse. If such cases are brought to their attention, they may not act, and if they do not act, the abuse will go unchecked. Furthermore, they could render themselves culpable of third party liability. It is worth recalling finally that in Chapter 1 attention was drawn to the procedural instrument on elder abuse at the Department of Health which, according to Horrocks in 1988, had never been used.

Apart from these fundamental issues of law and guidance which can only be solved adequately at a national level, GPs need additional undergraduate and postgraduate training in the management of elderly people and their carers, and in the early recognition of abuse and neglect. They only see what they are trained to see and they need also a strong reassurance from the National Health Service that if they do become involved in such cases, their input will contribute to an improvement in the quality of life of their elderly patients and their carers.

As long ago as 1984, Eastman (1984b) regarded the role of the GP in the United Kingdom as being of the utmost importance. This judgement has not changed. Wolf in the United States of America went further in 1988 maintaining that 'Physicians can make a major contribution to the advancement of knowledge, practice and policy, with regard to elder abuse and neglect' (Wolf, 1988: 761). The teaching of general practice in the medical schools and in the departments of postgraduate medicine must now, in the face of the growing evidence, ensure that the primary health care physician is enabled to take a lead role in the detection of the mistreatment, abuse and neglect of elderly people. 'It is important that physicians recognize and respond to the stresses of the families under their care' wrote Taler and Ansello (1985: 113) and similar observations have already been mentioned during the discussion of the role of the physician in Chapter 1. The current task is to develop this sensitivity at the heart of general practice. This will best be achieved by the establishment of multidisciplinary guidelines at a national level, which are reinforced by locally agreed policies based upon close liaison, discussion and agreement.

9
Carer–Dependant Relationships and the Prevention of Elder Abuse

Michael Nolan

This chapter advocates a proactive approach to the identification and prevention of elder abuse. It highlights, in particular, the vital role played by the relationship between carer and dependant and the need to consider potential abuse within the context of the wider caregiving situation. The arguments presented are supported by the results of a national sample survey of the Association of Carers (now Carers National Association) and a detailed evaluation of a respite care scheme for carers of the dependent elderly (Nolan and Grant, 1989, 1992; Nolan et al., 1990; Nolan, 1991). A model to aid the assessment of the whole of the caregiving situation is suggested and the implications of adopting such an approach for the implementation of community care policy are considered.

Chapter 1 highlighted the problems concerning the definition, identification and incidence of elder abuse and the lack of an adequate theoretical framework to aid our understanding. This, however, should come as no surprise as a similar situation is apparent with respect to the wider issue of caring itself. It seems reasonable to assume that if we are to extend our understanding in the specific area of abuse then we need first to develop models which explain the nature of caring in general. Biegel et al. (1991: 16) summarize the above situation in the following way: 'Caregiving has become such a ubiquitous term that its meaning is taken for granted, yet the definitions of what is included in the term care-giving are not always that clear.'

There exists a lack of conceptual clarity as to what constitutes caring, and accepted definitions have placed an undue emphasis on aspects of the carer's role to do with the act of providing physical care (so-called instrumental care) to the exclusion of more diffuse and subtle but potentially more important components (Gwyther and George, 1986; Bowers, 1987; Townsend and Noelker, 1987; Cox et al., 1988; Sutcliffe and Larner, 1988) to do with feelings, emotions and relationships (affective care). Moreover, the caring literature has focused almost exclusively on the stresses of caring to the virtual exclusion of sources of satisfaction and reward (Lawton et al., 1989; Motenko, 1989).

Some authors (Qureshi, 1986; Twigg, 1986) contend that caring is a mixed concept revolving around tasks of a supportive nature which involve both social and family relationships. There is also a range of complex affective/emotional issues concerning the nature of the interaction between carer and cared-for and the feelings which such interactions generate. Pearlin et al. (1990) argue that, for the sake of clarity, it is better to separate such affective components from the physical aspects of the carer's role and suggest that the term 'caring' be used for the emotional dimension and 'caregiving' for the tending. Dunlop (1986) follows a similar line of reasoning in highlighting both the practical and the emotional components of caring, but considers that the emotional elements are dominant and that caring is primarily a relationship of concern for the person being cared for. Empirical evidence would suggest that, while affection is not a prerequisite of care, in its absence the situation is more fragile and prone to collapse (Qureshi, 1986). Certainly there is now far wider acceptance of the central importance of the quality of the carer–dependant relationship in understanding the complex range of interactions that occur between carer and cared-for (Allen et al., 1983; Qureshi and Walker, 1986; Lewis and Meredith, 1988a,b; Morris et al., 1988; Stoller and Pugliesi, 1989).

Furthermore, increased attention has recently been turned to the potential rewards of caring and this is of interest for both theoretical and pragmatic reasons. Thus there is growing empirical support that carer satisfaction is positively associated with improved emotional health (Gilhooly, 1984; Cox et al., 1988; Motenko, 1989), an increased commitment to the caring relationship (Pruchno et al., 1990) and a reduced likelihood of institutionalization of the dependant (Hirschfield, 1981, 1983; Pruchno et al., 1990).

Kahana and Young (1990) present a strong argument outlining the need to look at the complexity of the caregiving situation and to consider the disparate interactions that can occur with potential positive and negative consequences for both care-recipient and caregiver. It is their contention that models must be developed which are flexible enough to allow for the diversity and multidimensionality of caring. They lay emphasis on the dynamic and changing nature of caring, as opposed to seeing caring as an essentially static situation. They suggest that such models are best advanced by linking them with general stress theory. In criticizing the models of caring that have been developed to date they state that: 'Caregiving theory and research have both generally centred on instrumental needs of the

frail elder and instrumental assistance provided by the caregiver.'
(Kahana and Young, 1990: 82). They advocate the development of
an expanded conceptual framework with a particular emphasis on
what they term dynamic and relational models, that is those that take
account of the changing nature of caring and give due prominence to
the quality of the relationship between the carer and the cared-for.
They use the term *congruence model* to denote an approach which
centres on the degree of agreement reached between carer and
cared-for about the sharing of caring roles and responsibilities. Such
a model would appear to be particularly useful for extending our
understanding of potentially abusive situations. As Kahana and
Young (1990: 86) themselves state:

> [the] literature on elder abuse . . . calls attention to the neglect of the
> elderly and the failure of some caregivers to attend properly to the
> legitimate dependency needs of the elders they do or should care for.
> [These] alternative expectations may be resolved if one considers a
> congruence model of interactions between caregivers and care-recipients.

Chapter 1 argued that increased attention should be given to the
study of family dynamics and to the potential for both positive and
negative outcomes. Recent literature on abuse has also highlighted
the importance of the relationship between the carer and dependant
(Kosberg, 1988; Steinmetz, 1988; Homer and Gilleard, 1990b;
British Association for Service to the Elderly, 1991; McCreadie,
1991; Royal College of Nursing, 1991), and as Phillips (1988) points
out abuse exists within the context of a relationship and reflects an
example of a caregiving relationship gone awry. If we are therefore to
be proactive in the identification and prevention of abuse, we need to
develop the type of comprehensive and dynamic models advocated
by Kahana and Young (1990).

One of the potentially most useful approaches in the area of abuse
has been suggested by Phillips and Rempusheski (1986). While
adopting a broad theoretical stance, their model is located primarily
within a symbolic interactionist perspective. The approach is essentially cognitive and is centred around a number of key variables which
are used to give meaning to the caring situation. Such meanings then
largely determine subsequent behaviour. The model highlights the
dynamic and interactive nature of caring and stresses the importance
of individual carer's evaluation of their behaviour. It is suggested that
carers hold an image of caring which determines both their role
relationship with the cared-for and the quality of the care given.
Factors considered influential in creating this image are the carer's
perception of their past relationship with their dependant and the
reconciliation of the present situation with this past image. Where

carers have a normalized view of their past relationship (in which both positive and negative factors are acknowledged but which remains positive overall) and when present interactions are consistent with this, then carers are more likely to be accepting of certain behaviours and less likely to adopt caring styles that revolve around the dependant conforming. Alternatively, if carers have a 'stigmatized' (only negative perceptions) or 'deified' (only see very positive perceptions) past relationship and if the stigmatized view remains or the deified relationship has been spoilt, then carers are less tolerant and have a greater expectation of conformity from the dependant. The carer's general beliefs as to what constitutes healthy living, a good quality of life and the nature of family relationships and responsibilities are also influential. Where there is congruence or fit between the carer's beliefs and the dependant's behaviour then carers are said to adopt a style of caring which is more open and protective and in which they have fewer expectations that the dependant will conform. Where behaviours and beliefs are incongruent or do not fit then carers are more likely to adopt a punitive style and expect the dependant to be more suppliant. In the latter circumstances the authors suggest that abuse is far more likely to occur.

This model would clearly fit into the type of framework advocated by Kahana and Young (1990) and is, moreover, entirely consistent with transactional approaches to understanding caring stresses and rewards, of which the congruence model is a good example. With regard to the understanding of stress reactions *transactional* approaches are now those generally accepted as offering the best way of framing individual responses. A transactional model is based upon the belief that each individual has a differing response to potentially stressful events (stressors) and that the degree to which any event is actually stressful is determined by the way in which each person views that event. What is stressful for one person is therefore not automatically stressful for another. Indeed, the same event can also be stressful to a person one day and not stressful the next. Central to the production of stress within the transactional model are the subjective perceptions of the carer as opposed to the objective circumstances of care. Such a model has received much support from recent caring literature (Poulshock and Deimling, 1984; Parker, 1985; Simmons, 1985; George and Gwyther, 1986; Zarit et al., 1986; Noelker and Townsend, 1987; Cox et al., 1988; Motenko, 1989; Kahana and Young, 1990).

Moreover, Steinmetz (1988) has also reached a similar conclusion with respect to abusive situations and her results add further support to the type of model suggested by Phillips and Rempusheski (1986).

She notes that abuse is not so much the result of instrumental dependency (that is, the need for physical care) but often arises when there is a conflict of values between carer and dependant. Situations are particularly fraught when dependants are demanding and resort to manipulative behaviour as a means of establishing control. She suggests that interpretation of interactions between carer and cared-for must be considered when attempting to predict abuse and that there are higher levels of abuse amongst stressed carers: 'In as much as a person's perception of a situation is a better predictor of behaviour than objective criteria, caregivers who report a sense of burden may have a greater potential for using abusive or neglectful behaviours' (Steinmetz, 1988: 70).

The usefulness of such general transactional models and the importance of subjective perceptions in determining both the stresses and satisfactions of caring has recently received empirical support from a national sample survey of members of the Association of Carers and an evaluation of a respite care scheme (Nolan and Grant, 1989, 1992; Nolan et al., 1990; Nolan, 1991). Using a combination of sophisticated statistical modelling and detailed content analysis of open questionnaire responses and in-depth interviews, the results of the above studies serve to reinforce the arguments already rehearsed.

The carer questionnaire survey used a large sample ($n = 522$) which, while non-random in nature, was not unrepresentative of more typical national samples (Nolan, 1991; Nolan and Grant, 1992). Therefore, while caution is needed in generalizing to carer populations the results are none the less instructive. In explaining those factors which predict carer stress the statistical model highlighted the unimportance of objective factors and the dependency characteristics of the cared-for. Indeed, the degree of assistance required with the major activities of daily living, the presence of incontinence (both urinary and faecal) and the confused behaviour of the dependant failed to account for any of the carer stress. Factors which were highly significant were to do with the carer's responses to the caring situation (particularly the experience of feelings of guilt, being constantly in demand and feeling out of control of events), the nature of the carer–dependant relationship (particularly strained when the dependant was perceived to be unappreciative, making unreasonable demands, failing to help the carer and adopting manipulative behaviour), the perceived adequacy of family support and the carer's financial situation.

The qualitative analysis of the extensive additional data from the survey (in the form of responses to open questions, appended comments and letters) entirely supported the causal model produced. The negative responses of carers were largely determined by their perceptions of the extent to which the dependant was seen to be manipulative, unappreciative or deliberately unhelpful.

The interview data from an entirely separate sample of carers ($n = 50$) using a respite care service produced results which were strikingly similar to those from the postal survey. One of the most frequently voiced stressors, and certainly the most problematic, concerned the extent to which the carer felt manipulated by a dependant. While the nature and degree of manipulation varied, it was often very destructive to the caring relationship, particularly where such behaviour was seen as being deliberate and wilful. This type of situation was further exacerbated when the dependant manipulated family interactions by playing one carer off against another. One of the most destructive situations was described by a daughter sharing the care of her mother with her sister. When the interviewee was providing care the mother would be totally un-cooperative, refusing to wash, dress or even feed herself. She was frequently deliberately incontinent, and prone to swearing and bouts of physical aggression. Moreover, she would accuse her daughter of stealing her money. However, when the interviewee's sister was providing the care the mother's behaviour would be entirely different and fully cooperative. Consequently, the sister could not see the interviewee's problems, and often hinted that these were overstated.

A lack of appreciation and 'not trying' often coexisted with manipulative behaviour. When this occurred it further heightened feelings of anger in a number of carers. This sometimes seemed close to spilling over into more physical manifestations of frustration:

> I can understand how people become aggressive and actually hit the person they look after. Sometimes mother just sits there demanding attention and wanting it there and then. I wouldn't mind so much but some of the things she could do herself if only she'd try. In any case no matter what I do it never seems good enough and she never says thank you. Things would be so much better if just once in a while at the end of a meal, she said 'Thank you, that was very nice'. (Nolan, 1991: 199)

Alternatively, equally trying behaviours could be perceived more positively when carers acknowledged the situation, confronted their dependant directly and made light of the situation, turning potential anger into humour:

> Of course, he becomes a bit 'demanding' now and again and I think if I let him he'd have me doing everything for him. I can understand how he feels, it must be very difficult having to rely on someone else all the time. But I don't let him get away with it and when I think he's going too far I

> say 'Anymore of that and you'll be on the street.' Then we have a good laugh and things are OK again.

> He's always been like that, you know wanting his own way, and I don't suppose he's going to change now. So I deal with it the way I always do, by pretending not to hear him. This is something of a joke between us, and after a while he'll shout 'Have you gone deaf again?' (Nolan, 1991: 200)

Other carers were able to look at events in a differing light so that they were not seen as being stressful. This was particularly apparent where carers saw difficult behaviour as a consequence of their dependant's illness, and therefore not deliberate.

> Sometimes I could cry when I look at him now and think of the man he used to be. But you have to see the humour in things or else you'd go mad. The other day he was hitting out at me and I said 'What are you doing that for?' He said 'Because you keep kicking me, what's the use in having a good woman if she kicks you all the time?' Well, what else could I do, I just laughed. I mean it's not his fault that he's the way he is, is it? (Nolan, 1991: 200)

This ability to consider similar events either in the context of past behaviours or to perceive them as non-deliberate was important in determining their stressful nature and is wholly consistent with the type of transactional approach to the understanding of stress that has been previously outlined.

Factors determining the quality of the prior carer–dependant relationship also influenced the degree of perceived stress. A good prior relationship was likely to minimize stress even in the face of manifestly heavy caring demands. Conversely, a poor or fragile relationship was soon exposed even by comparatively minor demands, with behaviour then being more likely to be perceived as demanding and deliberate, with the result that caring was all the more stressful:

> I think the main difficulty is that he's my second husband and we married more for companionship than love. We'd only been married a couple of years when he had his stroke and suddenly not only was he not a companion, he was a burden. I looked after my disabled mother for 15 years, whilst raising a family and working at the same time. Now there's no doubt that was far more demanding, but I didn't see it that way because I loved my mother and all that entails. (Nolan, 1991: 201)

Also consistent with the postal survey was the influence of family support in the caring process. Perceived stress was greater if the wider family were seen to be unsupportive. This situation was exacerbated when relatives lived some distance away, perhaps failing to appreciate the carer's day-to-day grind and sometimes being critical of the care given. Tensions were further heightened when the dependant, not having seen the visiting relative for some time, was openly affectionate towards them, ignoring the main carer. For this type of situation I have coined the term 'absent angel syndrome'.

It is important to point out that the above studies were not concerned with abuse *per se* but rather with the wider issue of carer stress and satisfaction. None the less, the factors described above mirror almost exactly those outlined by Steinmetz (1988) as being major contributors to abusive situations.

As noted above, there is now increased recognition of the need to consider the potential rewards of caring also. While space precludes a full discussion of this issue the results from the above two studies provide what is believed to be the most substantial body of empirical evidence in this area. Satisfactions were clearly identified by carers and were highly influential in ameliorating and contextualizing carers' responses to their situation. It is apparent that a holistic assessment of interactions between carer and dependant cannot be made without due attention being given to potential sources of satisfaction.

Returning to the suggestion of Kahana and Young (1990) that it is vital to develop new models of the caring situation if more comprehensive theoretical frameworks are to emerge, further advances can be made if the above findings are incorporated into the model suggested by Rolland (1988). He terms his approach 'the therapeutic quadrangle', so-called because it suggests that there are four major sets of factors to be considered if the caring situation is to be fully understood. He therefore advocates the need to see the situation from a number of perspectives including those of the service provider(s), the carer and the dependant, in addition to taking due account of the varying demands made by differing manifestations of chronic illness. He stresses that chronic illnesses do not form a homogeneous group but that differing types of illness make different demands that must also be adequately assessed. Other authors have also signalled the need to include such factors (Biegel et al., 1991).

The model is also important as it recognizes that service providers (both agencies and individuals) have complex ideological and professional beliefs of their own which often determine the type and level of help that a carer receives. If we add to this model some of the other factors previously discussed, such as those identified by Phillips and Rempusheski (1986) and Steinmetz (1988), together with those from my own work, the quadrangle approach provides a flexible framework which delineates those areas that need to be explored if real advances in our understanding are to be achieved.

The need for the type of comprehensive assessment suggested by this model is particularly apparent in the context of current British community care policy. Recent policy statements have outlined the philosophy behind the service response components of Rolland's expanded framework. The rhetoric of such policies reflects a marked shift in perspective with increasing emphasis being placed on the consumer and the notion of fitting services to people rather than vice versa. This suggests a strong element of choice. However, there is also an inherent tension in that the embracing of the community as the prime option has resulted in institutional alternatives becoming even more discredited. This, combined with the now rapid throughput and discharge rates from acute care hospitals, is likely to increase pressure on carers either to enter into or to remain in a caring role with the potential of creating or sustaining inappropriate caring relationships. In many cases, therefore, such policies may restrict rather than enhance choice.

The White Paper, *Caring for People* (Department of Health, 1989, para. 1.9) notes that the 'decision to take on the caring role is never an easy one', suggesting that an element of informed choice is in operation. However, as Steinmetz (1988: 61) points out, such decisions are often made in a time of crisis and are usually based on: 'guilt, love and a sense of responsibility rather than a careful evaluation of all the options and an acknowledgement of what is best for the elder, adult child and the family'. Such a contention is supported by the wider literature (Allen et al., 1983; Lewis and Meredith, 1988b; Pitkeathley, 1990). This would suggest that there is a need for a careful assessment of the caring situation before carers are expected to adopt such a role (Callahan, 1988; Kosberg, 1988), indeed 'the instinctive and uncritical use of family members as caregivers should not continue' (Kosberg, 1988: 44).

Community care should therefore not be seen as right for all, as it may burden the carer beyond endurance (Maclean, 1989). Nor should reluctant carers be forced into their role, especially when there is a poor caring relationship because, as Qureshi and Walker (1989: 247) note, when difficult or strained family relationships are added to powerful normative pressures then it can 'quite inappropriately force daughters and elderly people into potentially disastrous close physical and emotional relations'.

If this is to be avoided, it will be necessary to assess caring relationships before and during the caring history and to have acceptable available alternatives. The literature, reinforced by the studies discussed in this chapter, suggest that it is possible to predict which caring situations are most likely to be stressful and where there is likely to be a poor carer–dependant relationship. These involve situations in which the dependant is demanding, manipulative, unhelpful and unappreciative and where the carer perceives this as stressful. Where there is a history of a poor relationship or where the family member expresses doubts about caring, then questions should be asked about the advisability of that family member assuming the caring role. Thus, pressures should not be brought to bear on such individuals; nor should they be made to feel guilty for voicing doubts about caring, thus inhibiting them from asking for support (Morley, 1988).

As long ago as 1961, Farndale cautioned that services provided for carers should not sustain them in that role inappropriately. Yet there is evidence from recent work on respite care (Nolan, 1991; Nolan and Grant, 1992) that respite services can be used as an incentive to encourage reluctant carers either to take on or to continue in their role. Thus, for some carers who had voiced doubts about their ability and willingness to take a dependant home, there often appeared to be little choice in the matter. One carer described how she had been asked to come and see the consultant and then been 'given a good telling off', after which she felt obligated. Despite the relatively good functional ability of the mother in this case and the fact that she did not live with the daughter, the situation was one of the most fraught that was encountered during the carer interviews: 'I knew as soon as I started that things could only go from bad to worse. We'd never been very close anyway but I was surprised how, in just a couple of days, I could grow to almost hate my mother' (Nolan, 1991: 207).

Individuals often feel strong pressures to care, exerted by family and societal expectations of them (Qureshi and Walker, 1989; Pitkeathley, 1990) and, if we add to this implicit or explicit professional pressure, then real choice is all but absent. If this sort of situation is to be avoided, it is necessary to negotiate clear guidelines and ground rules from the start (Steinmetz, 1988). Failure to establish a realistic set of expectations results in carers being unable to set appropriate limits (Pratt et al., 1987) and only adds to the resultant guilt and frustration.

A comprehensive approach to assessment, such as that suggested in this chapter, is vital if potentially abusive situations are to be avoided. Particular attention must be given to the wide-ranging factors which make caring such a dynamic and individual situation. The quadrangle approach offers promise as a framework for assessment within which various instruments can be incorporated. Therefore Kosberg (1988) provides a useful pre-placement screening tool and two new instruments, the Carers' Assessment of Difficulties Index (CADI) and the Carers' Assessment of Satisfactions Index (CASI) (Nolan and Grant, 1992) can aid a comprehensive approach.

However, the issue of which tools to use is a technical and pragmatic one. What is more important, if we are ever to be proactive in addressing the area of abuse, is that we extend the way we think about caring. Failure to do so will only perpetuate the well-meaning but essentially superficial approach to the problem exemplified in recent guidelines for prevention (Tomlin, 1989).

10
Looking to the Future

Frank Glendenning and Peter Decalmer

During the course of this book we have drawn attention to a considerable number of difficult issues, the principal one being that of the definition of abuse. Insufficient attention has been paid to this in Britain, and Kingston (1990) has warned against the wastefulness of replicating the American debate. Our own inclination has been to settle for the time being with the definitions of Wolf and Pillemer (1989) which include physical, psychological and material abuse; and also active and passive neglect.

Development of guidelines for action

What is noticeable in the British situation is that a formal recognition of the existence of elder abuse has only recently been admitted. Age Concern England led the field with Cloke's report in 1983. The British Geriatrics Society (BGS) Conference in 1988 led to Tomlin's landmark report in 1989. In 1991, the BGS followed up its 1988 proposals with a leaflet, *Abuse of Elderly People: Guidelines for Action* (see Age Concern England, 1991), together with a further leaflet for carers. These were prepared in conjunction with Age Concern England, The British Association of Social Workers (BASW), The Carers' National Association, Help the Aged and the Police Federation of England and Wales. The Royal College of Nursing produced its own guidelines in 1991. Social services departments and health districts were slow to follow suit, led by Kent Social Services' guidelines, approved as long ago as 1987, and revised in 1989.

The BGS/Age Concern guidelines represented a major consensus because they embraced the views of those who work in the health service, social services, the police and the voluntary sector. Carers and older people themselves were also included in the process. The full text is included in the Appendix at the end of this book.

The principal headings are as follows:

1 *What is abuse?*: physical, psychological, deprivation, forcible isolation, sexual, misusing medication, misuse of monies etc.

2 *Who abuses?*: in the majority of cases it is the immediate carer, other family members or visitors may also abuse an elderly person.

3 *Factors which promote abuse*: when the elderly person is ill; has difficulty in communication; when there are behavioural disturbances; when the family is under stress through low income or poor housing; when the elderly person will only accept care from a particular person; when family relationships over the years have been poor; when violent behaviour within the family is common.

4 *The family at risk*. Family members who find themselves abusing their elderly relatives have certain characteristics which can help to identify 'at risk' situations. Some 15 factors are listed which should be of concern when identified in vulnerable carers.

5 *Physical indicators of abuse*, including unexplained injuries; finger marks; burns in unusual places; excessive repeat prescriptions or under-use of medication.

6 *Social and emotional indicators in elderly people*, including being withdrawn, agitated, anxious, isolated, being inappropriately dressed, unkempt; visitor has difficulty of access; carer always wishes to be present.

7 *Social and emotional indicators in carers*, including unremitting sense of anger, frustration and despair; feelings of victimization; anxiety, worry, loneliness; loss of self-esteem.

8 *Action for health workers to help prevent abuse*: lists simple actions to relieve sense of stress.

9 *Action when abuse has occurred*: careful instructions are given.

10 *Social services/social work departments' responsibilities and action*: need for local inter-agency guidelines on good practice; assessment and treatment by a qualified social worker; elders and carers to be interviewed separately; immediate action required through the medium of a case conference.

As Hildrew (1991a) has pointed out, some authorities have circulated guidelines that are based on the BGS pamphlet, although the authors of the pamphlet had not intended it to become a detailed model for departmental guidelines. Others have based their drafting on the Kent Social Services guidelines; others on Gloucestershire's *Adults at Risk*, which is detailed and procedural, involving an at risk register. It has been regarded by some as too rigid.

What emerges in general terms is that it is not at all clear that current decision-making about the abuse and neglect of old people is reliably research-based and the result of informed discussion. Indeed, Phillipson (1992b), referring to the Department of Health, Social Services Inspectorate report, *Confronting Elder Abuse*, suggested that 'it might well be argued that the area of abuse and neglect is now so muddled and ill-defined that departments should proceed with the utmost caution when trying to develop appropriate policies' (1992b: 2). This observation, however, has come after a number of social services departments and health districts have already implemented or drafted guidelines, often without reference to one another. What would have been helpful would have been to establish a compatible model first, which would then have enabled a national database to be more easily established, and to have assisted in the setting up of incidence and prevalence studies.

Additionally, it is not uncommon for child abuse to be linked in some way with elder abuse. The BGS/Age Concern et al. guidelines are a good example. The sentence that includes 'and draw on the experiences that agencies have in working together on child abuse' is unclear as it stands and introduces an element that may be misleading. It is inadvisable to make this linkage. Finkelhor and Pillemer (1988: 248) drew attention to elder abuse, within the context of family violence, being compared to child abuse more frequently than spouse abuse 'because of certain apparent similarities . . . The relationship between caretaker and elder in such cases is often thought to have a parent–child character in the extreme dependency of the elder.' As was suggested in Chapter 1, the carer may well be the 'dependant' and Breckman and Adelman (1988) have pointed out that even when it is the elderly person who is dependent, the conditions of dependency are quite different from those of young children. Kingston (1990) has shown that by 1990 four health districts in England had based their response to elder abuse on child abuse guidelines.

Local responses

According to Hildrew (1991a), by 1991 nine social services departments had implemented guidelines; two had approved guidelines which had not yet been implemented; a further 26 had drafted guidelines and 12 had working parties in existence. Thus, after a decade of published case examples and discussion, out of a total of 115, 66 departments appeared to have taken no action to advise, assist and support staff who encountered cases of suspected abuse or neglect among elderly people.

The chief elements of these local guidelines involve educating staff about the recognition of abuse and high-risk situations, knowledge of existing research, referral, investigation, subsequent action, case conferences and, possibly, at risk registers. (Hildrew points out that such registers in England and Wales at present are not favoured by

many authorities.) Little research is available about at risk registers
for elderly people, although Eastman (1984b) broaches the issue and
Aldrich (1989) mentions registers in relation to his flow chart for
procedures. The Association of Directors of Social Services (1990)
drafting procedural guidelines for adults (in general) at risk proposed
an 'Adults at Risk' register (based on guidelines devised by
Gloucestershire Social Services Department), which would be made
available to the district health authority. Some authorities have
shown interest in the Gloucestershire concept because it avoids the
charge of ageism. But others have rejected it as setting out too rigid a
framework, as we have already noted, in relation to its legalistic and
interventionist approach (Hildrew, 1991a). In any case, having
guidelines for 'adults' makes the assumption that elderly people are
no more at risk than members of the general population and could
well lead to a failure of local authorities to address the special needs
of elderly people who are at risk. When Hildrew reviewed the general
situation in 1991, she found that by that time only three out of 11
authorities with published guidelines had incorporated an at risk
register. In Chapter 5, some of the reservations from the social
services point of view have been expressed.

Kingston (1990) carried out a similar survey among the health
authority districts in England (again, briefly referred to in Chapter
1). Working through the 14 regional health authorities, the survey
revealed that of the 131 districts, only two claimed to have a policy
about elder abuse. Forty-three districts claimed to be aware of the
problem and 28 replied that they had no policy and did not explain
why or comment on their future expectations in this regard.

The Tower Hamlets guidelines (1991) are a useful introduction to
the concept of 'elder abuse/inadequate care', but present the usual
problems of obtaining information, using it appropriately and
implementing a planned response. The subsequent actions suggested
by most existing guidelines are either so general as to be unhelpful or
they cause the professional to reflect back on his or her own practice
and lead to more questions than answers. Furthermore, 'inadequate
care' as a term can lead to confusion between neglect and an
inappropriate identification of resources, where professionals may
set unreasonable standards and identify the observed discrepancy in
care as abuse.

The guidelines to be applied and which have been mentioned
concern people living in the community. Their result so far does not
appear to have taken us further in our understanding of the
mistreatment, abuse and neglect of older people. In Britain, there is
no national clearing house or database. However, it would be
possible to begin to deal with this locally by using instruments such as

the checklists described in Chapter 2 and the assessment tool in Chapter 6. This should be followed by a semi-structured interview undertaken by a trained professional in any situation where the mistreatment of an older person is suspected (see Wolf, cited in Phillipson and Biggs, 1992).

Guidelines for institutions

There is well-documented evidence from numerous official inquiries (see Chapter 1) of both active and passive abuse in hospitals and homes. Apart from increased resources, rigorous staff training and clear aims and objectives, it is necessary also to reinforce the resolve of those who, before and after the Wagner Report on residential care in 1988, were deeply committed to the provision of more than adequate care in residential settings and to the wiping out of abuse in all its forms.

At the very least, McCreadie (1991) suggests that there must be quality assurance programmes; a management audit and inspection of all homes (and she notes the risk area of very small private homes which remain outside the regulations); adequate levels of staffing; regular staff training; an independent advocacy scheme for all service users; a clear complaints procedure; a clear contract governing the provision of services to users, and their cost; public education about what constitutes acceptable and unacceptable practice in the care of elderly people; clear procedures for investigating alleged abuse in institutions; and services which meet the needs of a multiracial society.

While this list of suggestions applies more readily to residential homes for old people, the same principles apply to hospitals, which are even more entrenched in self-certainty. What is the implication for management of the institutional passive abuse 'on a massive scale' (Tomlin, 1989) that is implied in Horrocks' study of 12 Health Advisory Service (HAS) reports on long-stay geriatric wards up to 1987? His principal findings were detailed in Chapter 1 and he presented this material as a former Director of the HAS at the 1988 conference of the British Geriatrics Society. He commented at the time: 'We seem to be running institutions, not care programmes' (Tomlin, 1989: 12).

Home Life: A Code of Practice for Residential Care was a landmark text when it was published in 1984 by the Centre for Policy on Ageing and still provides an excellent base for those working in residential homes (Centre for Policy on Ageing, 1984). But in Britain we are still in the position of waiting to establish an up-to-date code of practice for institutional care, both in homes and in hospitals. A few social services departments (notably Enfield) are beginning to address this issue in their guidelines.

Under the present regulations, social services departments in Britain register rest homes and health authorities register nursing homes and homes for the elderly mentally infirm. This leads to the inherent problem of there being two registering authorities, which it is hoped will be addressed when the 1990 community care legislation is in place. When abuse is identified in a residential setting, the evidence has to be strong enough to be examined in a court of law, as withdrawal of registration may lead to challenge in the courts, with all its inherent costs. This will often have the effect that minor forms of abuse are not reported, or there may be a reluctance by some authorities to meet the potential escalating costs of litigation. The government may well need to address the issue of the advisability of appointing an ombudsman or commissioner, who can deal with complaints or issues of serious contention.

Inter-agency cooperation

Wolf and Pillemer wrote in 1989, 'cooperation between agencies is perhaps the most critical contributor to the success or failure of a project' (1989: 149). Such cooperation is an important part of working within the context of elder abuse. Health authorities are usually involved, as are social services, as may be voluntary organizations, housing departments or housing associations and the police. This cooperation may involve attendance at case conferences or the establishing of joint guidelines so that there is as little misunderstanding as possible concerning local procedures. Cooperation of this kind is the bedrock of everything that we mean by 'community care' and 'caring for people'. It will not be achieved unless each agency attempts to understand the role and ethos of the other and unless all are adequately resourced. Furthermore, it is essential that the infrastructure that will be required to make this possible is adequately resourced as well. Inter-agency cooperation implies in addition a complete rethinking of the content of existing professional, post-qualifying and in-service training.

Nevertheless, it has to be admitted that working together in a real sense is fraught with difficulty. The difficulty not only occurs because of attempting to meld the aspirations of different agencies who were previously autonomous and independent and in the case of social services accountable to local government, but because also of practical problems encountered through terms of service and professional attitudes. Far too little attention has been paid in recent years, by the makers of social policy in Britain, to such factors in the implementation of community care.

Matters of law

In addition to the setting up of guidelines and codes of practice, which should be moving towards universal compatibility, attention must be paid to legislative needs and requirements in relation to elder abuse and neglect. Griffiths et al. have demonstrated very clearly in Chapter 3 the areas in which action should be taken. It is also apparent that in Britain, social services departments should have available to them lists of lawyers who have a special expertise in this area, whose advice they can then draw on, when it is more appropriate to seek such advice, rather than routinely inform the police.

Some pointers from North America

Crystal (1986) declared his misgivings about mandatory reporting in the USA when he drew attention to the stereotypical language used to describe older people in state mandatory reporting legislation. Moreover, he suggested that there was a marked tendency for politicians to support mandatory reporting on the grounds that reporting and increased case finding was proving that elder abuse was being controlled and that there was no need for further substantial sums of money to develop new services. This illusory sense of progress, he concluded, was a real problem.

Kingston (1990) has concluded that it is important to understand the phenomenon of elder abuse before demanding solutions to it. A research base needs to be established in Britain which can establish incidence and prevalence. In the USA few attempted to do this until Pillemer and Finkelhor's prevalence study in 1988. Abused victims *can* be interviewed and we should not be afraid to attempt this method in Britain. There needs to be a study of those who perpetrate abuse and neglect and also a study of neglect and self-neglect. Since Wolf and Pillemer's findings in 1989, the issue of family violence has become of central importance.

Kingston (1990) also suggests that because the American literature on assessment tools far exceeds the entire British literature on elder abuse, British policy-makers need to learn from this. During the development of the study of the abuse and neglect of older people in America, a number of instruments were devised to assist in the identification of abuse and in the intervention procedures which were deemed to be appropriate. In Chapter 1, for instance, mention was made of O'Malley et al.'s (1983) identification table, which Wolf was still recommending in 1988. We noted lists of indicators by Breckman and Adelman (1988) and Podnieks's Canadian checklists (1988). Gnaedinger (1989) suggested guidelines which list the signs and symptoms of elder abuse for use by human service professionals, based upon Wolf and Pillemer's categories.

Chapter 1 referred to Breckman and Adelman's use of an eight-page protocol for identification and assessment, formulated by Tomita (1982). Tomita developed in considerable detail the technique and methodology of assessment, the mode of presentation of the signs and symptoms which have aroused suspicions about abuse and/or neglect, the physical examination and its recording and documentation, together with the necessary diagnostic procedures within a medical setting. These procedures are followed before the caregiver has been interviewed. At this stage, the interview with the caregiver takes place and the author includes a list of precise questions to be put, which will help to build up a social picture. The caregiver will be carefully observed as part of the attempt to determine whether there is a high-risk situation. Immediately there should be a follow-up of other personal contacts in order to avoid collusion. All this information should be integrated into a final assessment report. Intervention options should then be addressed, together with diagnostic, therapeutic and education/training plans. Environmental changes should be considered and links made for the elder with advocacy resources. Therapeutic, education/training plans and resource linkage should be provided for the caregiver. Parallel to these procedures there must be relevant staff training, and training should also be included for the natural helpers to be found within the elder's social system, for example, postal and utility workers, bank manager etc. Training should include follow-up and termination processes.

There is still time in Britain to avoid some of the more obvious errors that have occurred in the USA, where early state legislation was drafted at speed, frequently without expert advice. One outcome of this was the lack of standardization in terminology, for example, definitions of 'elderly' and 'elder abuse', and distinctions between different types of abuse. Other outcomes were the lack of a central database for reports, the lack of universally accepted guidelines for reporting, the lack of agreement about penalties for mistreatment or failure to report. Above all, there was financial under-resourcing, with all the consequences that are implied. In addition, the need for research will continue to be emphasized, based preferably on research designs which are compatible, so that we can begin to establish a cross-national database.

The debate in Canada still remains largely in the domestic sector, although Gnaedinger (1989) has produced evidence which indicates that attention may now be paid to abuse and neglect that takes place in institutions. The existence of family violence in general has captured the public's and the government's imagination. The Federal government has pledged $40 million for 1988–92 to help address family violence in general and half the provincial governments have responded with special legislation which recognizes elder abuse and have expressed a willingness to participate in an exchange of information.

Assessment procedures

It is clear that in Britain, we need to train both professional and voluntary staff in the recognition of abuse and neglect. A variety of ways has been suggested in the preceding chapters, together with the urgent need to develop effective tools for carrying out such assessments. There are other useful suggestions in Phillipson and Biggs (1992), as well as in the American texts just referred to. The issue for British readers is whether protocols travel comfortably across the Atlantic. It probably remains true that unless we can develop our own material, or effectively adapt material from North America, our responses to this major social problem will remain inadequate. Further, bearing in mind Nolan's conceptualization of carer–dependant relationships in Chapter 9, it would be useful to compare Kosberg and Cairl's 'The Cost of Care Index' (1986, cited in Bennett, 1992a) and Robinson's 'Caregiver Strain Questionnaire' and the 'High Risk Placement Worksheet' by Kosberg (cited in Phillipson and Biggs, 1992).

Continuing research

Throughout this book many issues have been raised which enter the category of matters for further research. McCreadie (1991) includes in her exploratory study an extensive list of suggestions and they are similar to the variety of topics that have been raised in the preceding pages. Among the most important are:

- a study of incidence and prevalence;
- a study of victims;
- a study of perpetrators;
- the consequences of abuse upon the perpetrators and upon the victims;
- the nature of family violence;

- the relationship between child abuse, spouse abuse, elder abuse and the abuse of other vulnerable adults;
- different perceptions of abuse;
- the issues of neglect and self-neglect;
- a study of caregiver stress;
- a study of abuse in institutions;
- an evaluation of intervention programmes;
- development of screening instruments;
- a study of standardization in recording;
- a study of different types of abuse.

These issues are all of common interest in Britain, North America and elsewhere.

Gnaedinger wrote in a paper for the Canadian Ministry of Health and Welfare:

> Without research, little can be done . . . The characteristics common to and different from other forms of family violence, clear and testable definitions, the incidence and nature of elder abuse, the relationship between abuser traits and type of abuse, the validity and reliability of research carried out to date, public awareness of the problem, the education and training of professionals who will increasingly have elderly people as clients, indicators of different types of abuse, legislation framed specifically to address elder abuse, appropriate intervention considerations and treatment models, prevention strategies at all levels – all of these issues require a sound knowledge base and this requires research. (1989: 20)

The difficulties are considerable. Victims are often socially isolated and unwilling or unable to report their abuse or neglect, but Wolf, Pillemer and their associates have been able to break through this previously imagined barrier. In addition, more clinical information in the form of case examples and case reviews is becoming available. With increasing public awareness as well, it is our hope that more elderly victims of abuse and neglect will find it possible to be heard and that we may, as a result of what we learn, find ways in which we may increase the quality of life of all older people.

APPENDIX   Abuse of Elderly People – Guidelines for Action

Prepared by Age Concern England, The British Association of Social Workers, The British Geriatrics Society, The Carers' National Association, Help the Aged, the Police Federation of England and Wales, and reproduced here with their permission.

These guidelines will help health and social services staff to identify elderly disabled people who may be at risk of abuse or people who may abuse. They also suggest how services can work together to prevent or protect vulnerable people. The guidelines are concerned about people living in the community; they do not tackle problems of institutional or random abuse.

What is abuse?

1 Physical abuse – hitting, slapping, pushing, restraining.

2 Psychological abuse – blackmail, blaming or swearing.

3 Deprivation of food, heat, clothing, comfort.

4 Forcible isolation of the elderly person – not letting others see or talk to them.

5 Sexual abuse.

6 Misusing medication.

7 Misuse of monies and property.

Who abuses?

The majority of abusing situations occur when the immediate carer, the person carrying the greatest responsibility, is no longer able to care in a loving and sensitive way. However, other family members or visitors to the household can also be abusing an elderly person.

Medical and social factors which promote abuse

Abuse is most likely to occur in the following situations:

1 When the elderly person has a physical illness, especially one which may affect performance of intellect or memory, control of bladder and bowels and impose severe limitations on mobility: for example, Parkinson's disease, stroke, senile dementia or Alzheimer's disease.

2 When the elderly person or his/her carer has difficulty in communication: for example, through deafness, blindness, loss or difficulty with speech and understanding due to strokes, poor memory and concentration span, because of senile dementia/Alzheimer's disease and other conditions leading to limited mental capacity.

3 When there are behavioural disturbances or major changes in personality and behaviour: for example, repetitive behaviour, wandering, questioning, aggression, lack of insight into own disability, lack of insight into the problems of the carer, inconsistent behaviour.

4 When the family is under extra stress because of living on a low income and/or in poor housing.

5 When the elderly person will accept care only from a particular person.

6 When family relationships over the years have been poor.

7 When violent behaviour within the family is common.

The family at risk

Family members who can find themselves abusing their elderly relatives have certain characteristics which can help identify risk situations. Any combination of the following factors should be of concern when identified in vulnerable carers who:

1 Have suffered an enforced, unplanned change in lifestyle which has changed personal aspirations.

2 Are or feel exploited by other family members and/or by health and social service workers.

3 Have found difficulty in making other family members and/or health and social service workers understand their stress.

4 Are physically or mentally ill, show depression or gross anxiety.

5 Are exhausted through heavy physical demands and/or disturbed sleep.

6 Have to live with a person who demonstrates major behavioural disturbances.

7 Are isolated and lack other adult relationships which give social, physical and emotional satisfaction.

8 Have financial difficulties including fears for the future, e.g. loss of pension rights, future earning capacity.

9 Are becoming dependent on alcohol or drugs

10 Make frequent contact with health, social services and other agencies' workers without any resolution of problems.

11 Have other dependants and responsibilities that are making demands, e.g. children, husbands, their own home or work.

12 Have no personal or private space, are in continuous close proximity to the elderly person.

13 Are subject to abuse by an elderly person who may be self-centred and/or intellectually impaired.

Other indicators are:

14 A historically poor relationship between carer and cared for.

15 Roles of carer and cared for have been reversed, e.g. the domineering mother becomes the dependent child.

Physical indicators of abuse

These include:

1 A history of unexplained falls or minor injuries.

2 'Pepperpot' injuries on chest.

3 Bruising in well-protected areas.

4 Finger marks.

5 Burns in unusual places.

6 Excessive repeat prescriptions, or under-use of medication.

7 Excessive consumption of alcohol by carer or elderly person.

Social and emotional indicators in elderly people

1 The elderly person appears to be withdrawn or agitated and anxious.

2 They may be isolated in one room of the house.

3 They are inappropriately and improperly dressed.

4 They are unkempt, unwashed, smelly.

5 They are overly subservient or anxious to please.

6 Professional and other visitors may have difficulty in getting access to the elderly person.

7 The carer always wishes to be present at interviews.

Social and emotional indicators in carers

Carers under stress express a range of feelings common to us all; it is the frequency and intensity of feeling which are important. Feelings expressed include:

1 An unremitting sense of anger, frustration or despair.

2 A sense of unfairness, of being victimized and/or resentment.

3 Grieving for lost personal ambitions and plans.

4 Anxiety and worry.

5 A sense of not being cared for themselves. Also feeling isolated, lonely and/or not respected.

6 Loss of self-esteem.

The carer often expresses a lack of time for self, an inability to see any end to the situation and no future. Besides grieving for the lost personality of their elderly relative, they are also often very hurt and upset by the elderly person's behaviour towards them. They feel they alone are in this position, that there is no relief and that they are seen as of secondary importance to the elderly person; basically, they feel the situation is beyond their control.

Action for health workers to help prevent abuse

Having identified a situation which could lead to abuse, some simple actions could relieve some of the stress. They are:

1 Be knowledgeable about factors which cause stress and lead to abuse.

2 Instigate medical investigations and treatment at early stages of illnesses that could lead to 'risk' conditions.

3 Prescribe drugs with care, ensure management and care of the condition as thought appropriate by the recipients.

4 Give all the information about the medical condition, its prognosis (even when time limits cannot be given), the effects of treatment, particularly side-effects of medication, be prepared to discuss alternative treatments.

5 Ensure that the elderly person and the carer feel listened to, understood and can act on advice; this takes time.

6 Ensure the carer's own health needs are considered.

7 Use the appropriate skills of other primary health care workers.

8 Always refer to social services/social work departments, giving comprehensive information including family structure, ages, diagnosis, prognosis and effects of treatment. Inform the elderly person and carer of your action.

9 Ensure the elderly person and carer know of self-help groups and other organizations that can share their problems. Refer and ask those organizations to contact them if those involved agree.

10 Help carers to accept their right to a life of their own and to have their own needs met. Do not reinforce the feelings that lead to isolation and stress.

11 Take regular opportunities to see the elderly person and the carer separately.

Action when abuse has occurred

When abuse is suspected, define the nature and degree for yourself. The carers must then be faced with your suspicions, remembering always that older people who come into the house may be responsible for it. Much abuse of elderly people is because of carers being stressed, exhausted and/or isolated. They would normally wish to care in a loving and sensitive way. But, however much concern is felt for the carer, abuse of another person is an offence and suspicions must be brought into the open and acted upon.

The following actions must be taken:

1 Interview the elderly person alone.

2 Tell the carer of your concerns and that you wish to help.

3 Tell the carer that a referral will be made to the social services/social work department and that a social worker will visit, discuss the problem facing everyone and try to find help which will benefit all.

4 Take any possible immediate action to relieve stress.

5 If there are identified injuries, if fraud is suspected, the police will have to be informed.

Social services/social work departments' responsibilities and action

Departments should ensure they have guidelines for the identification and treatment of abuse of elderly people. These guidelines should be drawn up by health, social services/social work agencies and the police, and draw on the experiences that agencies have in working together on child abuse.*

Such guidelines should state:

1 That a qualified social worker will be involved in assessment and treatment of potential and actual abusing situations.

2 That, on receiving a referral, the social worker will interview elderly persons and carers separately. The process of investigation is likely to take several interviews. The needs of both elderly person and carer must be assessed and care plans must take everyone's needs into account as much as possible.

3 That the social worker must take immediate action to prevent or stop abuse. The actions available to the social worker must include the possibility of finding alternative accommodation for the carer or the elderly person. It is not always appropriate to remove an elderly person from their own home.

4 That a case conference should be held in all situations of actual abuse, that the police should be invited, and that carers and the elderly person should be included in the conference.

* See pp. 32–3 and p. 161 in this volume which refer to the problems inherent in the use of child abuse literature (eds).

References

Age Concern England (1986) *The Law and Vulnerable Elderly People – Abuse in Institutions*. Mitcham: Age Concern England.

Age Concern England (1991) *Abuse of Elderly People – Guidelines for Action*. Mitcham: Age Concern England.

Aldrich, M. (1989) 'The Abuse of Elderly People: What are the Implications for Policy and Practice?' Unpublished MA thesis, University of Hull, Humberside.

Allen, I., Hogg, D. and Peace, S. (1992) *Elderly People: Choice, Participation and Satisfaction*. London: Policy Studies Institute.

Allen, I., Levin, E., Siddell, M. and Vetter, N. (1983) 'The Elderly and their Informal Carers', in *Elderly People in the Community: Their Service Needs*. London: HMSO.

American Medical Association, Council on Scientific Affairs (1987) 'Elder Abuse and Neglect', *Journal of the American Medical Association*, 257(7): 966–71.

Arie, T. and Jolley, D.J. (1982) 'Making Services Work, Organisation and Style of Psychogeriatric Services', in R. Levy and F. Post (eds), *Psychiatry of Late Life*. Oxford: Blackwell.

Association of Directors of Social Services (1990) *Adults at Risk*. London: ADSS.

Bailey, S.H., Harris, D.J. and Jones, B.L. (1991) *Civil Liberties Cases and Materials*. London: Butterworths.

Baker, A.A. (1975) 'Granny Battering', *Modern Geriatrics*, 5(8): 20–4.

Ball, C., Harris, R., Roberts, G. and Vernon, S. (1988) *The Law Report CCETSW Paper 4.1*. London: CCETSW.

Bardwell, F. (1926) *The Adventure of Old Age*. Boston: Houghton Mifflin Co.

Bebbington, A.C. and Davies, B.P. (1983) 'Equity and Efficiency in the Allocation of Personal Social Services' *Journal of Social Policy*, 12(3): 309–31. Cited in E. Ferlie, D. Challis and B. Davies (1989) (eds), *Efficiency-improving Innovations in Social Care of the Elderly*. Aldershot: Gower.

Bebbington, P.F. and Hill, P.D. (1985) *A Manual of Practical Psychiatry*. Oxford: Blackwell Scientific.

Bennett, D. and Freeman, M.R. (1991) *Community Psychiatry*. Melbourne/London: Churchill Livingstone.

Bennett, G.C.J. (1990a) 'Action on Elder Abuse in the '90s: New Definition Will Help', *Geriatric Medicine*, April: 53–4.

Bennett, G.C.J. (1990b) 'Shifting Emphasis from Abused to Abuser', *Geriatric Medicine*, May: 45–7.

Bennett, G.C.J. (1990c) 'Assessing Abuse in the Elderly', *Geriatric Medicine*, July: 49–51.

Bennett, G.C.J. (1990d) 'Getting through to the Abused Elderly', *Geriatric Medicine*, August: 25–6.

Bennett, G.C.J. (1990e) 'Abuse of the Elderly: Prevention and Legislation'; *Geriatric Medicine*, October: 55–60.

Bennett, G.C.J. (1992a) 'Elder Abuse', in J. George and S. Ebrahim (eds), *Health Care for Older Women*. Oxford: Oxford Medical Publications.

Bennett, G.C.J. (1992b) 'Elderly Victims – Time for Action', *Care of the Elderly*, 4(3): 102.

Bexley Social Services Department (1988) *Report of a Working Party and Seminar on Abuse of Elderly People*. Bexley: London Borough of Bexley.

Biegel, D.E., Sales, E. and Schulz, R. (1991) *Family Caregiving in Chronic Illness*. Newbury Park, CA: Sage.

Blessed, G. and Wilson, I.D. (1982) 'Contemporary Natural History of Mental Disorder in Old Age', *British Journal of Psychiatry*, 141: 59.

Block, M.R. and Sinnott, J.D. (1979) '*The Battered Elder Syndrome: An Exploratory Study*'. Center on Aging, University of Maryland. Cited in M.F. Hudson and T.F. Johnson (1986) 'Elder Neglect and Abuse: A Review of the Literature', in C. Eisdorfer (ed.), *Annual Review of Gerontology and Geriatrics*, Vol. 6. New York: Springer.

Bloom, J.S., Ansell, P. and Bloom, M.N. (1989) 'Detecting Elder Abuse: A Guide for Physicians', *Geriatrics*, 44(6): 40–56.

Blumer, H. (1969) *Symbolic Interactionism*. Englewood Cliffs, NJ: Prentice Hall.

Bornat, J., Phillipson, C. and Ward, S. (1985) *A Manifesto for Old Age*. London: Pluto Books.

Bowers, B.J. (1987) 'Intergenerational Caregiving: Adult Caregivers and their Aging Parents', *Advances in Nursing Science*, 9(2): 20–31.

Brazier, M. (1988) *Street on Torts*. London: Butterworths.

Brearley, P. (1982) 'Old People in Care', in V. Carver and P. Liddiard, (eds), *An Ageing Population*. London: Hodder and Stoughton/Open University Press.

Breckman, R.S. and Adelman, R.D. (1988) *Strategies for Helping Victims of Elder Mistreatment*. London: Sage.

Brillon, Y. (1987) *Victimization and Fear of Crime among the Elderly*. Toronto: Butterworths.

British Association for Service to the Elderly (1991) *Old Age Abuse: Lifting the Lid: A West Midlands Perspective*. Birmingham: BASE (Birmingham Branch).

Brubaker, T.H. (1990) 'An Overview of Family Relationships in Later Life', in T.H. Brubaker (ed.), *Family Relationships in Later Life*. Newbury Park, CA: Sage.

Burston, G.R. (1975) 'Granny Battering', *British Medical Journal*, 6 September: 592.

Burston, G.R. (1977) 'Do your Elderly Patients Live in Fear of Being Battered?', *Modern Geriatrics*, 7(5): 54–5.

Butler, R.N. (1975) *Why Survive? Growing Old In America*. New York: Harper Colophon Books.

Calcutt, D. (1990) *Report of the Committee on Privacy and Related Matters*. Cmnd 1102. London: HMSO.

Callaghan, D. (1987) *Setting Limits: Medical Goals in an Aging Society*. New York: Simon and Schuster.

Callahan, J.J. (1982) 'Elder Abuse Programming – Will it Help the Elderly?', *The Urban and Social Change Review*, 15 (Summer): 15–16.

Callahan, J.J. (1986) 'Guest Editor's Perspective', *Pride Institute Journal of Long Term Home Health Care*, 5: 3.

Callahan, J.J. (1988) 'Elder Abuse: Some Questions for Policymakers', *The Gerontologist*, 28(4): 453–8.

Carson, D. (1985) 'Registered Homes: Another Fine Mess', *Journal of Social Welfare Law*, March: 67–85.

Centre for Policy on Ageing (1984) *Home Life: A Code of Practice for Residential Care*. London: Centre for Policy on Ageing.

Chen, P.N., Bell, S., Dolinsky, D., Doyle, J. and Dunn, M. (1981) 'Elderly Abuse in Domestic Settings: A Pilot Study', *Journal of Gerontological Social Work*, 4 (Fall): 3–17.

Cloke, C. (1983) *Old Age Abuse in the Domestic Setting: A Review*. Mitcham: Age Concern England.

Clough, R. (1988) 'Danger: Look Out for Abuse', *Care Weekly*, January: 7.

Cochran, C. and Petrone, S. (1987) 'Elder Abuse: The Physician's Role in Identification and Prevention', *Illinois Medical Journal*, 171(4): 241–6.

Costa, J. (1984) *Abuse of the Elderly: A Guide to Resources and Sources*. Lexington, DC: Heath and Company.

Counsel and Care (1991) *Not Such Private Places*. London: Counsel and Care.

Cowell, A. (1989) 'Abuse of the Institutionalized Aged: Recent Policy in California', in R. Filinson and S.R. Ingman (eds), *Elder Abuse: Practice and Policy*. New York: Human Sciences Press.

Cox, E.O., Parsons, R.J. and Kimboko, P.J. (1988) 'Social Services and Intergenerational Caregiving: Issues for Social Work', *Social Work*, 33(5): 430–4.

Crystal, S. (1986) 'Social Policy and Elder Abuse', in K.A. Pillemer and R.S. Wolf (eds), *Elder Abuse: Conflict in the Family*. Dover, Mass.: Auburn Publishing Co.

Dalley, G. (1989) 'Professional Ideology or Organisational Tribalism? The Health Service–Social Work Divide', in R. Taylor and J. Ford (eds), *Social Work and Health Care*. London: Jessica Kingsley.

Daniels, R.S., Baumhover, L.A. and Clark-Daniels, C.L. (1989) 'Physicians' Mandatory Reporting of Elder Abuse', *The Gerontologist*, 29(3): 321–7.

Decalmer, P., Glendenning, F. and Marriott, A. (in preparation) 'A Retrospective Study of 150 Cases of Elder Abuse'.

Denton, F.T., Feaver, C.H. and Spencer, B.G. (1987) 'The Canadian Population and Labour Force: Retrospect and Prospect', in V.W. Marshall (ed.), *Aging in Canada*. Markham, Ontario: Fitzhenry & Whiteside.

Department of Health (1989) *Caring for People: Community Care in the Next Decade and Beyond*. Cn. 849. London: HMSO.

Department of Health Social Services Inspectorate (1991) *Hear Me: See Me. An Inspection of Services from three Agencies to Disabled People in Gloucestershire*. London: HMSO.

Department of Health Social Services Inspectorate (1992) *Confronting Elder Abuse: An SSI London Region Survey*. London: HMSO.

Derbyshire County Council (1979) Report of the Social Services Sub-Committee on its Investigation into the Alleged Ill-treatment of Residents and Other Complaints Relating to Stonelow Court Aged Persons Home, Dronfield. Matlock: Derbyshire County Council.

Dobash, R. and Dobash, R. (1992) *Women, Violence and Social Change*. London: Routledge.

Donovan, T. and Wynne-Harley, D. (1986) *Not a Nine to Five Job*. London: Centre for Policy on Ageing.

Doty, P. and Sullivan, E.W. (1983) 'Community Involvement in Combating Abuse, Neglect and Mistreatment in Nursing Homes', *Milbank Memorial Fund Quarterly/Health and Society*, 32: 222–51.

Douglass, R.L. (1983) 'Domestic Neglect and Abuse of the Elderly: Implication for Research and Service', *Family Relations*, 32: 395–402.

Downey, R. (1991) 'Waiting for Parity', *Social Work Today*, 13 June: 9.

Dunlop, M.J. (1986) 'Is a Science of Caring Possible?', *Journal of Advanced Nursing*, 11: 661–70.

Eastman, M. (1983) 'Granny Battering: A Hidden Problem', *Community Care*, 27 May, 413: 11–15.

Eastman, M. (1984a) 'At Worst Just Picking up the Pieces', *Community Care*, 2 February: 20–2.

Eastman, M. (1984b) *Old Age Abuse*. Mitcham: Age Concern England.

Eastman, M. (1988) 'Granny Abuse', *Community Outlook*, October: 15–16.

Eastman, M. and Sutton, M. (1981) 'Granny Bashing Signs are Passing GPs', *Pulse*, 24 October.

Eastman, M. and Sutton, M. (1982) 'Granny Battering', *Geriatric Medicine*, November: 11–15.

Estes, C. (1979) *The Ageing Enterprise*. San Francisco: Jossey Bass.

Farndale, J. (1961) *The Day Hospital Movement in Great Britain*. Oxford: Pergamon Press.

Featherstone, M. and Hepworth, M. (1991) *The Body: Social Process and Cultural Theory*. London: Sage.

Fennel, P. (1989) 'Falling through the Legal Loopholes', *Social Work Today*, 30 November: 18–20.

Fennell, G., Phillipson, C. and Evers, H. (1988) *The Sociology of Old Age*. London: Open University Press,

Ferlie, E., Challis, D. and Davies, B. (eds) (1989) *Efficiency-improving Innovations in Social Care of the Elderly*. Aldershot: Gower.

Filinson, R. (1989) 'Research Foundations: Introduction', in R. Filinson and S.R. Ingman (eds), *Elder Abuse: Practice and Policy*. New York: Human Sciences Press.

Filinson, R. and Ingman, S.R. (eds) (1989) *Elder Abuse: Practice and Policy*. New York: Human Sciences Press.

Finch, J. (1989) *Kinship Obligations and Social Change*. Cambridge: Polity Press.

Finkelhor, D. and Pillemer, K.A. (1988) 'Elder Abuse: its Relation to Other Forms of Domestic Violence', in G.T. Hotaling, D. Finkelhor, J.T. Kirkpatrick and M.A. Strauss (eds), *Family Abuse and its Consequences: New Directions in Research*. Newbury Park, CA: Sage.

Fisk, J. (1991) 'Abuse of the Elderly', in R. Jacoby and C. Oppenheimer (eds), *Psychiatry in the Elderly*. Oxford: Oxford University Press.

Foelker, G.A., Holland, J., Marsh, M. and Simmons, B.A. (1990) 'A Community Response to Elder Abuse', *The Gerontologist*, 30(4): 560–2.

Forbes, W.F., Jackson, J.A. and Kraus, A.S. (1987) *Institutionalization of the Elderly in Canada*. Toronto: Butterworths.

Forster, D.P. and Tiplady, P. (1980) 'Doctors and Compulsory Procedures: Section 47 of the National Assistance Act, 1948', *British Medical Journal*, 280: 739–40.

Froggatt, A. (1990) *Family Work with Elderly People*. Basingstoke: Macmillan.

Fulmer, T. (1984) 'Elder Abuse Assessment Tool', *Dimensions of Critical Care Nursing*, 3(4): 216–20.

Fulmer, T. and O'Malley, T. A. (1987) *Inadequate Care of the Elderly*. New York: Springer.

Gelles, R. (1987) *Family Violence*. London: Sage.

George, L. (1989) *Heroes of their own Lives: The Politics and History of Family Violence*. London: Virago.

George, L.K. and Gwyther, L.P. (1986) 'Caregiver Well-being: A Multidimensional Examination of Family Caregivers to Demented Adults', *The Gerontologist*, 26(3): 253–9.

Gesino, J.P., Smith, H. and Keckich, W.A. (1982) 'The Battered Woman Grows Old', *Clinical Gerontologist*, 1 (Fall): 59–67.

Gibbs, J., Evans, M. and Rodway, S. (1987) *Report of the Inquiry into Nye Bevan Lodge*. London: London Borough of Southwark Social Services Department.

Gilbert, D.A. (1986) 'The Ethics of Mandatory Elder Abuse Reporting Statistics', *Advances in Nursing Science*, 8(2): 51–62.

Gilhooly, M.L.M. (1984) 'The Impact of Care-giving on Care-givers: Factors Associated with the Psychological Well-being of People Supporting a Dementing Relative in the Community', *British Journal of Medical Psychology*, 57: 35–44.

Gioglio, G.R. and Blakemore, P. (1983) 'Elder Abuse in New Jersey: The Knowledge and Experience of Abuse among Older New Jerseyians'. Unpublished manuscript, Department of Human Services, Trenton, NJ. Cited in M.F. Hudson and T.F. Johnson (1986) 'Elder Neglect and Abuse: A Review of the Literature', in C. Eisdorfer (ed.), *Annual Review of Gerontology and Geriatrics*, vol. 6. New York: Springer.

Glouberman, S. (1990) *'Keepers' Inside Stories from Total Institutions*. London: King Edward Hospital Fund for London.

Gloucestershire Social Services Department (1991) *Adults at Risk: Procedural Guidelines for Professionals*. Gloucester: Gloucestershire County Council.

Gnaedinger, N. (1989) *Elder Abuse: A Discussion Paper*. Ottawa: The National Clearing House on Family Violence, Health and Welfare Canada.

Godkin, M.A., Wolf, R.S. and Pillemer, K.A. (1989) 'A Case-Comparison Analysis of Elder Abuse and Neglect', *International Journal of Aging and Human Development*, 28(3): 207–25.

Goldberg, D. and Huxley, P. (1980) *Mental Illness in the Community: A Pathway to Care*. London: Tavistock.

Grace, J. (1991) 'Warning: Ageism Can Damage your Patients' Health', *Geriatric Medicine*, October: 11.

Green, H. (1988) *Informal Carers*. London: Office of Population Censuses and Surveys, General Household Survey.

Green, M. (1985) 'Loss of Old Age', in *Loss Proceedings of the BASW Summer School on Loss*. London: British Association of Social Workers.

Griffiths, A. (1980) 'The Legacy and Present Administration of English Law: Some Problems of Battered Women in Context', *Cambrian Law Review*, 11: 29–39.

Griffiths, A., Grimes, R. and Roberts, G. (1990) *The Law and Elderly People*. London: Routledge.

Griffiths, A., Roberts, G. and Williams, J. (1992) *Sharpening the Instrument: The Law and Older People*. Stoke-on-Trent: British Association for Service to the Elderly.

Gwyther, L.P. and George, L.K. (1986) 'Caregivers for Dementia Patients, Complex Determinants of Well-being and Burden', *The Gerontologist*, 26(3): 245–7.

Halamandaris, V.J. (1983) 'Fraud and Abuse in Nursing Homes', in J.I. Kosberg (ed.), *Abuse and Maltreatment of the Elderly: Causes and Interventions*. Boston: John Wright.

Hall, P.A. (1989) 'Elder Maltreatment Patterns: Items, Sub-Groups and Types. Policy and Practical Implications', *International Journal of Aging and Human Development*, 28(3): 196–205.

Harman, H. and Harman, S. (1989) *No Place Like Home*. London: NALGO.

Hibbs, P.J. (1991) 'Freedom or Restraint'. Unpublished paper. Counsel and Care Conference, Autumn 1991, London.

Hickey, T. and Douglass, R.L. (1981a) 'Mistreatment of the Elderly in the Domestic Setting: an Exploratory Study', *American Journal of Public Health*, 71: 500–7.

Hickey, T. and Douglass, R.L. (1981b) 'Neglect and Abuse of Older Family Members: Professionals' Perspectives and Case Experiences', *The Gerontologist*, 21(2): 171–6.

Higgins, J. (1989) 'Defining Community Care: Realities and Myths', *Social Policy and Administration*, 25(1): 3–16.

Hildrew, M.A. (1991a) *Guidelines on Elder Abuse: Which Social Services Departments Have Them?* London: British Association of Social Workers.

Hildrew, M.A. (1991b) 'Safe in our Hands?', *Social Work Today*, 22(49): 15–17.

Hirschfield, M.J. (1981) 'Families Living and Coping with the Cognitively Impaired', in L.A. Copp (ed.), *Care of the Ageing*. Edinburgh: Churchill Livingstone.

Hirschfield, M.J. (1983) 'Homecare versus Institutionalisation: Family Caregiving and Senile Brain Disease', *International Journal of Nursing Studies*, 20(1): 23–32.

Hirst, S.P. and Miller, J. (1986) 'The Abused Elderly', *Journal of Psycho-Social Nursing*, 24(10): 28–34.

Hocking, E.D. (1988) 'Miscare – A Form of Abuse in the Elderly', *Update*, 15 May: 2411–19.

Hoggett, B. (1990) *Mental Health Law*. London: Sweet & Maxwell.

Homer, A.C. and Gilleard, C. (1990a) 'Abuse of Elderly People by their Carers', *British Medical Journal*, 301: 1359–62.

Homer, A. and Gilleard, C. (1990b) 'Elder Abuse in a Respite Care Population: Abusers Need Help'. Paper presented to BSG Annual Conference, University of Durham, September 1990.

Hooyman, N.R. (1983) 'Elderly Abuse and Neglect: Community Interventions', in J. I. Kosberg (ed.), *Abuse and Maltreatment of the Elderly: Courses and Interventions*. Boston: John Wright.

Hope, P. (1992) 'Point of View', *Nursing Standard*, 6(15/16): 43.

Horrocks, P. (1988) 'Elderly People: Abused and Forgotten', *Health Service Journal*, 22 September: 1085.

Hotaling, G.T., Finkelhor, D., Kirkpatrick, J.T. and Strauss, M.A. (eds) *Family Abuse and its Consequences: New Directions in Research*. Newbury Park, CA: Sage.

Hudson, J.E. (1988) 'Elder Abuse: An Overview', in B. Schlesinger and R. Schlesinger (eds), *Abuse of the Elderly*. Toronto: University of Toronto Press.

Hudson, M.F. (1986) 'Elder Mistreatment: Current Research', in K.A. Pillemer and R.S Wolf (eds), *Elder Abuse: Conflict in the Family*. Dover, Mass.: Auburn House Publishing Co.

Hudson, M.F. and Johnson, T.F. (1986) 'Elder Neglect and Abuse: A Review of the Literature', in C. Eisdorfer et al. (eds), *Annual Review of Gerontology and Geriatrics*, vol. 6. New York: Springer.

Humberside Social Services Department (1992) *Principles, Procedures and Practices in Abuse of Older People – A Discussion Document*. Beverley: Humberside County Council.

Hytner, B.A. (1977) *Report into Allegations concerning Moorfield Observation and Assessment Centre*. Salford: City of Salford.

Isaacs, B. (1971) 'Geriatric Families': Do their Families Care?', *British Medical Journal*, 30 October: 282–6.

Johnson, P., Conrad, C. and Thompson, D. (1989) (eds) *Workers versus Pensioners*. Manchester: Manchester University Press.

Johnson, T.F. (1986) 'Critical Issues in the Definition of Elder Mistreatment', in K.A. Pillemer and R.S. Wolf (eds), *Elder Abuse: Conflict in the Family*. Dover, Mass.: Auburn House Publishing Co.

Johnson, T.F. (1991) *Elder Mistreatment: Deciding Who is at Risk*. Westport, Conn.: Greenwood Press.

Johnson, T.F., O'Brien, J.G. and Hudson, M.F. (1985) *Elder Neglect and Abuse: An Annotated Bibliography*. Westport, Conn.: Greenwood Press.

Jolley, D.J. and Arie, T. (1978) 'Organisation of Psychogeriatric Services', *British Journal of Psychiatry*, 132: 1–11.

Jones, G. (1992) 'A Communication Model for Dementia', in G. Jones and B.M.L. Mieson (eds), *Care-giving in Dementia: Research and Applications*. London: Routledge.

Jorm, A.F. (1990) *The Epidemiology of Alzheimer's Disease and Related Disorders*. London: Chapman and Hall.

Kahana, E. and Young, R. (1990) 'Clarifying the Caregiving Paradigm: Challenges for the Future', in D.E. Biegel and A. Blum (eds), *Aging and Caregiving: Theory, Research and Policy*. Newbury Park, CA: Sage.

Kent Social Services Department (1989) *Practice Guidelines for Dealing with Elder Abuse*. Canterbury: Policy Officer, Kent County Council.

Kimsey, I.R., Tarbox, A.R. and Bragg, D.F. (1981) 'Abuse of the Elderly – the Hidden Agenda: I. The Caretakers and the Categories of Abuse', *Journal of the American Geriatrics Society*, 29: 465–72.

Kingston, P. (1990) 'Elder Abuse'. Unpublished MA thesis, University of Keele, Staffordshire.

Kosberg, J.I. (ed.) (1983) *Abuse and Maltreatment of the Elderly: Causes and Interventions*. Boston: John Wright.

Kosberg, J.I. (1988) 'Preventing Elder Abuse: Identification of High Risk Factors prior to Placement Decisions', *The Gerontologist*, 28(1): 43–50

Laslett, P. (1989) *A Fresh Map of Life*. London: Weidenfeld & Nicolson.

Lau, E. and Kosberg, J.I. (1979) 'Abuse of the Elderly by Informal Care Providers', *Aging*, 299–301: 11–15.

Law Commission (1991) *Mentally Incapacitated Adults and Decision-Making: An Overview*. Consultation Paper 119. London: Law Commission.

Lawton, M.P., Kleban, M.H., Moss, M., Rovine, M. and Glicksman, A. (1989) 'Measuring Caregiving Appraisal', *Journal of Gerontology*, 44(3): 61–71.

Lee, G. (1985) 'Kinship and Social Support: The Case of the United States', *Ageing and Society*, 5: 19–38.

Leroux, T.G. and Petrunik, M. (1990) 'The Construction of Elder Abuse as a Social Problem: A Canadian Perspective', *International Journal of Health Services*, 20(4): 651–63.

Lewis, J. and Meredith, B. (1988a) 'Daughters Caring for Mothers', *Ageing and Society*, 8(1): 1–21.

Lewis, J. and Meredith, B. (1988b) *Daughters who Care*. London: Routledge.

Lodge, B. (1991) *Whither Now? Planning Services for Elderly People*. Stoke-on-Trent: British Association for Service to the Elderly.

Lomas, G. (1991) *Middleton Elderly Resource Intervention Team (MERIT)*. Private Communication.

Lowther, C.P. and Williamson, J. (1966) 'Old People and their Relations', *The Lancet*, 31 December: 1459–60.

Lucas, E.T. (1991) *Elder Abuse and its Recognition amongst Health Service Professionals*. Hamden Court: Garland Publishing.

Lye, M. (1982) 'Geriatric Medicine and Medical Unemployment', *Journal of the Royal College of Physicians of London*, 16: 129.

McCall, G.J. and Simmons, J.L. (1966) *Identities and Interactions*. New York: Free Press.

McCreadie, C. (1991) *Elder Abuse: An Exploratory Study*. London: Age Concern Institute of Gerontology, King's College London.

McEwan, E. (ed.) (1989) *Age: The Unrecognised Discrimination*. London: Age Concern.

McEwan, J. (1989) 'Documentary Hearsay Evidence – Refuge for the Vulnerable Witness', *Criminal Law Review*, 629–42.

Maclean, U. (1989) *Dependent Territories*. London: Nuffield Provincial Hospitals Trust.

McPherson, B. (1990) *Aging as a Social Process*. Toronto: Butterworths.

Matthews, V. and Woods, R.T. (1980) *Abuse in Families of Psychogeriatric Patients*. Open University Course 253: *Conflict in the Family Block 3*. Milton Keynes: Open University Press.

Mechanic, D. (1989) *Mental Health and Social Policy*, 3rd edn. Englewood Cliffs, NJ: Prentice-Hall.

Medd, P. (1976) *Committee of Inquiry into Incidents at Besford House Community House*. Shrewsbury: Shropshire County Council.

Mildenberger, C. and Wessman, H.C. (1986) 'Abuse and Neglect of Elderly Persons by Family Members', *Physical Therapy*, 66(4): 537–9.

Millard, P. (1984) 'Views of a Geriatrician', in M. Eastman (ed.), *Old Age Abuse*. Mitcham: Age Concern England.

Mitchell, D. (1991) 'The Long and Short of it', *Community Care*, 7 November: 8.

Mixson, P.M. (1991) 'Self-Neglect: A Practitioner's Perspective', *Journal of Elder Abuse and Neglect*, 3(1): 35–42.

Monk, A. (1990) 'Gerontological Social Services: Theory and Practice', in A. Monk (ed.), *Handbook of Gerontological Services*. New York: Columbia University Press.

Morley, S. (1988) 'How Can We Help You?', *Community Outlook (Nursing Times)*, October: 32–7.

Morris, R.G., Morris, L.W. and Britton, P.G. (1988) 'Factors Affecting the Emotional Well-being of the Caregivers of Dementia Sufferers', *British Journal of Psychiatry*, 153: 147–56.

Motenko, A.K. (1989) 'The Frustrations, Gratifications and Well-being of Dementia Caregivers', *The Gerontologist*, 29(2): 166–72.

Murphy, J. (1931) 'Dependency in Old Age', *Annals of the American Academy of Political and Social Science*, 154: 38–41.

Nathanson, P. (1983) 'An Overview of Legal Issues, Services and Resources', in J.I. Kosberg (ed.), *Abuse and Maltreatment of the Elderly: Causes and Interventions*. Boston: John Wright.

National Health Service (1969) *Report into Allegations of Ill-Treatment at Ely' Hospital, Cardiff*. London: HMSO.

National Institute of Social Work (1988) *Residential Care: A Positive Choice*. London: HMSO.

Noelker, L.S. and Townsend, A.L. (1987) 'Perceived Caregiving Effectiveness: The Impact of Parental Impairment, Community Resources and Caregiver Characteristics', in T.H. Brubaker (ed.), *Aging, Health and Family: Longterm Care*. Beverley Hills, CA: Sage.

Nolan, M.R. (1991) 'Timeshare Beds: a Pluralistic Evaluation of Rota Bed Systems in Continuing Care Hospitals'. Unpublished PhD thesis, University of Wales.

Nolan, M.R. and Grant, G. (1989) 'Addressing the Needs of Informal Carers: a Neglected Area of Nursing Practice', *Journal of Advanced Nursing*, 14: 950–61.

Nolan, M.R. and Grant, G. (1992) *Regular Respite: An Evaluation of a Hospital Rota Bed Scheme for Elderly People*. London: Age Concern Institute of Gerontology Research Paper Series.

Nolan, M.R., Grant, G. and Ellis, N.C. (1990) 'Stress is in the Eye of the Beholder: Reconceptualising the Measurement of Carer Burden', *Journal of Advanced Nursing*, 15: 544–55.

Norman, A. (1987a) *Aspects of Ageism*. London: Centre for Policy on Ageing.

Norman, A. (1987b) 'Happy (Surrogate) Families', *Community Care*, 8 October: 22–3.

North Yorkshire Social Services Department (1992) *How to Complain*. Northallerton: North Yorkshire County Council.

Nusberg, C. (1985) 'Consumer Perspective on Quality of Institutional Care in the U.S', *Ageing International*, 12(3): 16–17.

O'Brien, J.G. (1986) 'Elder Abuse and the Physician', *Michigan Medicine*, 85: 618–20.

Ogg, J. and Bennett, G.C.J. (1991) 'Elder Abuse: Providing Answers to Some Questions', *Geriatric Medicine*, October: 15–16.

Ogg, J. and Bennett, G.C.J. (1992a) 'Screening for Elder Abuse in the Community', *Geriatric Medicine*, February: 63–7.

Ogg, J. and Bennett, G.C.J. (1992b) 'Elder Abuse in Britain', *British Medical Journal*, 24 October: 998–9.

O'Malley, H.C., Segel, H.D. and Perez, R. (1979) *Elder Abuse in Massachusetts: Survey of Professionals and Paraprofessionals*. Boston: Legal Research and Services to the Elderly.

O'Malley, T.A., Everitt, D.E., O'Malley, H.C. and Campion, E.W. (1983) 'Identifying and Preventing Family-Mediated Abuse and Neglect of Elderly Persons', *Annals of Internal Medicine*, 98: 998–1005.

O'Malley, T.A., O'Malley, H.C., Everitt, D.E. and Sarson, D. (1984) 'Categories of Family-Mediated Abuse and Neglect of Elderly Persons', *Journal of the American Geriatrics Society*, 32(5): 362–9.

Pahl, J. (ed.) (1985) *Private Life and Public Policy. The Needs of Battered Women and the Response of the Public Services*. London: Routledge and Kegan Paul.

Parker, G. (1985) *With Due Care and Attention: A Review of Research on Informal Care*. London: Family Policy Studies Centre.

Pearlin, L., Mullan, J.T., Semple, S.J. and Skaff, M.M. (1990) 'Caregiving and the Stress Process: an Overview of Concepts and their Measures', *The Gerontologist*, 30(5): 583–94.

Pfeffer, N. and Coote, A. (1991) *Is Quality Good for You? A Critical Review of Quality Assurance in Welfare Services*. London: Institute for Policy Research.

Phillips, J. (1990) 'The Reaction of Social Workers to the Challenge of Private Sector Growth in Residential Care for Elderly People', in B. Bytheway and J. Johnson (eds), *Welfare and Ageing Experience*. Aldershot: Gower.

Phillips, L.R. (1986) 'Theoretical Explanations of Elder Abuse', in K.A. Pillemer and R.S. Wolf (eds), *Elder Abuse: Conflict in the Family*. Dover, Mass.: Auburn House Publishing Co.

Phillips, L.R. (1988) 'The Fit of Elder Abuse with the Family Violence Paradigm and the Implications of a Paradigm Shift for Clinical Practice', *Public Health Nursing*, 5(4): 22–9.

Phillips, L.R. (1989) 'Issues Involved in Identifying and Intervening in Elder Abuse', in R. Filinson and S. Ingman (eds), *Elder Abuse: Practice and Policy*. New York: Human Sciences Press.

Phillips, L.R. and Rempusheski, V.F. (1986) 'Caring for the Frail Elderly at Home: Towards a Theoretical Explanation of the Dynamics of Poor Quality Family Care', *Advances in Nursing Science*, 8(4): 62–84.

Phillipson, C. (1992a) 'Challenging the "Spectre of Old Age": Community Care for Older People in the 1990s', in N. Manning and R. Page (eds), *Social Policy Year Book 1992*. London: Social Policy Association.

Phillipson, C. (1992b) 'Confronting Elder Abuse: Fact and Fiction', *Generations Review*, 2(3): 2–3.

Phillipson, C. and Biggs, S. (1992) *Understanding Elder Abuse: a Training Manual for Helping Professionals*. London: Longman.

Pillemer, K.A. (1986) 'Risk Factors in Elder Abuse: Results from a Case-Control Study', in K.A. Pillemer and R. Wolf (eds), *Elder Abuse: Conflict in the Family*. Dover, Mass.: Auburn House Publishing Co.

Pillemer, K.A. and Finkelhor, D. (1988) 'The Prevalence of Elder Abuse: A Random Sample Survey', *The Gerontologist*, 28(1): 51–7.

Pillemer, K.A. and Moore, D.W. (1989) 'Abuse of Patients in Nursing Homes: Findings from a Survey of Staff', *The Gerontologist*, 29(3): 314–20.

Pillemer, K.A. and Wolf, R.S. (eds) (1986) *Elder Abuse: Conflict in the Family*. Dover, Mass.: Auburn House Publishing Co.

Pitkeathley, J. (1990) 'Painful Conflicts', *Community Care (Inside)*, 22 February: 1–2.

Podnieks, E. (1983) 'Abuse of the Elderly', *The Canadian Nurse*, 79: 34–5.

Podnieks, E. (1985) 'Elder Abuse', *The Canadian Nurse*, 81 (December): 36–9.

Podnieks, E. (1988) 'Elder Abuse: It's Time We Did Something about It', in B. Schlesinger and R. Schlesinger (eds), *Abuse of the Elderly*. Toronto: University of Toronto Press.

Podnieks, E. (1989) 'Elder Abuse: A Canadian Perspective', in R.S. Wolf and S. Bergman (eds), *Stress, Conflict and Abuse of the Elderly*. Jerusalem: Brookdale Institute of Gerontology and Adult Human Development.

Podnieks, E. and Pillemer, K.A. (1989) *Survey on Abuse of the Elderly in Canada*. Toronto: Ryerson Polytechnical Institute.

Poertner, J. (1986) 'Estimating the Incidence of Abused Older Persons', *Journal of Gerontological Social Work*, 9 (Spring): 3–15.

Poulshock, S.W. and Deimling, G.T. (1984) 'Caring for Elders in Residence: Issues in the Measurement of Burden', *Journal of Gerontology*, 39(2): 230–9.

Powell, S. and Berg, R.C. (1987) 'When the Elderly are Abused: Characteristics and Intervention', *Educational Gerontology*, 13: 71–83.

Pratt, C., Schmall, V. and Wright, S. (1987) 'Ethical Concerns of Family Caregivers to Dementia Patients', *The Gerontologist*, 25(5): 632–8.

Pritchard, J. (1989) 'Confronting the Taboo of the Abuse of Elderly People', *Social Work Today*, 5 October: 12–13.

Pritchard, J. (1990a) 'Old and Abused', *Social Work Today*, 15 February: 22–3.

Pritchard, J. (1990b) 'Charting the Hits', *Care Weekly*, 19 October: 10–11.

Pritchard, J. (1992) *The Abuse of Elderly People: A Handbook for Professionals*. London: Jessica Kingsley.

Pruchno, R.A., Michaels, J.E. and Potashnik, S.L. (1990) 'Predictors of Institutionalisation among Alzheimer's Disease Victims with Caregiving Spouses', *Journal of Gerontology (Social Sciences)*, 45(6): S259–66.

Quinn, M.J. and Tomita, S.K. (1986) *Elder Abuse and Neglect: Causes, Diagnosis and Intervention Strategies*. New York: Springer.

Qureshi, H. (1986) 'Responses to Dependency: Reciprocity, Affect and Power in Family Relationships', in C. Phillipson, M. Bernard and P. Strang (eds), *Dependency and Interdependency in Old Age: Theoretical Perspectives and Policy Alternatives*. London: Croom Helm.

Qureshi, H. and Walker, A. (1986) 'Caring for Elderly People: The Family and State', in C. Phillipson and A. Walker (eds), *Ageing and Social Policy: A Critical Assessment*. Aldershot: Gower.

Qureshi, H. and Walker, A. (1989) *The Caring Relationship: Elderly People and their Families*. London: Macmillan.

Ramsey-Klawsnik, H. (1991) 'Elder Sexual Abuse: Preliminary Findings', *Journal of Elder Abuse and Neglect*, 3(3): 73–90.

Rathbone-McCuan, E. (1980) 'Elderly Victims of Family Violence and Neglect', *Social Casework: The Journal of Contemporary Social Work*, May: 296–304.

Rathbone-McCuan, E. and Voyles, B. (1982) 'Case Detection of Abused Elderly Parents', *American Journal of Psychiatry*, 139(2): 189–92.

Robb, B. (1967) *'Sans Everything': A Case to Answer*. London: Thomas Nelson.

Rogers, W.V.H. (1989) *The Law of Tort*. London: Sweet & Maxwell.

Rolland, J.S. (1988) 'A Conceptual Model of Chronic and Life Threatening Illness and its Impact on Families', in C.S. Chilman, E.W. Nunnally and F.M. Cox (eds), *Chronic Illness and Disability*. Families in Trouble series, vol. 2. Beverley Hills, CA: Sage.

Ross, M., Ross, P.A. and Ross, M.C. (1985) 'Abuse of the Elderly', *The Canadian Nurse*, 81 (February): 36–9.

Royal College of Nursing (1987) *Improving Care of Elderly People in Hospital*. London: Royal College of Nursing.

Royal College of Nursing (1991) *Guidelines for Nurses: Abuse and Older People*. London: Royal College of Nursing.

Royal College of Nursing (1992) *A Scandal Waiting to Happen?: Elderly People and Nursing Care in Residential and Nursing Homes*. London: Royal College of Nursing.

Salend, E., Rosalie, K. and Kane, M. (1984) 'Elder Abuse Reporting: Limitations of Statistics', *The Gerontologist*, 24(1): 61–9.

Sayce, L. (1991) 'Registering: A Risky Business', *Social Work Today*, 4 July: 12–13.

Schlesinger, B. and Schlesinger, R. (eds) (1988) *Abuse of the Elderly: Issues and Annotated Bibliography*. Toronto: University of Toronto Press.

Sengstock, M.C. and Barrett, S. (1986) 'Elderly Victims of Family Abuse, Neglect, and Maltreatment: Can Legal Assistance Help?', *Journal of Gerontological Social Work*, 9: 43–60.

Sengstock, M.C. and Liang, J. (1982) 'Identifying and Characterizing Elder Abuse'. Unpublished manuscript, Wayne State University Institute of Gerontology, cited in M.F. Hudson and T.F. Johnson (1986) 'Elder Neglect and Abuse: A Review of the Literature', in C. Eisdorfer et al. (eds), *Annual Review of Gerontology and Geriatrics*, vol. 6. New York: Springer.

Sengstock, M.C. and Liang, J. (1983) 'Domestic Abuse of the Aged. Assessing some Dimensions of the Problem', in M.B. Kleiman (ed.), *Social Gerontology*. Basel: Karger.

Sharpe, G. (1988) 'The Protection of Elderly Mentally Incompetent Individuals who are Victims of Abuse', in B. Schlesinger and R. Schlesinger (eds), *Abuse of the Elderly: Issues and Annotated Bibliography*. Toronto: University of Toronto Press.

Shell, D.J. (1982) *Protection of the Elderly: a Study of Elder Abuse*. Winnipeg: Manitoba Association of Gerontology.

Shell, D.J. (1988) 'Elder Abuse: Summary of Results – Manitoba', in B. Schlesinger and R. Schlesinger (eds), *Abuse of the Elderly: Issues and Annotated Bibliography*. Toronto: University of Toronto Press.

Simmons, S. (1985) 'Family Burden: A Qualitative Study'. Paper presented at Royal College of Nursing Research Society Annual Conference, University of Nottingham.

Solomon, K. (1983) 'Victimization by Health Professionals and the Psychologic Response of the Elderly' and 'Intervention for the Victimized Elderly and Sensitization of Health Professionals: Therapeutic and Educational Efforts' in J.I. Kosberg (ed.), *Abuse and Maltreatment of the Elderly: Causes and Interventions*. Boston: John Wright.

Soule, D.J. and Bennett, J.M. (1987) 'Elder Abuse in South Dakota', *South Dakota Journal of Medicine*, 40(10): 7–10 and (11): 5–8.

Sprey, J. and Matthews, S. (1989) 'The Perils of Drawing Policy Implications from Research: The Case of Elder Mistreatment', in R. Filinson and S. Ingman (eds), *Elder Abuse: Practice and Policy*. New York: Human Sciences Press.

Stathopoulos, P.A. (1983) 'Consumer Advocacy and Abuse of Elders in Nursing Homes', in J.I. Kosberg (ed.), *Abuse and Maltreatment of the Elderly: Causes and Interventions*. Boston: John Wright.

Stearns, P. (1986) 'Old Age Family Conflict: The Perspective of the Past', in K.A. Pillemer and R.S. Wolf (eds), *Elder Abuse: Conflict in the Family*. Dover, Mass.: Auburn House Publishing Co.

Steingal, H.D. and Peraz, R. (1979) 'Elder Abuse', in *Massachusetts Survey of Professional and Para-professionals*. Boston: Boston Legal Research and Services to the Elderly.

Steinmetz, S.K. (1983) 'Dependency, Stress, and Violence between Middle-Aged Caregivers and their Elderly Parents', in J.I. Kosberg (ed.), *Abuse and Maltreatment of the Elderly: Causes and Interventions*. Boston: John Wright.

Steinmetz, S.K. (1988) *Duty Bound: Elder Abuse and Family Care*. Beverley Hills, CA: Sage.

Steinmetz, S.K. (1990) 'Elder Abuse: Myth or Reality?', in T.H. Brubaker (ed.), *Family Relationships in Later Life*. Newbury Park, CA: Sage.

Steuer, J. and Austin, E. (1980) 'Family Abuse of the Elderly', *Journal of the American Geriatrics Society*, 28(8): 372–6.

Stevenson, O. (1989) *Age and Vulnerability*. London: Edward Arnold.

Stoller, E.P. and Pugliesi, K.L. (1989) 'Other Roles of Caregivers: Competing Responsibilities or Supportive Resources?', *Journal of Gerontology (Social Sciences)*, 44(6)S: 231–8.

Sutcliffe, C. and Larner, S. (1988) 'Counselling Carers of the Elderly at Home: a Preliminary Study', *British Journal of Clinical Psychology*, 27: 177–8.

Sutton, C. (1992) *Confronting Elder Abuse: An SSI London Region Survey*. London: HMSO.

Taler, G. and Ansello, E.F. (1985) 'Elder Abuse', *Association of Family Physicians*, 32(2): 107–14.

Thomas, K. (1978) *Religion and the Decline of Magic*. Harmondsworth: Penguin.

Tomita, S.K. (1982) 'Detection and Treatment of Elderly Abuse and Neglect: A Protocol for Health Care Professionals', *Physical Therapy and Occupational Therapy in Geriatrics* 2(2). New York: Howarth Press Inc.

Tomlin, S. (1989) *Abuse of Elderly People: An Unnecessary and Preventable Problem*. London: British Geriatrics Society.

Tower Hamlets Local Authority and Health Authority (1991) *Guidelines: Elder Abuse/Inadequate Care*. London: Tower Hamlets Social Services Department.

Townsend, A.C. and Noelker, L.S. (1987) 'The Impact of Family Relationships on Perceived Caregiving Effectiveness', in T.H. Brubaker (ed.), *Aging, Health and Family*. Beverley Hills, CA: Sage.

Townsend, P. (1962) *The Last Refuge*. London: Routledge.

Townsend, P. (1963) *The Family Life of Old People*. London: Penguin.

Townsend, P. (1981) 'The Structured Dependency of the Elderly: Creation of Social Policy', *Ageing and Society*, 1: 5–28.

Twigg, J. (1986) *Carers: Why do they Pose Problems for Social Services Departments?* University of Kent, Personal Social Services Research Unit, Paper no. 433.

Twigg, J., Atkin, K. and Perring, C. (1990) *Carers and Services: A Review of Research*. London: HMSO.

Ungerson, C. (1987) *Policy is Personal: Sex, Gender and Informal Care*. London: Routledge.

United Kingdom Central Council for Nursing (1984) *Midwifery and Health Visiting Code of Professional Conduct*, 2nd edn. London: UKCC.

United States Department of Commerce (1990) *Statistical Abstract of the United States*. Washington: Bureau of Census.

United States Department of Health and Human Services (1980) USDHEW Publication OHDS 79–3021. 47–8. Washington, DC: USDHEW.

United States Department of Health and Human Services (1987) *Urban Report*. Washington, DC: USDHEW.

US Government Printing Office (1990) *Aging America: Trends and Projections. An Information Paper to the Special Committee on Aging, United States Senate*. Washington, DC: Serial no. 101–J.

US House of Representatives: Select Committee on Aging, Sub-committee on Health and Long Term Care (1990) *Elder Abuse: a Decade of Shame and Inaction*. Washington, DC: Government Printing Office.

Vadasz, M. (1988) 'Family Abuse of the Elderly', in B. Schlesinger and R. Schlesinger (eds), *Abuse of the Elderly: Issues and Annotated Bibliography*. Toronto: University of Toronto Press.

Victor, C. (1991) *Health and Health Care in Later Life*. Milton Keynes: Open University Press.

Vousden, M. (1987) 'Nye Bevan Would Turn in his Grave', *Nursing Times*, 83(32): 18–19.

Wagner, G. (1988) *Residential Care: A Positive Choice*. London: National Institute for Social Work/HMSO.

Walker, A. (1980) 'The Social Creation of Dependency in Old Age', *Journal of Social Policy*, 9: 45–75.

Wenger, C. (1984) *The Supportive Network: Coping with Old Age*. London: Allen and Unwin.

Whitehead, T. (1983) 'Battered Old People', *Nursing Times*, 79(46): 16–22.

Wigdor, B.T. (1991) *Elder Abuse: Major Issues from a National Perspective*. Ottawa: National Advisory Council of Aging.

Wilkin, D. and Thompson, C. (1989) *User's Guide to Dependency Measures for Elderly People*. Sheffield: Joint Unit for Social Service Research, University of Sheffield.

Williams, E.I., Bennett, F.M. and Nixon, J.V. (1972) 'Socio-medical survey of patients over 75 in general practice', *British Medical Journal*, 2: 445–8.

Williams, G. (1982) *Learning the Law*. London: Stevens.

Williams, G. (1983) *Textbook of Criminal Law*. London: Stevens.

Williams, G. (1989) 'Did She Fall or was She Pushed?', *Nursing Standard*, 4 February: 23.

Williams, G. and Hepple, B.A. (1984) *Foundations of the Law of Tort*. London: Butterworths.

Winkler, F. (1990) 'Bridling the Market', *Community Care*, 18 October: 26–7.

Wolf, R.S. (1988) 'Elder Abuse: Ten Years Later', *Journal of the American Geriatrics Society*, 36(8): 758–62.

Wolf, R.S. and Pillemer, K.A. (1989) *Helping Elderly Victims: The Reality of Elder Abuse*. New York: Columbia University Press.

Worsam, B. (1991) 'Assessment', in M.W. Shaw (ed.), *The Challenge of Ageing*, 2nd edn. Melbourne/London: Churchill Livingstone.

Zarit, S.H., Todd, P.A. and Zarit, J.M. (1986) 'Subjective Burden of Husbands and Wives as Caregivers: A Longitudinal Study', *The Gerontologist*, 26(3): 260–6.

Index